©Sean Bair-Flannery 2021

www.seanbairflannery.com

All Rights Reserved

Cover photo & design by Rudy Schultz

ISBN: 978-0-578-39720-7

Places I Can't Return To

An Accidental Memoir

by Sean Bair-Flannery

This book is dedicated to all the people who threw me out of these places. The bouncers, the professors, the owners, and all the other rule-followers who said, screamed, or shoved that I needed to leave.

But this is no rebuttal.

This is not some long "I told you so!"

This is an "I heard you so."

Table of Contents

Foreword by CJ Sullivan   6
Preface/Apologia   10

Yak-Zies   12
Batteries Galore   24
McDonald's PlayPlace   31
Cleveland Municipal Stadium   40
Kinney Shoes   65
Pat Joyce's Tavern   74
The Gas Lamp Inn & Saloon   82
Comp USA   95
Social Security Office   105
Have A Nice Day Cafe   114
77 North   130
Web Clout Solutions   145
Guy's Party Center   156
Allstate   167
Janet's Boss's House   180
Ripley's Believe It Or Not Wax Museum   210
The Birds Nest   233
SLAMMABLEDICKCAVES.COM   235
Yankee Stadium   253
Keith Building   266
Hi-Tops   271
Cleveland Public Auditorium   282
Long John Silver's   294
Taco Bell   307
Lake County Memorial Hospital   331

WinCit Finance	348
Acknowledgments/Thank Yous	360

Foreword
(and Forewarned)
by CJ Sullivan

"We have to start hanging out with Sean Flannery."

This was something I was told around 2003 in a Chicago bar called The Long Room. It was stated in a matter-of-fact tone, by a fellow comic and good friend, the late Pat Brice. "Yea, I saw him go up at the Den," I replied, "he was funny, I guess."

"Oh, he is," Pat responded, "but who cares about that shit…have you actually *hung out* with him? He's a hell of a time." He made direct eye contact with me then repeated: "A Hell of a Time."

For Brice to command *appointment drinking* with someone meant that we weren't talking about an ordinary blotto bro. This was serious. It was almost like someone saying, "Hey, we got to start betting on Tom Brady every Sunday…this could be beneficial to all of us!'

So, we T9Word-texted him on a Nokia and had him join us for an unannounced audition for debauchery, and he did not disappoint. The Long Room bar is exactly that: a long room. It had two private, but spacious bathrooms in the middle of the aforementioned long room that, appropriately, had locks. Sean disagreed with this feature. He believed that Men's public bathrooms should be open to several patrons at a time, so he went ahead and removed the doorknob with a Phillips head screwdriver that he kept in his briefcase (more on that later). The problem, other than the petty vandalism, was that in the throes of his boozy vigilantism he had actually removed the handle on the *Women's* bathroom door instead, creating a whole new set of crimes. When we pointed out Sean's error, he "corrected" it by removing the other doorknob, so now it was equal! I knew right then: I was going to be in the Sean Flannery business for the next 20 years. It's not a profitable business, but it's never dull.

The Chicago comedy scene in the early 2000s was undeniably explosive, equally for the stars that emerged from it and for the carnage it left behind. Yes, there were great names like Hannibal Buress, Kyle Kinane, Kumail Nanjiani, etc. All well documented, and all talents whose greatest achievement might have been surviving the nightly combat drinking that was Chicago comedy. A lot of us owe our lives to Sean for guiding us through the battlefields of stages and bars and then for having the decency to burn it all to the ground so no trace was left behind. Like all great leaders, he believes in his troops, even if he doesn't believe in what he's telling them.

Sean is a walking paradox in many ways, and it's what makes him uniquely qualified to pass on these stories of places he can't return to (how he didn't title this book "Oh, the Places You *Won't* Go" is beyond me). He has a legitimately brilliant mind that he uses to bail out his dumb mouth.

Sean's intelligence combined with a genuine curiosity in people's lives is also what makes his stories fascinating. In the wrong hands, these tales could easily be dismissed as boorish regrets doused in cheap beer with no charm whatsoever. Luckily for us, his advanced, but skewed brain power along with his deep, blue collar Cleveland roots allows us to ride along with him from one hilarious exit to another. He's like if Matt Damon's character, Will Hunting, was real and fun to hang out with instead of that dick who assaults people at Little League games and ghosts co-eds. Sean is the condescending everyman done right!

Sean's live comedy storytelling show, "The Blackout Diaries," which I occasionally take part in, is a great summation of why these stories are so good. The show has performers and civilians alike telling outrageous true tales usually related around dumb drunk decisions. It's his championing of people that not only relates but draws our rooting interest as well. He guides city workers, plumbers, and whoever else through their regrettable trials of intoxicated mayhem, and promises it's okay, because he has done worse. Way worse. Sean is a public defender for the fascinatingly dumb.

Sean even wears the public defender's uniform of a cheap wool suit and briefcase to go out drinking. Oh, right, that briefcase. Almost forgot. In order to keep within his allotted $20 drinking budget set by his patient wife, Jessica, Sean would load an actual leather briefcase with assorted beers and a full wet bar in order to drink on the cheap. Sean would have to fake important business calls with Japan every twenty minutes and go into the bathroom stall to make his libation. They never throw a guy out in a suit, he claims.

Speaking of claims, there will be times during this book where you will ask yourself if this is real. To that, I say, Sean is never one to lie, but he doesn't need truths to slow down a ride. He is never as wrong as you think he is, and that's half the battle. Flannery doesn't have time to be corrected—"Beautiful Mind"-style—and you're slowing down the journey to the good part. The only damn part that matters!

Very few comics pull off being hysterical both on and off the stage, because nobody wants to be around someone trying to be funny. It's sad and exhausting. Sean's brilliant stage act is still actually tame compared to his real-life résumé; you get the feeling he is saving his best material for himself. I'm extremely envious of that and equal parts excited that for the first time we get to experience the Full Flannery, from a safe distance. Sean never forces anything, he doesn't need to seek adventures at night, because he IS the adventure. Like Pat Brice said, "We have to start hanging out with Sean Flannery."

—CJ Sullivan, October, 2021.

Preface/ Apologia:

This book is true stories, but it is not a memoir. It is a more an illustration—maybe a warning —of what your life will look like if you decide to live every day like it's your last. Because I followed that advice. I followed it for a good fifteen years.

I can't re-enter most the places I visited in that time.

Many of these stories happened in Cleveland Ohio, in the 1990s. I was (and still am) a huge baseball fan, to the point where—as you will soon learn—I spray-painted the logo of my favorite team, The Cleveland Indians, on to my car. Yes, I drove around with Chief Wahoo on the hood of my car.

This will become a big part of the book. It was my car and my team.

Growing up watching that team, I never thought anything weird about spray painting a highly caricatured Native American face on my car. It was the logo I cheered for each night and I was proud to be from Cleveland.

That logo, Chief Wahoo, was racist. The name, The Indians, was racist. I was racist to put that logo on my car.

I made a decision in this book that I will discuss these topics—"The Indians" and "Chief Wahoo"—as though they were normal during the story. I do not apologize or address the inappropriateness of it in the text of the book because, at the time, they were normal to me.

But I wanted to be abundantly clear, since you won't read it in the book: that name, "The Indians," and that logo, "Chief Wahoo," were racist.

Finally, I made a decision in this book to portray drinking and driving as mostly a struggle against bad civic planning and that I stand by.

-S. B-F.

Yak-Zies
Chicago, IL

The word "Chicago" is thought to derive from a Native American term, "shikaakwa," which means "smelly onion." The land Chicago occupies is a natural swamp; it floods extensively in the spring, is a hazy, mosquito-filled sauna in the summer, and the winters—which are legendarily brutal—last for nine months. People have lived in America since before the pyramids were built, yet in all that time, none of them settled in Chicago. Then white people showed up, and—within two generations—would build what would at one point be the fifth biggest city in the world in the very area that everyone else had studiously avoided. I think it's a pretty good insight into our priorities.

I imagine the first Swede, lost, sunburnt, and soaked in mud, emerging from a thicket of reeds and asking, "What's this place called?"

"Chicago," comes the answer. "Means smelly onion."

"It's PERFECT! All we have to do is dredge 5,000 cubic miles of swamp mud, reverse a river, raise the tableland about ten feet somehow, and then this will be the port city for the entire region."

"Your children will die from illness."

"Yeah, but think of the shareholders!"

People I'd Like to have a Drink With: *George 'Cap' Streeter*

It's often said of great men, "He built this town!" but that has never been truer than of George 'Cap' Streeter, a two-faced hustler who literally built part of this town: his conniving brought in the very soil where "Streeterville," an affluent neighborhood on the near north side of Chicago, now stands.

In July of 1886, Streeter purchased an enormous steamboat and was intending to become a gun-smuggler down in Honduras, but was so incompetent a captain that, during a storm, he grounded his newly-purchased vessel on a sandbar just outside Chicago. Most captains would ask for help. Streeter went the opposite way; he decided living on this sandbar would be just as good as Honduras and declared the sandbar "The United States District of Lake Michigan."

His boat settled into a permanent footing on the sand bar and Streeter started a speakeasy and brothel out of it, claiming neither the laws of Chicago nor Illinois applied to him, as he was in the aforementioned newly created district.

Streeter then sold dumping rights to Chicago waste management companies who surely understood this was all illegal but as they also loved the idea they could chuck all their garbage into the lake, they decided to ask no follow-up questions. Streeter's district was quickly filled with enough garbage to make the footing solid enough to build houses, allowing Streeter to then sell land rights.

Americans like to think that all successful people willed themselves into victory and, put in other circumstances or different eras, they too could have achieved the same results. I disagree and think a lot of it is having the right plan at the right time and George 'Cap' Streeter is a perfect example of that because the entire success of his plan hinges on how fucking crazy Chicago was in the late 19th century. His success was only possible back then; his swindle was allowed because, frankly, the city was so insane it needed him as a pressure release.

Take the early success of Streeter's brothel: it shows that some men in Chicago were so cheap and hard up for a good time, they were willing to wade through a shallow lake of shit and, upon reaching their destination, excited to sleep with the kind of woman who's willing to sleep with a man who swam through a shallow lake of shit. Does that sound like someone you want in the city "proper"? If you just opened a new bed and breakfast with a tavern on the bottom floor, do you want the guy who will swim through shit for a cheaper beer at your home/business? No, you thank the gods of commerce that Streeter is out there, beached in Lake Michigan and willing to take these crazies.

Similarly, Chicago did not want to "solve" its garbage problem by planning and designing city dumps; no, it wanted to just dump it all in the lake, but it knew Canada, Wisconsin, Michigan, and maybe even Illinois itself (the goddamn back-stabbers) would object, so it probably liked having Streeter to blame.

Streeter's biggest mistake was probably in accepting so much trash, so much money, that eventually grass grew over everything and the area looked respectable, meaning the city of Chicago was now ready to take it over.

Chicago sent in a platoon of cops and there was a battle at Streeter's steamboat, where Streeter's forces beat back the police by dousing them with boiling water and shooting bird shot at them. After the battle, Streeter was arrested for assault with a deadly weapon and, at the trial, he told the jury the truth: that he owns a brothel on a shifting pile of garbage that he considers to be outside the realm of Chicago and, therefore, when Chicago police showed up, he felt he had the right to shoot them and drop boiling water on them. Because the Constitution gives you the right to a jury of your peers and, because this was Chicago in the 19th century, Streeter's peers immediately decided, "Agreed! Not guilty on all counts!"

> What I find most hilarious about this story is that the city itself resisted official memorizations of George Streeter, because he was a lying, cheating, real estate swindler, yet, in 2010 a private group constructed a statue to finally cement his legacy. The group that funded it? Yep, they are a real estate investment company.

Chicago is still a city of hilarious, reckless hustlers. One of the first bars I entered in Chicago had a bartender banning a regular "for a good six weeks" after the guy went around collecting money for his dad's funeral, only for his dad to walk in and order a beer during the collection.

I was a bit of a grifter myself when I moved here. We would go to all-you-can-drink charity events (thirty dollars to enter, unlimited beer, all profits go to charity) but we drank so much at them, it felt like we were setting the cure for cancer back five years. I realized that when a bar offers an all-you-can-drink deal, they are playing the numbers. Most people probably won't view it as a challenge to see how much they can drink; they just want to have a fun night—maybe drink two or three cocktails. Not I. Have you ever attended a birthday party at Chuck E. Cheese? They have this big wind tunnel that the birthday kid enters and it blasts free tickets around and the kid has thirty seconds to spin around in this windy vortex and grab as many tickets as they can hold. That's how I order drinks at an open bar. Like a kid in The Ticket Blaster.

On one particularly rainy night in Chicago, my roommates and I attended such an event —a $30 all-you-can-drink "fundraiser"—and, due to the inclement weather, many guests canceled, leaving my roommates and I to have the bar nearly to ourselves, on an open tab; a Chuck E. Cheese party where each invitee is thrown into The Ticket Blaster. We drank and drank and drank, until the event ended and we had to decide: stay here and pay for each new drink or try a new place?

"Let's try a new place," I suggested.

"HAVE YOU LOOKED OUTSIDE?" my roommates questioned.

It was a driving, monsoon-like rain and the few people we saw on the streets were sprinting to shelter.

"It's perfect," I answered, "let's go."

Everyone has a favorite kind of drinking; maybe day drinking or drinking at a ballgame. My favorite kind of drinking is disaster drinking. I like to drink in the kind of situations where you see a lot of local news vans parked on the streets: power outages, devastating blizzards, floods, and so on.

On New Year's Eve, they will warn you: "Watch out; it's amateur night at the bars!" Well, when you go out during a flood, it's professional night. No one approaches the bartender and orders like, "Hmm, let's see…what's good here? What do I want?" at a bar three hours after the national guard was activated.

We were walking down Diversey Avenue in

Chicago into a mighty rain. The news later called what we were walking into a "derecho" which is essentially a tornado that also dumps waves of rain; a once-in-a-decade, overachieving weather event that turned to its rain cloud buddies and proposed, "Ya know, I'm already going to Chicago—to destroy some old houses and what not—why don't I take all your rain over there for you too? Save you a trip?"

I learned "derecho" the next morning, watching the news, when the weather forecaster confidently used the term like it was as common as "thunder": "Good morning! And, wow, do we here at News Channel Four hope your basement is okay after that *derecho* we had last night!"

This is a consistent trick the news media plays upon us. They make you believe that a weird, scary story is not to be worried about because they have a word for it; a precise, scientific term that explains this exact situation, and they pretend we all know this word and because we know it and they know it, the event is normal. When a tornado arrives that is so angry that after it blows off all the roofs it sticks around to piss inside each house, you start to question why nothing like that has ever happened before in your family's eighty years in the area. "Maybe it's related to global warming?" you wonder. And maybe it's something you need to be concerned about? Maybe it will become more common? But then the news says, "Nope; it's a derecho. Standard 'derecho.' See? It's so normal, we have a word for it. No need to worry."

They did the same thing when Vice President

Dick Cheney shot a guy in the face with a shotgun. In fact, it was about the same time as the derecho, and I remember the news reports all explaining the shooting with, "The Vice President was surprised by a covey of birds causing him to shoot one of the members of his hunting party" and I further remember my friends thinking I had lost my sanity:

"This is a conspiracy!" I'd yell, "The incident is far worse than they are admitting! Maybe Cheney was drunk!"

"No, Sean, you're reading too much into it. You think everything is a conspiracy. It was just a 'covey' of birds," they'd reassure me.

"Exactly! That's my point! That's the conspiracy! When did we all start to act like we know what the word 'covey' means? None of us have ever used that word before last week. *Ever!*"

After leaving the first bar, we walked for a block and the conditions were not good.

"This is a terrible idea!" one of my roommates screamed into the wind. "Let's go into that motel; it has a bar!"

We were all new to the city and, given how unfamiliar we were with Chicago, my roommates were ready to enter the first place with shelter.

"No!" I dissented, "Trust me! There's a basement bar not three blocks away. And it's open late!"

They relented and we reached the bar, sopping wet. The bar was called Yak-Zies and as we passed through the doorway, it was as though we entered, not a bar, but the lower deck of a sinking pirate ship; a ship whose crew was so well stocked with rum and so tired of sailing they wanted to go down with her.

Water was emerging, splashing, leaking into the bar in every direction. Men were swimming, in the building, in about shin-deep water, to order new pitchers of beer. One guy was crab-walking through the water on all fours, singing, "UNDER DA SEA! UNDER DA SEA!"

Most amazing was the owner of the bar, the captain of the sinking ship, who had made no SOS calls. Not only was Yak-Zies staying open in over a foot of water; not only were they continuing to sell beer by the pitcher in over a foot of water; but they had also not disabled a single electrical device. Their popcorn machine was on. People were backstroking to the jukebox to play songs.

We took this all in—absorbed all the chaos—as we entered. My roommate straightened his arm across my chest, to stop me from walking into the impromptu pool and said, "I've been to a lot of bars. And this...this is A BAR!" and he released me into the flood like I was being baptized in Chicago street water.

We drank and drank and the water rose and rose, and was now hitting our knees. My roommate finally noticed all the electrical gadgets still operating in a flooded room.

"Whoa! Shouldn't they unplug all this? Couldn't we be electrocuted?" he asked loudly.

"No, no need to unplug, friend," a guy one table over answered. "Name's Donut. Former master electrician," he introduced his soaking-wet self, "there's no reason to unplug."

"Oh, nice," my roommate responded, "so this isn't an electrical hazard?"

"No, it's a *huge* hazard," Donut replied, while "Little Pink Houses" played on the jukebox, "it's just that, once the water reaches the outlet, unplugging the appliances is actually more dangerous; it's the water at the outlet that is bad so"—here he pointed at the air—"we might as well listen to some Cougar while we die!"

After Donut assured us we need not worry about the glowing lights, we drank even more and the water seemed to rise with each pitcher.

I started dancing with this gorgeous woman. We had a chemistry on the verses, then as the chorus hit I dipped her but I forgot we were standing in water and her head submerged for a second. I immediately pulled her up:

"We're all going to die in here!" she yelled.

"I know! It's the perfect way to go out," I shouted back.

I married that woman.

That was seventeen years ago. We have three kids now and whenever I do something that nearly kills me at home, I hear Jess mutter to herself—but loud enough that I'm pretty sure the kids also hear it—"This is what I get for marrying someone I met in a bar."

One of the better ways to summarize my wife's

confidence in me is that throughout the first seven years of our marriage, she increased the life insurance policy on me each year. Meaning, each year she saw some event—me trying to change lightbulbs on an office chair with wheels or me reaching into a fire to get a hotdog that just dropped—that made her think, "I need to prepare for a life without Sean."

    I am a stand-up comedian who mostly performs for drink tickets at bars and my wife has me insured like I run Wells Fargo. I always tell her she better hope I don't die because there is no way the police won't think she killed me, given the ludicrous insurance policies she's opened on me.

    "I'll just explain the truth," she'll reply, "that you were a jackass and that's why I insured you like that."

    "Yeah, well babe," I'll rejoin, "the problem with jackasses is: we die the same way murdered husbands do. Ya know, falling from penthouses. Poisoning. Antique sword accidents."

    When you make major changes to your life insurance policy, the insurance company sends a nurse to give you a physical and I was amazed at how cursory the examination was. The representative asked if I smoked, if I did drugs, then weighed me, measured my blood pressure and left. That was it! I was worried there would be more probing questions that would highlight risk-prone behavior, such as:

    "What's the weirdest thing you've ever drank?"

    And I would have to answer that when my buddies and I were on Put-In-Bay Island, on Lake Erie, we opened the closet at the house we were renting and there was a two-liter plastic bottle of dark beer with a handwritten label that said "BEER?" To be clear, the question mark was on the label; even the container wasn't sure what was in it. We opened it and tested it and confirmed it was beer and drank the whole thing even though it was probably eighty degrees warm.

And if this hypothetical medical examiner were to ask, "How old were you when you did this?" and I would have to be honest and say, "That was last summer." At which point the examiner would probably turn to my wife and say, "No, we can't insure this man."

I have always been surprised that "jackass" is not a formal risk level in insurance products, listed somewhere above healthy adults but below people with high blood pressure. Insurance companies could even tailor how the policy covers them (jackasses): flu shots are not covered but all hospitals become in-network during NFL home games. And the death benefits! Cancer, heart attack: zero payout. But, electrocuted in a basement bar during a *derecho*? Your wife would never have to work again. Drinking buddy shoots you after a covey of birds surprises him? No problem. You sustain an injury while repelling the local police from your self-declared trash town? No co-pay, no deductible.

I'm proposing the first ever insurance plan that caters exclusively to jackasses, one underwritten by the official insurance company of The United States District of Lake Michigan. Our motto is: "We don't offer absolution, but we *do* cover electrocution."

Batteries Galore
Summit Hall, Fairlawn, OH

Everyone has had job interviews they wish they could forget; answers you bungled; jokes you flubbed; names you muddled. But have you ever had an interviewer ask you a technical question, and then knocked yourself unconscious?

I have.

When things go bad for me in a job interview, it's never in a way that you would find covered in a career advice book, where a simple rewording of an answer could have saved the situation. When they go bad for me, they don't go bad at the "employment" level; they go bad at the *human* level.

I was interviewing at Batteries Galore, a narrow kiosk in the center of a mall that sold all kinds of batteries, some of which were fairly obscure. The store did very little business and made most of its money—meager though it was—from changing the batteries of out-of-warranty watches and supplying odd, hard-to-find appliance batteries.

The manager took me to a pizza shop next door and asked a few opening questions; general inquiries about life and work. It went well and, after we ate, she took me inside the kiosk to show me more of the store. Her assistant manager knew me from a previous job—we were essentially drinking buddies at this point—and recommended me. Things were looking up. The manager began showing me inventory as though I were to be her next employee.

Before we advance further, I should share a detail of my childhood that is essential to this story: my brothers and sisters and I used to lick nine-volt batteries.

If you place a nine-volt battery on your tongue—if you squish both terminators against the ol' licker—your body completes the circuit and a quick, silly electrical charge can be felt inside your mouth. We thought it was hilarious and would dare each other to do it if we got a Christmas gift with a nine-volt battery. What's more, my father would routinely ask us to lick the batteries of our smoke detectors in order to verify that they still worked. My dad trained us to learn about the world of electronics the same way babies learn about the objects in their cribs: put it in your mouth.

We were now inside the kiosk and the manager opened a drawer of unmarked, rectangular batteries—they looked like nine-volt batteries, maybe a fingerbreadth bigger—and she asked, "How would you describe your overall level of battery knowledge?"

I knew next to nothing about batteries. I had been lying through my teeth during the entire interview. But, when she asked me to rank my battery savvy, I answered her, confidently:

"I would rate myself as an expert. Or, if I may: above."

I grabbed one of the rectangular batteries from

the drawer, and lifted it up toward my mouth.

At this point I should probably mention that, as it turns out, these were *not* nine-volt batteries. They were sixty-five-volt garage-door-opener batteries. So I had miscalculated the energy in this cube by about 700 percent. I then asked my would-be boss a question of my own:

"You ever do *this*?"

I placed the battery square against my tongue and immediately electrocuted myself unconscious. I threw it back into my mouth like a spy trying to commit suicide before capture.

The next few minutes were related to me later by various participants who were at the scene. One detail I was unaware of at the time was that there was a display case of watch bands that had been on the floor to make room for the inventory tour. My unconscious body fell onto that case and shattered it completely.

I was further told there had been a customer present waiting to get his watch battery replaced, standing there with his two daughters. He swept both of them into his arms and ran away like people were being shot. Likely, he assumed I had died and, as a dad on a tight schedule of errands, felt he couldn't afford the time to get pulled into a police report.

The manager—a woman so young she had probably never given a job interview before, let alone witnessed someone assassinate themselves right in front of her—panicked. Previously, her biggest worry had been running out of AA Duracells; now she had an unconscious body on the floor of her kiosk and

the only identifying info she had was my high school résumé. I often wonder how that 911 call sounded:
"A man just electrocuted himself inside my store!"
"Is he breathing? What can you tell us about him?"
"He once worked at Lady Foot Locker and types forty-five words a minute."

The social dynamics of electrocuting yourself in a kiosk, as opposed to a full retail store, are interesting. Unlike a store, where everyone can see your unconscious body on the floor and immediately realize there is a problem, in a kiosk you collapse behind the counter and you kind of just *disappear*. So, to passersby at the mall, all they saw was a woman at the register of a battery kiosk freaking out for no visible reason; like she was having the world's most fervent panic attack about a battery that wouldn't recharge.

The next day I got a phone call from the assistant manager of that kiosk (my drinking buddy who had recommended me for the job). She was livid.

"I told them you were the smartest person I know! I talked you up like you were so smart I was lucky to even know you. And then you put a fucking *battery* in your mouth?"

"Listen," I responded calmly, "that battery was unmarked and, I want you to know, that is the first thing I plan on changing as your employee."

She laughed as I continued to joke that, in my

27

eyes, the interview went quite well:

"At a minimum, you now know those batteries still work and there is no reason to discount them. I performed a service!"

Two days later, I'm not sure who was laughing—maybe God—when the manager of the Batteries Galore called and said, yes, I was the best candidate she interviewed. She offered me the job.

I was dumbstruck, silent for the first time in a long time (probably since I knocked myself unconscious). Who, I wondered, were the other people interviewing for this job? Did someone outright decapitate themselves? How did a man who electrocuted himself unconscious become the top candidate?

"So, do you not accept?" she asked after a delay.

"Yes! Of course! Thank you! Sorry. I accept! I'm just surprised…I mean, I nearly killed myself in the interview and, on top of that, I think we can both agree I was—at minimum—exaggerating about being a battery expert, so…well, I guess, I wasn't expecting to hear back."

"Look," she answered in a deeper, very deliberate tone, "this job doesn't pay well; for you or me. So what's the point, if you're not having fun? I'm offering you the job because it seemed like, assuming you don't kill yourself, you'd be fun to work with."

"Well, that is my goal."

"To have fun?"

"No, to not accidentally kill myself."

When one looks back on an old job, you always wonder what happened to certain people: "What could he or she possibly be doing nowadays?" you ask yourself. When I look back at Batteries Galore, I usually wonder what happened to that man who ran away with his daughters after seeing me electrocute myself during a job interview. More generally, I often ask: how many strangers, over the years, thought they had just seen me kick the bucket?

The clearest victim of all my bad decisions is myself—the bones I've broken, the jobs I lost, the tongues I've electrocuted—but I often reflect on those downstream, forgotten sufferers: the bystanders who just returned from the mall; the Browns game; the turnpike; all convinced they had just witnessed a death. Hell, half the time I had done something so stupid, they probably assumed I was committing suicide.

Imagine taking your kids out to run errands... and if you are a parent you know there is no fate worse than bringing your kids on errands. When you see a parent running a weekend errand with multiple kids you can safely assume the purchase is so important the family will die without it. You may even assume the other parent is dead, because that's about what it would take for my wife or I to agree to take all three of our children to the hardware store alone.

Have you ever seen a cartoon where one of the characters is sleepwalking, so the other character is constantly running ahead, putting down boards to save the sleepwalking character from falling into a well? Running errands with kids is a bit like doing that but you're also looking for the paint aisle. One child is about to topple headfirst out of the grocery cart; the other is touching a power saw; and, as to you try to navigate the store without one of your offspring dying, the eldest is asking non-stop questions about where money comes from or if the store is allowed to kill robbers and did dinosaurs ever eat cavemen?

Imagine balancing all that and, just as you're about to accomplish one of the errands—to finally cross *something* off the list—an employee puts a battery in his mouth and shocks himself dead in front of your kids! So you run outside of the mall because you don't have time to have the police ask you a bunch of questions, but in the excitement you can't recall where you parked and your kids are asking:

"Is that man dead?"

"Is he in heaven?"

"When are we gonna eat?"

You can't find your car, you now have to explain the afterlife and, worst of all, your watch still doesn't have a battery.

McDonald's PlayPlace
Berwyn, IL

In high school, I worried that my friends and I had normalized vomiting. It was occurring every time we hung out: a friend would puke in some antique vase or unused aquarium (they never puke in the sink or toilet; it's always the biggest vessel in your house not connected to plumbing). And it was odd to me, that none of us found this odd.

Years later I had a kid and learned we were mere amateurs. I discovered that there is no wino, no hopeless barfly, no troubled celebrity, that will ever puke more than the average toddler. Kids puke *constantly*. And that's because—at the end of the day—kids fucking *party*.

You have never, even at the height of your college-years confidence, shown up to a party with a fraction of the nerve that a kid does. A child will walk past a dozen adults, all looking for hugs, and say, "I have no memory of you," then reach the end of the room, turn and ask, "So where's this bouncy house?"

My kids will run up to me at a party and say:

"Hey, my best friend...um, I forgot their name..." (it's someone they met ten minutes ago), "but...well, they want to come over some time so I need to know where we live."

"We live in Oak Park."

"What? I thought we live in America?"

"Oak Park is a city in-" and before you can explain further, they interrupt: "Hmm, that's weird," and they hold their stomach for a second—and that's all the warning you will get, a momentary rub of the stomach—and then they let loose and vomit like a garden hose set to "JET."

Once you are past your first kid, you learn to recognize the twitch, the warning—the way a mongoose knows when a snake is about to strike—and you get out of the way, or you pick up the kid and point them away from the carpet and furniture, almost like they're a blender that's running without its top on; you are redirecting the stains to a preferred, cheaper place.

When kids are done vomiting, much like a drunk, they show zero remorse. A few seconds of silence will pass, then they will break the tension with something along the lines of:

"I may have had too many brownies."
"How many did you have?" you'll ask.
"What comes after ten?"
"Eleven."
"I had two elevens."

On this occasion, my family was visiting from Ohio and due to a nearby factory fire our house lacked power for several hours. We took the kids to a McDonald's with a PlayPlace for breakfast to entertain them while we waited for the zoo to open. The adults were mostly occupied with using the restaurant's Wi-Fi (since we had not been online for half a day due to the power outage) when we heard it: a child's shriek, the grossed-out kind that usually means that one of these families is going to leave a lot sooner than they were planning.

"Oh my God," yelled one of our kids, "I can't believe you just did that, right there! Of all the places!"

We looked up and saw kids jumping out of the play structure (which seemed about three stories tall) like their lives depended upon it; as if they were leaping from the burning wreck of the Hindenburg.

"What's going on?" my sister asked.

"John just took a *shit* in the attic of the playground!" her oldest answered.

Somehow, kids know to wait until the most public moment possible to reveal that they know a particular swear word. They never let the word slip privately in the car; it's always when your boss or three generations of your family is visiting that they decide to debut a new vulgarity.

"What?" my sister replied.

"'Shit,'" her youngest explained, "it means 'feces.' You might know it as a"—and here he changed his voice to impersonate an adult)—"'bowel movement.'"

"I KNOW WHAT IT MEANS, CONNOR!"

By this point the besmirched John had now descended, at his own leisurely pace, and alighted on the ground.

"John, what happened?" someone asked.

"That did not go like I planned," he answered, gesturing back toward the top of the playcenter, and then began the lizard-legged walk of a person who has just made a great mistake.

"Jesus," said his dad.

We looked into the corner of the playcenter where a McDonald's employee, who was sweeping the floor with a broom, had overheard everything. We gave him a kind of "What's the protocol here?" look, and, before we could even form a question, he announced, unsolicited:

"I make seven dollars an hour."

This is one of my favorite dead-end job responses: when someone asks you to go unreasonably past the requirements of your job, and you immediately silence them by letting them know your salary.

"Jesus!" my brother-in-law murmured again. This is something my dad would also do when one of us upset him profoundly: he would stare into the distance, repeating "Jesus," every few seconds, almost like he was reviewing every decision in his life that led to him hearing the news he was presently hearing.

"Hey!" my sister screamed, breaking him out of his trance. Her and my brother-in-law then exchanged that chilly glare you see couples do after one of their children has done something horribly disgusting; that piercing, contemplative glance you trade, attempting to recall who dealt with the last such incident or who—in general—has to debase themselves most often for the kids. Because, if the answer is, "I did the last one," or, "I do this stuff all the time," that means the other person is about to climb up a playcenter designed for people a third their size, to clean up their kid's diarrhea.

Some couples fight about this but not my wife and I. We have a floating agreement that because of the people I surrounded myself with during my twenties, my skill set for solving issues of bodily mistakes is uncommonly well-developed; that I am to puking what Liam Neeson's character in "Taken" is to hostage situations, and therefore I handle all child-related biological disasters.

I do it so regularly that I am often called upon to walk other dads through it. And so too in this case.

"I'll help," I told my brother-in-law as he started to plan his ascent up the playcenter, adding, "but first we need to grab a *lot* of napkins." And I picked up a nearby napkin dispenser.

"Good idea," he said.

"And a garbage bag. The trip down will be a lot easier if we have a garbage bag."

I began climbing up while my brother in law took the mostly empty garbage bag from the nearest bin and joined me.

At which point a different McDonald's employee opened the door, and, seeing us start our ascent, admonished us: "No one above the age of twelve in the playcenter, gentlemen!"

"Let them go," said the seven-dollar-an-hour broom sweeper. "Trust me."

We showed the new employee the napkins and garbage bag we were holding and they immediately put it all together and waved us on.

We had worried that it would be difficult to reach the top—that there would be a tube or web of netting we couldn't fit past—but we scaled it easily. The architects at McDonald's had clearly accounted for such eventualities; realizing that the entire structure would have to be incinerated within forty-eight hours if they didn't make all spaces large enough for adults to enter for when a child inevitably relieved themselves inside. I wondered how many generations of playcenters existed before this adjustment was made?

We reached the top and began dealing with the situation. From down below, we heard my sister ask, "Is it going to be...easy to clean up?"

"No one shits themselves with a dry, solid poop, dear!" my brother-in-law screamed back, as though to convey: "No, it is not looking easy up here at the summit."

We cleaned it as best as we could, descended with the trash and, as we reached the bottom and exited the playcenter we noticed all eyes upon us: the two McDonald's employees, my sisters, my wife, and some new lady and her two kids, who had also been forced to seek refuge under the Golden Arches due to the power outage.

"Is it cleaned?" my sister asked my brother-in-law.

"We should leave a tip," was his answer. Which everyone correctly understood to mean: that top floor is still disgusting and it's going to take more than two dads with napkins to solve it.

The new lady was the first to react, grabbing both her kids by the arms and yanking them back towards their car, snapping, "This is why I never go to McDonald's!"

My sister looked at the employees, who would

probably have to sort out the rest of it, and came closer to us, asking, "What's the appropriate tip for this kind of situation?"

"All of it," my brother in law answered, "all the cash we have. They have to get a mop to the top of a jungle gym."

We left McDonald's and were heading back to our place, wondering who should stay home with John while the rest went to the zoo.

"Why?" John wondered. "I feel fine now. I just needed to poop."

This is the area where the analogy of kids acting like drunks does not align well because, unlike drunks, kids return to being totally normal after shitting or puking all over a room. It's miraculous, as though they expelled a demon from their body with the food. My kids will pace around whining at a party—"When are we going to leave? Do we even know these people?"—then puke into a piano, and when I rise to apologize and leave, they quibble:

"Whoa? Why are we leaving? I'm having a great time!"

"You just threw up into a piano!"

"I feel great now. And dad, the correct word is 'vomit.'"

Kids will go to a party, have a dozen fights with other children about toys, fall off a table, get sick from the food, and their first question at breakfast the next day will be, "When are we going back there? That was a blast."

After the McDonald's debacle, we went to the zoo, John included (and, indeed, he was fine for the rest of the day). As none of us wanted to deal with traffic and parking, we took the train, which excited the kids. When the train arrived, we entered and my sister's youngest boy immediately ran up to the first pole inside the car, stuck his tongue out and licked that metal pole—on a Chicago public train that runs twenty-four hours a day—from top to bottom.

I have been at sporting events where a grotesque injury happened and the crowd groaned; I have been at standup shows where the performer seemed to get each audience member laughing at the same cadence; but I have never heard a more uniformed response then when my nephew licked a pole on a crowded CTA Blue Line car. It was a guttural, Jungian, shared, "UUUGGH!" You know that strep test, where the doctor shoves a long swab down your throat until you choke? It was like a hundred people got a simultaneous strep test.

My sister cried out: "God! No! COONN-NOORR!"
Believe it or not, this happens a lot with kids, where you disagree with their actions so deeply that you find yourself screaming the name of your god before you get to "NO!" If my Catholic parents were disgusted enough with what I was up to, they may even get to all three members of the Trinity first:

"What? Jesus! Are you dangling your brother out the window? Holy Ghost! God dammit, NO!"

We found some seats and sat down. Everyone was looking at us, holding back laughs. My brother-in law obviously felt the collective stares, because he said, loud enough for the entire car to hear:

"I wish I could say that was the grossest thing one of my sons did today."

Cleveland Municipal Stadium
Cleveland, OH

Cleveland Municipal Stadium was a cavernous, 80,000 seat stadium built in the 1930s on the shores of Lake Erie. It was built as part of a bid to win the Summer Olympics. When I think of the peak moment of American optimism, I do not think of the moon landing. No, I think the most optimistic act in American history was Cleveland building a giant stadium next to the most polluted lake in the world, thinking it could land *the Olympics*.

If only the Olympic bid had worked! What a sight those Games would have been! Municipal Stadium—which would go on to be home to both the Cleveland Indians and the Browns—was so close to the lake that swarms of mayflies and midges would descend into the venue every summer like some kind of London fog, often affecting the outcome of games. Cleveland always seemed to win those games and visiting press came to think of it as a home field advantage; that Cleveland players were more accustomed to playing inside a blight of insects. I never bought that. I don't think anyone becomes used to having a cloud of bugs around them, and it's not like the players on Cleveland's roster grew up near Lake Erie and thus developed a tolerance. Most of the players came from sunny, southern places. No, instead, I think when someone moves to Cleveland and lives there for a decent period of time, they just start to believe something will always go wrong. When they begin their day, they assume they will end up inside a car that won't start or get stuck in a broken elevator, or that a flying soup of ticks will engulf them and, because they have already made peace with this, they are less bothered by the problem; minor disasters become normalized.

Visiting players did not find it normal. Seattle pitcher Jim Bounton once said: "If you are going to die in a plane crash, have it be on an inbound flight to Cleveland." Opposing players began calling the stadium "The Mistake By The Lake" and, to them, it must have seemed like some terrible accident of architecture or even nature was responsible for these playing conditions, particularly during Mayfly Season.

Mayflies emerge from Lake Erie by the cloud; billions of what appear to be large, ugly butterflies landing everywhere. Near the lake, they blanket the ground so thoroughly—deeper than snow—that your car sounds like it's driving on top of peanuts as it advances over them. And mayflies only live a few minutes in the air. So imagine the oddity of these visiting players not only being engulfed in a gathering of the world's ugliest butterflies but also learning that, as you swat them away, most of them are choosing to land on you to die. Even the bugs in Cleveland are despondent.

All the same, the local fans were not bothered. Not so much because they were used to the flies or the humidity or, during the winter months, the freezing, whipping winds off the lake. No, they were too drunk to care. I have never seen drinking like that at Municipal Stadium: She seated 81,000 persons and I don't think a soul ever entered it sober. 81,000 people! When I was growing up, Cleveland only had 400,000 adults living in the city which meant twenty percent of the city's population was at the game drunk. Attending a game was less like attending a sporting event and more like entering a living, breathing painting by Hieronymus Bosch.

Parties I Wish I had Attended: *Ten Cent Beer Night*

There have been 139 forfeits in Major League Baseball history and all but ten of them took place before the advent of night lighting. The first forfeit of the modern era that was not due to an inability to light or officiate the game was when the city of Cleveland decided to sell beers for ten cents.

In 1974, the Cleveland Indians were a losing team averaging around 10,000 fans a game in a stadium designed to hold 80,000 people. To boost ticket sales for their game against the Texas Rangers, the Indians announced that drafts of beer would sell for only ten cents. Almost 30,000 people showed up; 20,000 more than their average attendance and you have a pretty good idea what brought them. And the key thing to remember here is not just that they attracted twenty thousand people who were only there to drink beers for ten cents; it's that they attracted twenty thousand people who could drink ten cent beers on a Tuesday night with no discernible impact on their schedules.

Believe it or not, Ten Cent Beer Nights were common to baseball in the 1970s. Several cities—Milwaukee, Arlington, and others—regularly staged them to improve attendance. It was one of those traditions—like smoking on airplanes or the way zoos used to have lions in cages that you could reach into—that no one had questioned yet. And just as we needed Ralph Nader to come along and show us that seatbelts in cars are a good idea, we needed the city of Cleveland to show us, yes, if you sell beer for ten cents, you will get a riot.

All drunken debacles end terribly but Ten Cent Beer Night is unique in that it also *started* horrifically. There was never a moment during the entire fiasco where the crowd, the baseball players, the press, or the police thought this plan could work. Twenty thousand extra fans arrived, many carrying firecrackers. Smoke covered large swaths of the stadium before the first pitch. Sensing a rowdy crowd, the Indians decided to impose a beer limit: you could buy as many drafts as you like, but no more than six beers at a time.

That limit is an amazing indicator of what the city of Cleveland considers safe, versus what the rest of the world considers safe. Doctors define binge drinking as five drinks in one day. The city of Cleveland was not willing to limit a round of beer as aggressively as the medical community defines a whole day of unhealthy drinking.

The six-beer limit was useless. The beer was being served from Stroh's trucks near the outfield and the crowd was so drunk, so menacing that the staff tending the trucks decided the aggression wasn't really worth whatever pittance they were being paid and abandoned their posts. Fans were left to pour their own beers, now for free.

That's right. Ten Cent Beer Night, an already bad idea with an equally ill-conceived six beer limit, was now: All-You-Can-Drink Free Beer at the Stroh's Truck Night.

Dan Coughlin, a hilarious, legendary Cleveland sports reporter, covered the Indians beat back then and the most definitive summary of the game comes from him:

2ND INNING: *A woman jumps over the wall and runs to the batter's on-deck circle. She takes her shirt off, flashes the crowd and then tries to kiss the umpire who refuses.*

3RD INNING: *A father and son—baseball has always been about dads and sons—descend the outfield wall, run to centerfield and moon the bleachers together.*

4TH INNING (top): *Texas pitcher Fergie*

Jenkins is hit in the stomach by a line drive and as he is being attended to by training staff the fans start cheering, "HIT HIM AGAIN, HARDER!"
   4TH INNING (bottom): Tom Grieve of the Texas Rangers hits a home run. As he is rounding the bases, a naked fan bounces on the field. The naked fan slides into second base before Grieve.
5TH INNING: Fans are throwing tennis and golf balls on the field to distract players.
6TH INNING: Fans throw firecrackers into the Texas Rangers bullpen and it is evacuated.
9TH INNING: The seventh and eighth innings are interrupted by a continued stream of fans running on the field, but the crowd is getting no worse than it was in the previous innings. The game is nearly over; it looks like the teams will be able to leave mostly unscathed.

   Then the Indians did the unthinkable, particularly for a team this talentless: they tied the game.
   After the tying run scored, a young fan rushed to centerfield and tipped the cap off Rangers centerfielder Jeff Burroughs. Burroughs spun to confront him, lost his balance and fell, and this was misread by the Rangers dugout as him being attacked. The Texas Rangers left their dugout, armed with bats, to confront the man they believed assaulted their teammate.

In a normal city, this fan would explain the misunderstanding and apologize to the wave of professional athletes who are descending upon him with baseball bats. But this being Cleveland, he signaled for help and a mob of other fans armed with knives and chains and broken steel chairs descended to the field to confront the Rangers. The motto of the actual Texas Rangers, the legendary law enforcement agency, is "one riot, one ranger"; fate, having a great sense of humor, now decreed that all twenty-five Texas Ranger baseball players would find themselves fighting a single riot with the city of Cleveland.

Luckily the Texas players, who were assisted by Cleveland players in their exit, were all able to leave the field with nothing more than minor injuries. In photos almost every starting player had some visible wound from the game with the worst injuries sustained by Umpire Nestor Chylak. Chylak, who was bleeding badly from being hit in the head by both a chair and rock, called a forfeit after fans ran away with all the bases.

Chylak's post-game interview is hilarious and, as a man who grew up in Cleveland, one of the more spot-on descriptions of how the city parties:

"They were uncontrollable beasts! I've never seen anything like it except in a zoo. Fucking animals! You can't pull back a pack of

> *animals. When uncontrolled beasts are out there, you gotta do something. I saw two guys with knives and I got hit with a chair. If the fucking war is on tomorrow, I'm gonna join the other side and fight Cleveland!"*
>
> I have always felt Cleveland should adapt that into a mural at the airport for visitors to read after they land:
>
> "WELCOME TO CLEVELAND: I've never seen anything like it except in a zoo."

My first memory of Cleveland Municipal Stadium was tailgating before a Browns game. We were drinking beer and eating venison. My cousin's drinking buddy, Ern, provided the venison. People would ask Ern where he could possibly hunt deer in Cleveland. "I got a special system," he'd reply.

"Discovered it by accident," Ern would explain. "I got drunk and lit off some fireworks too close to the forest preserve one night; all of sudden a herd of deer bolt out of the woods and run straight into the highway. 'Bout five of them died: Hit by cars immediately. I figured, Hell, those commuters and truck drivers ain't gonna want 'em, so...I made some chili."

I once read that humans may have supplanted

Neanderthals because humans were able to hunt larger game due to our intelligence. One such example is the "special system" humans used to hunt mammoths at night: Early humans would light torches and scare mammoths to run off cliffs. Scientists, I'm sure, assumed it was the geniuses in those early groups of humans who developed the plan to scare mammoths with fire, but, as I ate venison in the parking lot of Municipal Stadium, I wondered: maybe it was the jackasses? What if it was two morons, drunk from rotten peaches, screwing around with fire who accidentally stumbled into a way to kill whole herds of mammoths.

"Hey Ugg! Hold me fermented fruit broth! Me making an idea!"

Perhaps we displaced the Neanderthals not because humans had more brains in our group but because we had more jackasses—more Erns—who were stumbling into new foods, new hunting methods, new inventions, purely off drunk horseplay.

As I drank in the parking lot of the Cleveland Municipal Stadium surrounded by grown men dressed as dogs for a Browns game, the following conclusion dawned on me: We are not a race of adventurers and tinkerers but of jackasses. And Cleveland is our capital.

We drank and ate until almost kickoff before starting for the stadium. During football season there were always two games being played simultaneously at Cleveland Municipal Stadium: One was the Browns, on the field against their opponent; the other was the Browns' fans against stadium security, trying to sneak as much booze as possible into the venue.

This was the golden age of Municipal Stadium booze smuggling; it was the early days of The Dawg Pound and decades before terrorism-related security checks. Fans started dressing up like junkyard dogs for games and every aspect of those costumes was chosen with the end goal of surreptitiously ferrying outside alcohol into the stadium. One group would always bring a doghouse into the game and raise it into the air after touchdowns. Unbeknownst to security, this doghouse was filled with beer, a sort of drunkard Trojan horse. My buddy's group would attend with his uncle, who was older. They would put him in a wheelchair, cover him in blankets—like FDR doing a fireside chat—and push him past security. Under the blankets, the man was actually sitting on a keg of beer.

Architects have a term, a word dating back to the Romans, for the repeating tunnel-like exits below seating areas: "vomitoria." What a perfect word to describe both the architecture and the aroma of Cleveland Municipal Stadium. The catering staff could have served the fans raw meat and I don't think it would have induced more vomiting than was being induced by alcohol. Turns out the number one method of slipping booze into Municipal Stadium was to hide it in your stomach.

Today, it is impossible for me to return to Cleveland Municipal Stadium because, like all places of great, natural lawlessness, America paved something fancier over it. The Indians left Municipal Stadium for a small, glassy field in 1994 and the Browns departed for Baltimore shortly after. Four years later, football returned to Cleveland but only after the city agreed to bulldoze Municipal Stadium and build a trimmer, more elegant venue in its place. Cleveland Municipal Stadium sits at the bottom of Lake Erie, demolished to an artificial reef.

Worse yet, the dashing complexes that replaced Municipal Stadium were financed by a sin tax! The horror! Not only did we replace one of the rowdiest, good-timing stadiums in America, but we agreed to raise the cost of a beer while doing it! Most people prefer the newer, sleeker venues, but not me. I believe the story of Cleveland Municipal Stadium is more a story on the taming of the American drunk.

Cleveland Municipal Stadium was built after voters, in the 1920s, approved $2.5 million in bond financing to construct it. It was called Municipal Stadium because the public owned it; they paid for it cleanly, via bonds. Do you know what would have happened if you suggested to voters, in the 1920s: "Rather than all of us paying for this stadium evenly, how about we just raise the cost of cigarettes?" City Hall would have been burnt down before the mayor's press conference ended.

Drunks in America used to show amazing levels of organization. Politicians used to fear drunks as a voting bloc the way current ones fear the gun lobby or evangelicals. The surest way to see a riot in your town was to suggest that alcohol should cost more.

A (Brief) History of Politically Active Drunks:

The Whiskey Rebellion (1791): How determined were the drunks in the 18th century? Well, they formed an actual militia rather than agree to pay more for whiskey.

Laden with huge debt from The Revolutionary War, Congress enacted a six to eighteen cents tax on every gallon of distilled spirits. The western half of Pennsylvania more or less tried to secede, and George Washington himself—the fucking *president*, no less—had to leave the Oval Office and lead an army against a huge militia forming outside Pittsburgh. It remains the only time a sitting U.S. President has led troops into battle. That's right. The only time we forced a president to get off his ass and actually lead a war was not to fight a foreign adversary but something much scarier: our own drunks.

The Whiskey Rebellion is often taught in elementary schools in America due to its historical importance: It was an early test of the Federal Government's will and ability to collect country-wide taxes. Washington's response showed that the Government is going to get its money. But I also enjoy the secondary effect of teaching kids: Man, adults do like their whiskey.

Eggnog Riot (1826): The only riot in West Point

history occurred when a keg of eggnog was smuggled into a dormitory on Christmas Eve. Not only is The Eggnog Riot the greatest name of a riot, it is also the best example of how truly explosive alcohol is: A single keg of spiked holiday punch turned the greatest, most-disciplined fighting force in the world into an aimless, two-day-long donnybrook. Outside of a bomb, alcohol is probably the most destructive thing an enemy can hope to land in its opponents' barracks.

The riot started when cadets were told the eggnog at their holiday party would be alcohol-free due to recent drinking infractions. Rather than face Christmas sober, the cadets rowed to nearby taverns, purchased whiskey and rum to spike their eggnog and then proceeded to riot for two days.

Nineteen cadets were expelled for their participation in the riot which, at its height, involved a third of all cadets. Interestingly three "heroes" of the Confederacy—Robert E Lee, Jefferson Davis and eventual Supreme Court Justice John Archibald Campbell— were all in the barracks that rioted but none were disciplined as they did not participate. I can't help but wonder if, in an alternate timeline where those three party, does the Civil War last half as long? Could we have made the war shorter by making better eggnog?

The Lager Riots (Chicago, 1855): In 1855 Chicago elected as their mayor Levi Boone, an avowed racist and member of the Know Nothing Party. He closed taverns on Sundays and raised the cost of a liquor license six fold, from $50 to $300 a year. It was seen as an attack on German and Irish immigrants and they immediately rioted.

They formed such a frightening mob—-it had its own fife and pipe band—that the city of Chicago raised its drawbridge while the rioters were on it, to prevent them from storming the Court House. The rioters and police battled until cannons were finally deployed by police to disperse the crowd.

I once calculated at a bar that Boone's licensing increase probably made the average beer about two cents more expensive.

Portland Rum Riot (1855): Maine became a dry state in 1851 and four years later—about a month after Chicago's Beer Lager riot in fact—the city of Portland, Maine, which had not had a drink in almost half a decade, heard the mayor was hiding his own personal stash of rum and they straight-up lost it.

The riot was said to be particularly fueled by Portland's large population of Irish immigrants. That is a sentence you encounter over and over when reading about these incidents. Mass public disobedience over the price of alcohol is almost always explained as: "Bear in mind a bunch of Irish people recently moved to the city so we kind of didn't have a chance at passing these alcohol taxes."

I love that historians, even today, talk about the Irish of the 19th century as a roaming bacchanalia that devours your town's liquor the way locusts eat wheat. I remember reading a book in a sociology class ("Beyond The Melting Pot" by Daniel Patrick Moynihan and Nathan Glazer) where the authors argue—after sharing the statistic that over a quarter of all Irish people reported being drunk enough to hallucinate at least once in their life (the next highest race was Scandinavians at 7.6 percent)—that organized Irish crime probably collapsed because the Irish were too drunk to do it effectively:

"Bookmaking, policy-making and drugs are complex, serious, exacting trades. They are not jobs for heavy drinkers."

That is, by far, the most hilarious backhanded compliment a race could receive: you are too drunk to be dishonest.

I must mention: Cleveland has a lot of Irish people.

So to me, seeing the old stadium replaced via a new one, financed by a sin tax, was particularly dispiriting; not only would we lose that giant, splurging rumpus we called a stadium but, also, it showed the politicians didn't fear us anymore. The drunks, as a political bloc, have gone the way of the Whigs.

In modern America, big bills are paid by small sinners.

But, for a short time before Municipal Stadium was razed, I did see fear and consternation from politicians. In the winter of 1995 the owner of the Cleveland Browns, Art Modell, blindsided the city by announcing he would relocate the football team to Baltimore. The people of Cleveland threatened to expel or rip apart anyone who helped Modell move the team. Fans cataloged every company that advertised with the Browns and stopped shopping there; it was the most effective boycott I have seen. Within a few days McDonald's pulled their ads from Browns games, citing declining sales. Do you know how mad the average American needs to get in order to quit eating McDonald's?

Soon, all sponsors left. The boycott was so effective, no commercials were aired during the remaining games. Instead the announcers would either remain on air kibitzing loosely where commercial breaks would normally appear or, better yet, stations would air government-produced public service announcements. It was an odd sensation: To go from the loud, often-idiotic clamor of a NFL game to a speaker in a mid-Atlantic accent reminding you to look both ways before crossing train tracks; or to hear instructions on how to safely install a car seat, where once a man was screaming for you to buy a bigger television.

The boycott grew so large it started swallowing incidental businesses. My buddy Tyson and I drove down to Columbus to visit friends at Ohio State shortly after Modell announced the Browns were moving. We went to a small, family-run liquor store off High Street. There was no parking so I was sent inside to grab a case of cheap beer while Tyson idled in the street. As I approached the entrance, I noticed a customer exiting violently. The customer opened the door with a punch, lingered for a moment, then yelled, "You're never gonna see us again!" before walking off. A second customer, a friend of the first, followed, stopping to scream "ASSHOLES!" back into the store.

I entered the liquor store and quickly saw the problem: there was a giant display of Dog Pound Beer greeting customers. The customers were upset because they were Browns fans and, by seeing this giant display of Cleveland Browns-affiliated beer, they felt this store was stabbing them in the back by not honoring this giant, state-wide boycott of Browns merchandise.

Behind the registers, I heard the owner, thin and defeated, complaining, "These people are so angry. What a disaster! I just bought two pallets of this beer. How am I going to get rid of it?"

This moment—me entering the store the exact instant the owner was lamenting about needing someone to finish all the beer—seemed preordained. I knew I was going to be part of something special, like in those Western movies, where the owner of a saloon asks, "How are we ever going to clean up this town?" just as John Wayne saunters in.

"I'm your gunslinger," I said to the owner.

"What?" he asked.

"What's the cheapest you can sell all that beer to me?"

"Where would you fit it?"

"That will be *my* problem".

"If you can take it all, I'll sell it to you for state minimum".

"What would that be?"

"$1.88 a case"

I ran back to the car. Tyson, who had been idling on the street the whole time, asked, "Where's the beer?"

"We're gonna need a bigger car," I replied.

We went to a hardware store to rent a large work truck. Hardware stores always rent big trucks for super-low rates, but the catch is you have to return it within an hour, and what job can you complete in under an hour? We had such a job.

We returned to the liquor store with the truck and purchased every last container of Dog Pound Beer. The owner thanked me like I had just saved the store from marauding gangs. They threw in the eight-foot-tall cardboard cutout of a dog in shoulder pads.

Tyson and I drove the van to meet two close friends at Ohio State. Our visit was unplanned—a surprise—and we were denied entry. Ohio State was on quarters at the time, not semesters, and it turned out that Tyson and I were visiting during their Finals week. When our friends saw us arrive with a commercial vehicle full of Dog Pound Beer, the day before they were to start their final exams, they locked the doors and more or less pretended to not be home.

"Where do we go now?" Tyson asked.

"Ya know," I answered, "I worked a factory job last summer with this guy called Frank. He goes to Ohio State. He's a lot of fun. Let's see if he answers."

We looked up Frank in the student directory, drove to his place, and I reminded him that we worked together last summer. Frank invited us in. We mentioned that we brought some beer and started what was to be the craziest twenty-four-hour bender of my life. When the Lotto hits a huge jackpot, say $300 million, and people around me speculate about what they would do with the money, I always counter: "Purchasing a stack of Dog Pound beer at $1.88 a case nearly killed me, so I'm not positive I want three hundred million dollars."

Tyson and I thought it was great that Frank let us enter, when our two closest friends at Ohio State treated us like barbarians at the gate.

"Do you have finals this week, Frank?" I asked, trying to understand if he was under a different schedule.

"Doesn't everyone?" he answered, popping open a Dog Pound.

That is, very closely, the last coherent sentence I remembered before waking up, two days later in an unfurnished apartment above an auto body repair shop. As I woke up, I felt a terrible soreness along my forehead. Reaching up, I discovered I was wearing a hat. I pulled it off and took a look. It did not belong to me; I'd never seen it before; and it was way too small to fit my head.

I heard Tyson grunting from another corner of the apartment as he began to move.

"Where are we?" I asked.

"Kent State, dude!" Frank answered confidently from what sounded like a separate room.

I turned to Tyson, "I must have fallen asleep with some hat that doesn't fit me. Man, you'd be surprised how sore it's made my forehead."

At this point Tyson turned and looked at me for the first time and opined, "I don't think a hat did that to you, dude."

"What?"

"You need to find a mirror, bro."

I found the bathroom, flipped the lights and that's when I saw I had a grapefruit sized bruise in the exact middle of my forehead. It looked like someone batted a softball as hard as they could and, rather than catch it, I headbutted it back to the batter.

"How did we get up here?" I asked.

"I think my girlfriend drove us up here," Frank answered, "but she and her friends split pretty quickly after they saw how much Dog Pound beer we had in the trunk".

"OK, well, I gotta get out of here," I explained. "I have to work in Akron later today."

"Yeah, me too," Tyson agreed and we started to locate our shoes and wallets when we heard, from whatever room Frank was in:

"You're not gonna believe this. I can't find my leg."

It's here that I should point out that Frank only had one leg. He was born with one and he used a prosthetic leg on the other side.

"*What*?" we asked.

"I can't find my leg," he repeated. "Normally I put it right next to my bed."

"Is it possible you left it at the bar?"

"I've never done that before."

"Well," Tyson added, "we did drink two pallets of Dog Pound beer last night." It was said in such a way as to suggest that, having consumed such a high quantity of such low-quality alcohol, one could not expect the normal rules governing life and limb to apply.

Frank entered the room we were in, hopping on one leg while holding his jeans in the air, like a magician trying to prove the top hat is indeed empty: "Look…no leg!"

"Fuck," I moaned. "I don't even know what bars we were at last night."

Tyson walked into Frank's room to verify, as though someone—no matter the hangover—could miss an unattached leg inside an unfurnished room.

"Yep," he concurred. "There is definitely no leg

in here."

"Fuck!" I yelled again and bolted up from the chair. I was wearing a shirt, a winter jacket, a baseball cap that didn't fit me, socks and underwear…no pants. I stormed about the place looking for my own pants while yelling for the guys to "get serious."

I found my pants in the bathtub, grabbed them forcefully and tried to put them on in one move while still yelling at the guys, like a fireman who'd been woken up by all five alarms:

"We gotta find this leg! That's priority one, and then…what the hell?!"

As I shoved my leg into the pants they just bounced right off me. Frank's leg was inside them. Apparently he had taken his pants off in the bathroom; I had thrown mine in the hallway and he mistook my pants for his.

Despite a ninety-minute search for our car, the guys got me to work on time, whereupon my boss promptly fired me.

As it turns out, I was supposed to have been working all of the previous day and that morning. I had actually arrived (to get fired) as my day off was officially starting. I told them I had no idea and I think they believed me. But I think they also felt pretty confident about firing a guy with a huge welt on his head.

I was fired so quickly that Frank and Tyson, who drove me there, were still in the parking lot, returning to the car with two coffees as I left the building. "Well," I thought, "at least I won't need to call for a ride home."

"I thought you were working?" Tyson asked, upon seeing me at the car.

"They fired me."

"Why?"

"Why not?" I replied, waving my hands in the air, as though the absurdity of the last twenty-four hours had not hit them.

"You want a coffee?" they asked.

"I need something stronger than a coffee." I got a Dog Pound Beer out of the glove compartment.

We sipped our drinks against Frank's car and, as I pulled my can down, I noticed—for the first time—how peculiar the can was. What initially caught my attention was that it was spelled "Dog Pound" beer, and not—as Browns fans spell it—"Dawg Pound." Then I further noticed that the football uniform on the dog—each can had a dog wearing shoulder-pads and holding a football above a pile of bones—was oddly generic. The dog's uniform did not have, as you would expect, the number of a famous Brown player, like 32 or 19, or even a valid NFL number; rather, it said "DP," as if to avoid any purposeful likeness to a real player. I turned the can over and read the small print that said:"Brewed in Indiana and not affiliated with the NFL or any of its teams."

I began laughing at the top of my lungs.

"What's so funny?" Frank asked.

"This beer had nothing to do with the Browns," I said, "it's a fraud."

"What do you mean?"

"Look at it. It's spelled wrong. The images are purposefully vague."

"So?"

"Yep. We rented a commercial truck to buy two pallets of a beer that, technically speaking, never needed to be boycotted."

"Doesn't that just make us lucky?"

I was holding the beer against my forehead because it made the bruise feel better, outside the store that just fired me.

"I don't know that I feel lucky," I answered. "But," I continued, starting to laugh, "there's something kind of perfect about even the beer being meaningless this weekend."

We sipped on our drinks a bit longer, laughing, until Frank announced, "All right, let's go."

"Hold on, we don't want an open container in the car," I said, pointing to the empty can, "I'll have to throw this out." I hustled to the nearest trashcan I was familiar with, which happened to be inside the Famous Footwear store I'd just been let go from.

One of the sales associates greeted me, a bit confused, saying "Hey, Sean?" After I had been fired, she and I had a brief, but nice, conversation on how much we enjoyed working together, and were disappointed to probably not see too much of each other again.

"Hey, I just need to use your trash can," I explained, showing her the can of Dog Pound Beer.

She gave out a kind of hiss, a loud, judgmental

inhale of air.

"Oh, no," I assured her as I threw the can in the trash bin, "it's not what it looks like."

It was 10 a.m.

"What do you mean?" she asked.

"It's a fraud beer. It's not really sponsored by the Browns."

I turned and began to exit.

"It's some swindler out of Indiana, if you can believe it."

Those were my last words at that store.

Kinney Shoes
Akron, OH

I am colorblind. As handicaps go, it's not burdensome. In fact, the biggest annoyances have nothing to do with colors and more with how people react when learning you are colorblind. Say you are at a party and you've been asked to grab the red bottle but you only see brown bottles. So you share that you are colorblind: The people at the party will react like you just announced you competed in the last Olympics. Some won't believe it; others demand proof; scads of questions are immediately thrown upon you:

"What color is this carpet to you?"

"How do you know what light is on at an intersection?!"

"Can you see the future?"

Several times, a party-goer has approached me and, in all seriousness, announced: "I have bad news. You can't be an astronaut. It's a rule. NASA won't allow colorblind people to steer their shuttles."

On one occasion, someone said this—that I cannot be an astronaut—right after I had shot a champagne cork into my face. As though I could even reach a point in the interview process where NASA is testing my eyesight. I've run out of gas on the highway three times, in major cities; I simply don't look at the gauge. My college won't release my grades until I pay parking tickets. I don't see NASA saying, "Action-wise, we like how this kid manages travel and learning; let's just hope his eyes come in good".

Color blindness is, in most cases, not as dramatic as the public believes. The world is not black-and-white to us. We see colors and pure shades. Things like sky blue or grass green are easy to identify, but mixed, in-between shades are tough to identify: a dark red may appear brown; light greens are difficult to separate from light reds or khaki. The point being: unless you are formally tested for it at school or the doctor's office, you can live a long time—maybe your whole life—without knowing you are colorblind.

I learned I was colorblind the way most people do: Aged fourteen, working at a shoe store.

A group of women entered our store (Kinney Shoes) to collect the shoes and handbags they had specially ordered and customized for their wedding party. "Of course, ma'am," I told the future bride then exited to the back, to fetch her shoes and handbags.

I started working at the store this same week and was mostly hired to dye shoes. My cousin managed the store and my father asked him to hire me. I was a talented artist; nothing prodigious, but a few of my paintings at both grade school and high school advanced to being on display at academic art workshops at the local college. My cousin told my dad that I was not old enough to sell shoes and their stockroom needs were light, but, if I could paint that great, they needed someone to dye shoes.

This wedding party was my first party.

I returned to the counter, placed boxes on the table, and removed a pair of shoes for her to approve the dye job they had requested: a bright pink.

"What the fuck is this?" asked the bride.

"Your party's shoes, ma'am. Five pairs of pumps and five purses, correct?"

"Are you fucking with me?" she demanded.

I looked back, confused.

"Today is not the day to be fucking with me," she asserted.

This is how I learned I was color-blind. When I ruined a bride's wedding shoes, twenty-four hours before the ceremony.

The shoes I had presented were not pink; they were gray. They looked perfectly pink to me but I was later told by my manager that they looked "grayer than my fucking marble counter top!"

To this day, I have many problems with pink and gray, but that moment, I had a bigger issue: this bride's shoes were not the correct color and the two people dealing with the problem were me—a teenager who doesn't know he is colorblind—and her, an anxious bride who thought everyone is trying to fuck with her.

I attempted to defuse the tension by opening the other four shoe boxes, along with the packages containing the purses. Each was equally gray.

"You will notice how consistent everything is," I affirmed to her.

I then took out her swatch. When a wedding party needs shoes dyed to match a dress, they provide a swatch of the material to the store to use as a reference. I put the bright pink scrap of fabric on top of the gray pumps and confidently declared: "You will notice how perfect the match is."

At that point, the bride became so angry she had to walk away.

The assistant manager of the store walked to the counter and calmly asked, "Sean, do those shoes look pink to you?"

"Yeah, of course. They don't to you?"

The bride walked back: "Bro! That shoe is grayer than a fucking *dolphin!*"

At this point, my manager (also my cousin) heard what was going on. He walked over and looked at the shoes.

"This looks pink to you?" he asked.

"Isn't it?" I answered.

Initially he looked confused, staring at several hundred dollars of now-worthless, grey inventory. Then it hit him:

"Oh, FUCK! He can't see colors!!" He hired me expressly for my artistic ability and I was asked to dye three other wedding parties that morning.

"What do you mean?" asked the bride.

"It means, we're screwed!" he yelled as he ran back to the stockroom to see how badly I had dyed the other shoes for all the other wedding parties.

The following week, I asked the school nurse if I could be tested for colorblindness. The nurse administered what they call the Ishihara Test, where you are asked to identify numbers within circles of many-colored dots. As a man who has flunked thousands of tests (failing an eye test is no different than failing a history exam) you know it's not going well as you are taking it.

The nurse would ask: "What number do you see inside the circle?"

"There's a number in there?"

"Whoa, so you don't see anything?"

After the final page in the test, the nurse consulted a chart and summated:

"You are color-blind. Red/green to be exact. Normally, this is where I tell the student they can't be an astronaut but, well Mr. Flannery, I'm assuming you don't see yourself in outer space, given your grades."

Over the years, I have been fired from multiple jobs due to my color blindness; which I consider to be unfair and a potential violation of the American With Disabilities Act. Of course, my previous employers might counter that my only real disability is that I was a jackass; the mix-ups on color merely served as reminders that they had been meaning to fire me.

I worked at a restaurant in college that required us to wear a white shirt with black pants. My manager hated me; I constantly arrived late, joked around, bungled orders and, in addition to those frustrations, owned so few white shirts that I frequently had to substitute a light blue or pale beige one.

One day, on which I was late, mis-entered several orders, and broke a chair laughing with other employees—all while wearing a blue shirt—my manager laid down the law: "If you come in next shift either late or without a white shirt, don't even bother clocking in because you don't have a job."

I drove to an Old Navy that night to get white dress shirts and, fortuitously, they were on sale for the incredible price of $2 a shirt. I bought every large in stock: fifteen shirts. The next day, I was late again by about twenty minutes, but I hoped my crisp white shirt might be enough to quell my boss's anger. I entered, said "Hi" to the hostess as I passed down the main hall, at which point I noticed my manager staring at me hotly. I raised my arms defensively,

"I know I'm late! I know I'm late. But"—I pointed at my shirt—"this ought to make you happy."

What I didn't know is that the reason Old Navy had these dress shirts on sale for only $2 is that they were all hot pink. I was wearing a shirt that looked white to me but to everyone else looked like something a bullfighter would wear. Which means, not only was I arriving late again, but my manager believed I purposefully dressed myself in a flamingo blouse purely to taunt him.

The most recent time I was fired for color blindness, my boss felt even more disrespected. I was working for a consulting company who flew me out to Dallas each week to develop software for a telecommunications firm. I drank with coworkers until last call on most nights and, when I am hungover or sleep-deprived, I get these large, dark bags around my eyes. Because of how pale I am, it can sometimes be confused for a black eye. This was one of many things that my manager hated about me: That

I would go before clients, who were paying a lot of money for what they thought were the best software developers in America, looking like I had lost a bar fight about three hours earlier.

One morning, after I had strolled in late, he confronted me:

"Sean, if you come in tomorrow with those damn black eyes, it will be your last day. We are meeting with their head of new business and I can't have you looking like you just arrived from the emergency room."

I think he expected me to acquiesce, but, back then, I never missed an opportunity to disagree with management.

"Legally," I responded, "you cannot fire me because my eye sockets are flawed."

"Damnit, I know you look like shit because you're out drinking every night. I approve the damn expense receipts each morning, so I see what you are doing. Don't act like you have some facial deformity for Christ's sake!"

I doubled down: "The way I behave—what I do outside of company time—it's part culture, part religion, and all my choice."

I walked away, leaving him to chew on that rather confusing evasion.

About two hours later my manager approached me.

"I think I have a solution," he began, apprehensively. I'm not positive who he consulted to help devise this proposal—a woman in Human Resources; his wife; a mob fixer; somebody—but he continued: "I don't want you to have black eyes, but you want to stay out all night, correct?"

"Correct."

"Well, what do you think of makeup?"

"What do you mean?"

"Makeup can hide a black eye. What if you buy makeup for tomorrow's meeting? I'll let you expense it."

"I think that's a fair request."

We shook hands, feeling this was a great business compromise and perhaps the start of a new, more-agreeable relationship between us.

The next morning, I arrived late and barged straight into this important meeting. Per request, I had used make-up to cover my dark, sunken eye sockets. Make-up that was bright green, but which I thought matched my skin-tone perfectly. As my coworker would put it later: "You looked like Ziggy Stardust-era David Bowie opening the wrong office door."

I sat down and introduced myself, having no idea that I have two giant, green ovals around my eyes. I then turn to my manager, delivered a big grin, and proudly pointed to my face.

I was fired.

I once read that colorblindness occurs at such a high rate—almost one in ten males—that it most likely had some evolutionary benefit. The theory is that tribes with a few colorblind members hunted better since those people, the colorblind people, could identify quarry that appeared camouflaged to everyone else. There is even some modern evidence of this effect: During World War Two, the Allies specifically stationed colorblind soldiers amongst their spotters because the colorblind guards often detected threats that appeared hidden to people with normal vision.

Maybe my people—color-blind jackasses—peaked in the Stone Age. We could wake up late, hungover on fermented prunes, roll out of our burrow, spot some grouse that's hiding in a tree that no one else can see, point it out and let the athletes of the tribe go kill it, then return to bed, a hero.

Which is why, when someone at a party announces that I am colorblind and people begin telling me that I cannot be an astronaut, I now respond:

"Well, you better hope we don't have to *hunt* up there, amigo."

Pat Joyce's Tavern
Cleveland, OH

Growing up, if St Patrick's Day fell on a weekday, my dad would pull us out of school to go watch the parade. More correctly, he would pull us out of school angrily, since he was forever livid that our Catholic school did not declare it a holiday.

"What do the Irish have to do to get a holiday?" he would ask.

Almost all of my dad's arguments contradicted themselves but my favorite was his assertion that the Irish still faced intense discrimination despite the fact that (according to him) we had invented almost everything you use on a daily basis:

"The battery? Ever use one of those, hmm? Well the Irish invented that. Amazing when you consider we weren't allowed to have jobs until ten years ago. How about TV? You guys ever watch TV?"

"I thought the first television was invented in Scotland, dad," I chimed in. Challenging one of his claims was fun because he always fell back on the same defense:

"Oh yeah? Well, ever heard of the *English language*? I doubt they could have invented it in Scotland if the Irish hadn't saved the entire English language in the Middle Ages!"

Both my parents were incredibly proud to be the son and daughter of Irish immigrants. And the stories my grandparents, great uncles and aunts told about immigrating from Ireland were amazing:

"It was 1908 and we had a bad harvest on the farm in Cork, so my pa says: 'You're going on a ship to America because we can't feed you. You'll land in New York, then you must get on a train to Cleveland where you have an uncle living as a roofer.'"

"'How will I know when I've reached Cleveland?' I asked. And my pa says, 'The conductor will announce it. Plus, your uncle Timmy says it smells like it's on fire.' I was ten years old."

I used to wonder why old people were so serious, then I learned: Half of them escaped starvation by entering and navigating a foreign country by themselves at age ten. I'm not sure I had used a public restroom by myself at that age.

When I was growing up in Cleveland, it seemed like each person was but a generation or two removed from immigrating to America; and they all believed that

a) Their ancestral country was responsible for most major inventions and works of art.

b) Thank God they didn't come from whatever country dominated the next neighborhood over because they did everything 'wrong' over there.

Better yet, was how closely these complaints matched their own behavior: "Heaven help us, if we lived along 25th Street next to those Germans, Sean! They're crazy!" my uncles would lament. "All they do is drink beer! All day long!" and then, without irony, my uncles would open their fourth bottle of whiskey for the day.

But, having complained about a neighboring race, they would always—perhaps out of fear of appearing racist before their nieces and nephews—follow that criticism with what they thought was a compliment:

"I will say *this* for those Germans, though: As drunk as they get, I've never seen them make a mistake measuring a porch. You need a roof put up, a floor re-planked? You call some Germans! Doesn't matter how much beer they've put-back, they will fix whatever you need fast and it will last a lifetime."

c) They each believed that the best day of the year was whatever religious holiday they had converted into a drinking party since immigrating to America. The Irish had St. Patrick's Day, which is known nationally, but in Cleveland each month saw a different party being thrown by a different immigrant group for hilarious, lesser-known holidays.

There was Oktoberfest of course, and The Feast of The Assumption, when Italians celebrated the miracle of Mary, mother of God, being summoned to heaven so her body would not perish on earth. Yes, Catholics believe that Mary was tractor-beamed into the sky like Captain Kirk, right in the middle of lunch. They celebrate that perfectly normal moment by covering Little Italy in beer tents and carnival rides so unsafe they could slingshot the believers into the clouds to meet the Madonna in time for some heavenly tiramisu.

Weirder and more debauched was Dyngus Day, a Polish holiday the Monday after Easter where everyone gets drunk and the boys throw water on girls and spank them with pussy willows. The girls respond by throwing dishes. That was a true holiday in Cleveland, Ohio: a giant wet tee-shirt contest that ends in dueling acts of domestic violence. As though the city wanted to prepare an entire generation to be arrested as a couple on an episode of "COPS."

But the biggest of these holidays was always St. Patrick's Day. Each year, we attended mass in the morning, then dropped my sister off at the start of the parade route, as her Irish dancing school always marched in the procession. We would then hurry over to St. John's Cathedral and watch the festivities from the top of the cathedral steps. The cathedral was next to where the judges sat, so all the participants would do their best routine when they got in front of it. We would cheer loudest for my sister's Irish dancing company, then as soon as they passed my mom would turn around and say, "OK we have to go pick up your sister before we go to the pub, to Pat Joyce's," which is when she would realize: we had lost at least two of my brothers.

I was the eldest of six kids and my impression of the 1980s was that if you entered any event that erected temporary fencing, you were losing half your kids at that event. Have you seen nature documentaries where the mother bobcat knows her kittens are old enough to hunt for themselves and be independent so she roams farther and farther and tries to lose them? That's how parents in the '80s walked with their kids. Parents would walk at top speed, trying to find an open picnic table for lunch and, after spotting one, they would turn to announce that we have to hurry even faster to claim that table before anyone else and, in that instant, realize that were only talking to half their kids.

"Where the hell is Kevin?" my mom asked.

A mom turning to notice a missing kid has a timeless dynamic because she always asks her husband for an insight and, if he's anything like my dad, he confidently and reassuringly says, "He's right here," and points, without looking, to an area behind him that contains nothing but blank, humanless concrete.

"Shit, he's lost!" my mom yelled after dad predictably gestured to an empty stretch of sidewalk.

"Where did we lose him?" she asked us and we all shrugged. Actually, all except for my other sister—still a toddler—who was able to state the exact place Kevin wandered off.

"Why didn't you say anything?" my dad asked.

"I did," she answered. "I said 'Kevin is leaving us' and you told me to quit complaining."

My dad was so inured to his kids asking "Are we there yet?" that he learned to globally ignore us while commuting, to the point where we could say, "Dad, our brother just disappeared into a crowd of strangers", and he would automatically respond, "I already told you, we will be there in ten minutes!"

Today, you can give a child an electronic device while traveling and, if the battery lasts long enough, you could drive them to Mount Rushmore without hearing a complaint. In fact, you could drive the wrong kids to Mount Rushmore without a complaint.

I often wonder what we would need to pass on the highway, for my kids to stop watching their device and look out the window instead. I know it's not a mountain or an ocean or even a flying bald eagle. We would have to see something that, if we were filming, would change history. Something like a mountain collapsing or bigfoot running alongside the vehicle.

"He can't be far," my dad assured my mom. This is, without exception, the first response by a father after he's lost a kid and it's always hilarious because it wholly contradicts every experience you've had of that kid. A momentarily unobserved child will bolt like a prisoner who's just heard the guards are out of ammo. A kid is always further away than you realize; it's practically a scientific constant, like the speed of light. If you lose focus on a kid for more than four seconds, they will somehow cover more terrain in that time than a wildcat could.

Kids love to run; it's the only speed they know. My wife and I sleep in the downstairs bedroom, and we are never alerted to the fact the kids are up by a few random pitter-patters in the morning. No, they have a biological need to run everywhere and from the moment they rise it sounds like a field hockey game is being conducted on mahogany mere feet above our heads. You know how kids run when they are trying-on new shoes? Sprinting and zigzagging, asking if you have ever seen someone move so fast? That's how my kids get a glass of milk.

"You stay here, I'll go back," my dad proposed. He took me and my two, non-missing brothers to go look for Kevin. We descended the steps, turned the corner and, within a block or two, realized we were outside of Pat Joyce's Tavern, which all of us knew to be the second destination.

"He might have gone in there!" my dad suggested and escorted us inside. We walked inside and saw what is, to this day, one of the most arresting visuals I have encountered. Kevin was seated at a table with my dad's boss. At the time, my dad worked for Catholic Charities and reported directly to His Holiness, The Bishop of Cleveland. So, yes, my brother was at a seat next to a Bishop who was wearing a giant white miter, like Kevin had pulled Excalibur out of a stone near the Cuyahoga River and was now the Child King of Cleveland, assembling his court and Royal Advisors at Pat Joyce's Tavern.

My dad and the bishop both start guffawing upon seeing each other. This was a pretty standard greeting for my dad. Whenever he 'found' friends at a public event, they were usually holding one of his lost kids, laughing hysterically. They would hold up the errant child and say, "Lose something?" and laugh uproariously.

We had lunch at Pat Joyce's and then drove home. Somewhere well before the midpoint of our thirty minute drive—but far enough into the drive for it to be a hassle—we realized my other brother, Brendan, was not in the car. He was still at Pat Joyce's Tavern, playing with our cousins.

"Damnit," my dad cursed, as he turned his blinker on to signal a U-turn. We were returning to Pat Joyce's to recover the second lost Flannery of the day.

The van was silent, except for the sound of the blinker and my dad muttering, "these kids, these kids" over and over.

"Well, maybe he'll be sitting next to the pope," my mom joked as we started back towards downtown.

The Gas Lamp Inn & Saloon
Cincinnati, Ohio

I don't think I have a friend who hasn't almost killed me by accident at some point. I sometimes think male friendships are closer to a coordinated stunt-show than a real interpersonal relationship. When I announced to my then-fiancée which male friends of mine would be standing next to me as groomsmen at our wedding, she reflected on all the stories she had heard about each one and asked, "Hasn't each of these people tried to kill you?"

"I wouldn't say they were *trying*," I assured her, "rather they reached a place in the evening where miscalculations happened."

"I see," she replied, "but, as a comparison, none of my bridesmaids caused an explosion that burned all the hair off my face."

She was, of course, referring to my buddy Jeff who had once nearly killed me in what I've chosen to call a pyrotechnicality. But I don't blame him. It wasn't his fault. We were day drinking.

It was in Cincinnati. We had been on a bender for a few days. After waking late one morning, Jeff led us to a new bar, in a new neighborhood.

"This is a good, proper bar," Jeff told me while opening the door. We quickly and happily began drinking.

Around 2 p.m.—with the sun still beaming outside—Jeff asked if I wanted to get food.

"Not quite yet," I answered. I am philosophically opposed to leaving dive bars in the afternoon, as I think both Nature and The Almighty want you to remain inside that bar until all the normal people—the folks traveling as part of commerce—go home. That's why God blinds you with sunlight if you leave too early.

"But!" I told Jeff, "don't let me go too long without food! This night could get ugly if we don't eat."

My next memory was the bartender slapping me awake while screaming, "IT'S LAST CALL! The both of you have to leave!"

I looked around.

Jeff was under the dartboard, dancing. We were the only two people in the bar.

I apologized and asked to close my tab.

"Where are we?" I asked Jeff.

"Same bar, my man," he answered, while trying to do the splits.

The bill came: $40.

"I love this fucking state!"

The bartender looked at me, mystified.

I explained that I was from Ohio originally but had been in Chicago for a couple of years and that if my friend and I were to get equally drunk in Chicago, the tab would be ten times the amount.

However, I later learned from credit card statements that the bill I was celebrating as such a cheap triumph was actually the fourth tab I had opened and closed at that bar that day. Every time a new bartender clocked in, I settled my tab with the previous server, and, thinking that was my only bill for the day, would start telling everyone how affordable Ohio was, and buy a(nother) round for the house. I was spending money like an amnesiac lottery winner and didn't realize it until the following month when my credit card statement informed me that I had emptied my checking account into a dive bar along the Ohio River.

Back then, reading my credit statements was like listening to the tapes from the black box recorder on a crashed airplane: however horrific, they were the only way to discover what really happened. Sometimes the amounts seemed impossible, given how cheap the bars and cities were: "$350 at RUMORS in Cedar Rapids, Iowa? Did I get drunk and purchase one of their ovens?"

Jeff and I stumbled out of the bar, and the fullness of how much time had elapsed hit us: it was now pitch black. The streets—bustling with activity when we entered—were now empty. The wind was howling around the corners, and, most noticeably, a wholly new shift of animals was working and caroling: a full chorus of owls and crickets and tree frogs where once was just the odd yelp from a bored dog.

We meandered away from the bar and turned a corner, whereupon we were stopped by the most arresting sight: an amber orb glowing brightly but a foot or two above our heads. It was beautiful, imbued with a strange, hypnotic-gravity, as if it were speaking to us from some ancient and ethereal plain.

"That streetlamp," I said to Jeff, "it's gorgeous.

We should take it home."

"How?" he asked.

"I think if you get on my shoulders, we can unscrew it."

"Okay, but what would we do with it?"

"Easy," I replied, "we turn it into a chandelier!"

Some people, when they become drunk, think they are sexy; others believe they are good at fighting; still others think they have somehow become incredibly witty, but my preferred delusion when inebriated is something that will get you in far more trouble: I think I am *handy*. I will carry home loose bits of abandoned wood believing I can turn them into a coffee table. I will begin projects that I would never consider sober, such as replacing the fuse in the dishwasher. And, on this night, I believed that I could convert a public street lamp into a chandelier, despite zero experience in either glass-working or electricity.

Unquestioning, Jeff clambered on to me, balanced himself against the light's pole, and readied to unscrew the bulb.

He began twisting the glass to take it off, but paused after just a few revolutions, saying, "This glass is HOT."

"These are old light bulbs," I answered back, "we can't expect them to be energy efficient."

Which was an incorrect characterization as to why the orb was hot; an error likely caused by the fourteen hours of drinking. See, we were not merely unscrewing some ordinary lightbulb; we were removing the top of a gas street lamp. Some

Dive Into Science:
Beer Goggles

Since the beginning of time humans have noticed, that alcohol, very often, leads to more sex. Ovid wrote, "Wine prepares the heart for love... unless you take too much," making it, at around 10 B.C.E., one of the earliest references to both beer goggles and whiskey dick.

Multiple studies have shown that people are usually more sexually active after drinking than when not drinking; and hooking up with a stranger is particularly correlated to drinking. And we are not the only species for which this is true: fruit flies that drink fermented fruit have more babies than fruit flies that do not imbibe alcohol. But what science has been less clear on is "beer goggles"; the idea that a person becomes more physically attractive as you drink.

Studies on beer goggles are somewhat conflicting, but the general picture seems to be, no, there is no such thing as beer goggles. That does not mean you will always wake up the next day proud and happy about who you chose to couple-up with: it just means that, when you made that decision the previous night, your eyes were not seeing them any differently then you are in the morning.

Several early studies on beer goggles asked

drinkers and non-drinkers at a bar to rate the attractiveness of other customers, and researchers found that the drinkers rated people more attractive than the non-drinkers, which they took as an indication that beer goggles might exist. But follow up studies—early in the morning and outside of bars—on the same group found that drinkers always rated people more highly, even when sober. The implication being: drunks see more *beauty* in the world.

Besides seeing more beauty in others, drunks also (and more importantly) see more charm in themselves. Many studies have shown that people are more confident about their own looks after two drinks. Most interestingly though, that confidence you have after two drinks—when you are bold but haven't had enough drinks to trip down a flight of stairs yet—is actually more in line with how other people rate you. That is to say: when you get a little buzzed and start feeling sexy and noticing how good you look, that image you are celebrating is how the world normally views you.

Plus, beer goggles seem impossible at a physiological level. Your senses dull with drinking, but eyesight is near the last to go so the idea that you can be so drunk you see the world incorrectly, yet can still form words and understand sentences—both higher-level tasks—is unlikely.

> We know that alcohol principally affects the inhibition center of the brain, which causes us to do things when drunk that our sober mind would reject as a plan. Which further suggests that what we call "beer goggles" may just be our attraction to a person that the higher level of the brain would normally reject. Which brings me to my final point on beer goggles: I do not like the term. "Beer Goggles" is an ugly phrase, the greatest sham "respectable" society duped us into believing: that the people we meet and enjoy when drunk are not the people we should be fraternizing with when sober.
>
> For these reasons, I have dropped the phrase "beer goggles" from personal usage and, instead, say "I turned on the old brew-noculars" to better suggest I am seeing people more accurately and choosing more attractive people when drunk.

Jeff was still struggling to free the unwieldy glass globe from its fixture, wincing from the pain of the hot surface.

"Lick your fingers!" I yelled up at him.

"What?"

"It will insulate you a bit from the heat!"

Jeff licked his fingers, turned the globe a bit, then licked again, turned again, and so on.

Eventually we heard a distinct *pop*.

It was at this point I think we realized that what

we had here was a gas streetlamp: the instant the bulb came off, wind and oxygen rushed in, and turned what had been a small flame into a giant ball of fire that exploded toward Jeff, instantly singeing his eyebrows clean off. He dropped from my shoulders as the flame leapt out above, igniting the leaves of a nearby tree.

We reacted the way any reasonable people would after discovering that they have ruined a street safety device and possibly caused a fire; we ran for a taxi.

There was a cab sitting at the end of the block, outside a different bar. I hurried Jeff and I over to it, opened the back door, threw Jeff in and screamed, "GO!"

This is one of the moments that you see all the time in old movies that does not work in real life, but you don't realize it doesn't work until you have the audacity to try it. In movies, the hero jumps into a taxi and barks "Go!" or "Follow the red car!" and the cabbie dutifully puts the car in drive, hits the gas, and says something like, "No problem, Mac. Who we following?"

But this is how it works in real life:

"Go!" I yelled again.

"Where to?" the cabbie asked, confused.

"Just go!"

"I need an address!"

"This town is toast, amigo! We need to ROOOLLLL!!!"

The cabbie reached down into the glove compartment and pulled out a can of Mace.

"Address or get out of my cab!"

"Art Museum!!"

And with that, we were on our way to the Cincinnati Art Museum. At 3 a.m.

Whenever I visit a new city, I like to see their art museum, their zoo, and dive bars. I had not yet seen the art museum so, when an exact destination was demanded, that popped into my head.

After a few stoplights, we merged onto a highway.

"Ya know," Jeff piped up as we climbed the on-ramp, "Cincinnati has a really gorgeous art museum." He had no eyebrows and appeared sunburnt.

"Jeff, I don't think they're gonna be open."

Jeff put his hand through his hair and a bundle of charred, curly stubs fell upon the back seat of the cab.

"What the hell *was* that thing?" I fumed, after seeing how much of Jeff's scalp had burnt off, "I mean, it's the 21st century! You can't be surprising people with gas street lamps! Those are death traps! This town needs to put some warnings on those things!"

I was very much trying to make the case that we were the victims in this incident.

"We probably have grounds to sue this city," Jeff concurred.

"It's a real case!" I agreed, "I'm definitely going to sue that bar for not warning us!" As I railed against the perceived injustice, we were deposited outside a lightless art museum.

Weeks later, when I received the credit card statement and realized I had closed six tabs that day, I also learned the name of the bar that I intended to sue for not warning me about the possibility of life-threatening illuminations: The Gaslamp Inn & Saloon.

I spent fourteen hours inside a bar named after the gas streetlamps around us, yet still felt there was no realistic "warning."

Hemingway once told a friend, "Always do sober what you said you would do drunk; that will teach you to keep your mouth shut." Of all my drunk plans that were never carried out sober, suing the city of Cincinnati for not warning me of gas streetlamps is the one I regret most, as the trial would have been a great demonstration of how many facts you can miss when drinking. Realistically, the process of just finding a lawyer willing to take-on our case would probably be enough to make us rethink day drinking again:

"You want me to sue the city of Cincinnati because you guys were able to unscrew a gas bulb that was ten feet high and had a clear, burning flame inside it? And you did this after spending twelve hours in a bar named after these gas lamps?"

"I wouldn't word it exactly that way, but, yes."

The next day we woke up, Jeff missing his eyebrows and much of his hair, and me with no money; not only from the drinking but taxi rides to and from the Art Museum. Seeing all this, I offered a summation of the previous evening:

"I think last night might have been a milestone."

"How so?" Jeff asked.

"I think it's the first time two people caused more damage to the neighborhood by walking home drunk, rather than driving home drunk."

"Driving would have been a bad idea," Jeff replied.

"Agreed. But I'm not sure walking was a 'great' idea, either. We nearly started a bush fire in Cincinnati!"

"Okay," Jeff conceded, "what should our plan be for tonight?"

"Easy!" I answered. I begin all my bad plans with, "Easy!"

I continued: "We walk to the bar, right? Responsibly. But when we get there, we tell them we drove. We even show keys! Then when we get super drunk, they'll say: 'Hey fellas, let us call you a cab home; you can pick up the car tomorrow.' They'll even pay for it!"

"It's bulletproof!" Jeff agreed.

That night, we walked to a bar ten blocks from Jeff's house, got hammered, claimed that we had driven there and, as planned, the bar ordered us a cab upon seeing how drunk we were, and even agreed to and pay for it

"Isn't it beautiful when a plan comes together?" I nudged Jeff as we entered the cab.

We made it one turn in the cab before Jeff puked all over the back seat. The driver told us we owed him $200 or he and his cousin would break our arms.

It took us a while to get the payment together; in the end we offered him all that we could muster: $150. He agreed but not without griping, "You shouldn't even be in my cab! Why the hell do you need a ride for a few blocks?"

"We're working on a system," I answered calmly. There was a pause, and I added, "It's not going well."

The Day the Music Died:
When Puking in a Taxi Became Illegal

In 2009, Chicago taxi drivers asked the city to approve a 22 percent increase in passenger fares to offset higher fuel costs. Mayor Daley quickly vetoed the proposal, stating that the economy was still recovering from the housing crisis and Chicagoans could not afford higher taxi fares. But as a compromise, Daley offered to green light the taxi industry's separate request for a $50 fee when a passenger vomits in the cab.

Only. In. Chicago.

Only in Chicago could a major transportation industry ask for a 22 percent overall raise in revenue and, because of how drunk everyone is, the mayor counters with, "Don't you think you'd make as much money in vomit fees?"

The fee was approved, making Chicago the first city in the U.S. to institute a fee for puking in a cab. Upon its passage, Chicago newspapers reached out to civic leaders in other big cities, asking if they had a comparable fee. My favorite response is Boston's:

"No, we do not have a puking fee. To my knowledge it's free to puke in a cab." –Boston Police spokesman Joe Zanoli.

Only in Boston—the one city that is perhaps crazier than Chicago—would the lead police spokesman talk about puking in cabs like it's walking in a nature preserve: "Free, as far as I know!" As though you'd be a fool to not take advantage of that great, local price.

This is one of the reasons why I love Chicago: we trail blaze in workers' rights. Chicago created unions, the five day work week, and the right not to have a Grand Slam Breakfast spewed at you while you drive a 1.5-ton vehicle.

Comp USA
Fairlawn, OH

"Why did you get fired this time?" my dad asked after seeing that I was not dressed for work.

"Dad, hand to God," I replied, "I was fired for having too big of a vocabulary."

"Sean, if that's the full story, then I'm Saint Peter, walking the Earth."

I have always maintained that that *was* the full story, but the manager who fired me probably tells it differently.

And perhaps I was focused on the vocabulary issue to soften my dad's frustration. My dad has the largest vocabulary of anyone I know and he had recently come to notice that, for a kid in high school (as I was at the time of this story), my own vocabulary was growing impressively. He enjoyed quizzing me on words and etymologies, probably because—given how terrible my grades were and how often I was fired from jobs—phraseology was one of the few topics where he could have a conversation with me and walk away with the impression that I might be employable one day.

My dad started to notice my vocabulary during a disagreement we'd had about the SAT. He wanted me to prepare diligently for the test.

I told him: "You either know it or you don't. Nothing can change it."

"Sean," he countered, "those questions; they might *seem* impossible, but with training you can break down the etymology and structures. Maybe guess a few right. For instance, they showed me words I had never seen before or since. Try this one on for size, Sean. What's a 'fetlock'?"

"Going down from the hip, it's the second joint on the leg of a horse," I answered.

"*What?*"

My dad was amazed I had answered that question correctly. He couldn't believe I might test better than him—it was the only question he got wrong on the verbal portion—and he was therefore annoyed by the possibility that I might know more words than him.

He never pestered me about the SAT again.

I didn't have the heart to tell him that the reason I knew that word was because I regularly skipped high school to bet on horses and 'fetlock' featured frequently on injury reports.

When I did eventually take the SAT—or at least, when I was supposed to—I was out of my mind with a hangover, walked into the wrong room by mistake, and took a citizenship test instead. To this day, I have no SAT score and, if I'm being honest, I don't think my vocabulary grew much after high school. I can diagram the hell out of a horse, though.

Maybe my vocabulary stopped growing after high school because I lost a job due to the size of it, and I realized the world hates a person that sounds too elitist. But, again, that's according to *my* version of the story as opposed to my manager's. He probably says he fired me because I was a terrible employee.

At the time, I worked at a CompUSA and I entered the store one day to find another employee, Randy, speaking with a frustrated customer in the cable aisle. The customer needed a cable to connect his monitor to a computer, but inadvertently purchased the wrong cable (a cable extension rather than a replacement). Randy was trying to explain the difference, but the customer kept insisting that both cables were the same:

"No sir, you bought *this* cable," Randy explained while holding the extension-cable in the air. "This cable makes the *other* cable reach farther. But you still need the other cable for it to work."

"But they look the same."

"No, see, the pins are different." Randy rotated both cables around to show the clearly different configurations: that the extension cable was male-to-female while the replacement cable was male-to-male.

"No, you're not understanding it, kid! I need a totally different kind of cable!" the customer insisted.

At this point Randy noticed me and exclaimed, "Oh, there's Sean! He's our cable expert; perhaps he can explain it better than me."

At each computer store I worked at there was a tradition whereby employees tried to pass stupid customers on to the next team member in a funny or creative way; a kind of "idiot hot potato." Whenever you heard another employee identify you as an expert on a topic you knew nothing about, you knew they were trying to unload a moron.

Occasionally though, an employee would dump their idiot in such a *creative* way that you didn't realize what was happening until it was too late. Once a boss paged me over the loudspeakers by announcing:

"Sean Flannery to customer service. We have a gentleman with an I-D-TEN-T error."

It wasn't until later I realized that "I-D-TEN-T" spells out "IDIOT" when written down.

Other times someone might say: "Sean, would you come over here? I'm dealing with a really fascinating PMAC error," which you would later learn stands for "Problem exists between Monitor And Computer," that the user is the problem. But on this particular day at CompUSA, I was summoned over via the most common method: being introduced as a subject-matter expert. This was a popular maneuver mainly because it worked like a charm; a moron always believes they are correct and is waiting for an expert to join the conversation so that someone else is operating at their rarefied level.

"Thank God!" the customer said to me after Randy flagged me down. "This idiot has been trying to get me to repurchase the same bad cable for the last twenty minutes!"

Randy smiled, with that wide, sinister grin people have when they know their terrible problem is now someone else's, kind of like a guy who's just sold a haunted house. Randy exited backwards, waving to me and laughing impishly.

"OK, sir," I said, "you need a cable to connect your new monitor with your computer, right? And you bought this cable that doesn't work, right?"

"Yes!" he cried with relief.

"It's the terminators, sir," I explained politely. "This one has the two ends you need, see? Same ends on both sides. Look at that, versus the one you got?"

I showed him the cables. The correct cable had fifteen pins sticking out of a trapezoidal port on each end. The incorrect cable, that he bought, had fifteen pins on one end, and fifteen *holes* on the other, not pins, so it can't be inserted into the computer; only connected to another cable with the corresponding pins. It even said *"EXTENSION CABLE"* in capital letters on the packaging.

"Damn it you don't get it either?" he sighed. "I need a different *kind* of cable."

I pressed on. I was an "expert" after all.

"Sir, it's just the terminators. It's a common mistake; they are very similar, and you purchased the incorrect one. You need a male-male cable. Not female-male."

"What the hell are you talking about?"

"Male-male." I showed him the cable with the pins sticking out on both sides.

"I don't know all your computer terms!" he snapped, exasperated.

"OK, no problem sir," I continued, trying a different tack, "how about this: I want you to *not* think of this as a computer problem, and, instead, let us just do word association."

I showed him the replacement cable with pins on each side again, "See how each end of this cable has pins that are EEE-*RECT*? That's a MAAALE, sir."

At this point I was speaking to him so loudly, and with such condescension—the way a jerk might teach English to a classroom full of non-English speakers—that a small crowd had gathered, including my manager, who, it should be noted, had been looking for an excuse to fire me for a few days.

"Now I want you to look at the end of this cable sir," I said, showing him the female end of the extension cable he had purchased. "Notice how the holes are *ENVAGINATED*? That's a FEEEEMALE, sir."

I don't know how the man reacted to that explanation because before I could register his expression my manager grabbed me and pushed me through the door of a nearby office, while yelling something about having another employee fix the problem. My manager followed me into the office and slammed the door behind him.

"That's it!" he growled. "I can finally fire you *with cause!*"

'With Cause' was a phrase I heard a lot when being fired and I always found it hilarious. Of course the firing has a cause. Even illegal firings technically have a cause, like: "Well, I am a racist and he is black," or: "I am a creep-ball and she will not sleep with me."

I started smiling at the idea of a causeless firing—a firing born of pure chaos—and what that might be. Maybe a carpet beetle that lives in our store controls my manager's thoughts and body and has decided to fire the first employee it sees. That seemed pretty causeless: "A solid case" as lawyers say, and I smiled wider.

"No," I thought, "that still technically has a cause: the angry beetle."

Oblivious to my inner monologue about the staffing practices of insects, my manager continued:

"You *cannot* talk to a customer that way! Not only was it condescending; not only did it have borderline, sexual connotations but, also…'*ENVAGINATED*'? That's not even a word!"

It should be added, he was doing violent air quotes as he said "envaginated."

Internally, I knew my manager had every right to fire me and I was also beginning to think I might have made-up "envaginated," but I also felt: I should leave this job the way I worked it- by arguing with my boss.

"Oh no," I countered, "'envaginated' is most *certainly* a word. It's used rather commonly in engineering documents."

We began to argue for several minutes about the correctness of 'envaginated' and, somehow, I was able to convince him that, under Ohio employment laws, he could not fire me if we determined that 'envaginated' was a real word. Because in that case, the firing becomes "causeless" (which is another word I had just started using).

"Fine! Should be easy enough to prove!" he yelled, and picked up the office phone. "Warehouse? Warehouse, I want you to walk over to customer service, take fifty dollars out of petty cash, and go to Borders and buy me a dictionary! Yes. A fucking *dictionary!*"

Now, I knew for a fact that every time petty cash was used, a detailed expense report had to be completed and sent to corporate headquarters to justify the expenditure. Even as I was being fired, I always wondered how they would justify this; why a computer store in the mid-1990s needed to spend fifty dollars on a dictionary. And further, I knew those expense reports, physically, had very little room for someone to write in the explanation, and *this* situation was too complex to sum up concisely. And you certainly wouldn't dare include the word "envaginated" in official documents. So I hoped that the only reason cited for laying out fifty bucks to buy a dictionary would be, simply: "FIRE EMPLOYEE!"

A few minutes later (there was a Borders in the same plaza as our store) an employee from the warehouse appeared with a dictionary and gave it to my manager. My manager handed the dictionary to me and, smiling like someone holding a straight flush, commanded: "OK, let's see you find it."

I opened the dictionary to "vagina." My reasoning was: If this *is* a word, it will be a part of speech listed next to the body part. But no such luck; it wasn't listed.

"It's not there, is it Sean?" my manager asked.

"This dictionary may not have it," I offered weakly, which is the only time that sentence has been stated outside of a game of Scrabble.

"It was the most expensive dictionary they had," the employee who purchased it added. That's going to look even better for the expense report, I thought.

"Hold on," I interjected, "maybe it has become its own, stand-alone word? You know, due to how *incredibly common* it has become? Like 'dishearten'?"

I flipped the pages, desperately, to "E" to see if "envaginated" was indeed its own word:

"**env.** envelope
envapor (en vā' pər), *v.t.* to surround with vapor.
enveil (en vāl'), *v.t.* to cover with a veil; place a veil upon."

It wasn't there.

"I'll walk you to the breakroom, Sean," said my manager, trying to conclude the meeting. "You can collect any personal effects."

"Wait!" I yelled, suddenly remembering just how terrible my instincts for spelling were. Maybe, I thought, just *maybe*—the word in question actually starts with an "I." I re-opened the dictionary, flipped the pages to that section and finally there I saw, defined in big, bold print:

"**invaginate** (in vaj'a nāt), v. **-nated, -nating,** *adj.* —*v.t.* **1** to fold or draw (a hollow structure) back within itself; introvert; intussuscept. **2** = sheathe."

I turned the dictionary around to face my manager, pointed to the word, and stood confidently, saying: "Well, if you'll excuse me, looks like I have a sales record to go set."

I left the room, my final remark all the more confident considering I did not work on the sales floor and had yet to make a sale.

I was fired two days later for being late.

"So you were fired for your vocabulary, Sean?" my dad confirmed again, with no small amount of doubt in his voice.

"Yeah. Well, I suppose, if we were to get into the"— here I winked, to indicate I was about to slip into begin fancy talk—"*'frippery'* of it, Dad, I think it was more that management found my vocabulary so annoying, they searched for *any* reason to fire me."

"And what did they find, Sean?" my dad asked. My mom, who had been working in the living room, entered to hear this answer.

"I was three and a half hours late for work on Monday."

My mom started laughing loudly. My dad shook his head, staring at the carpet. I heard him mumble, "Jesus, not one, not two…" and he trailed off.

"Sounds like you need a clock," my mom chuckled as she headed back to the living room. "Or maybe," she added, turning around, "as you two geniuses probably call it, 'a chronometer.'"

Social Security Office
Chicago, IL

"So, are you really going to do this?" Jessica asks after I get out of bed.

"Yeah, it doesn't seem weird to me at all."

"That's why I love you!" she says and kisses me.

I throw some clothes on, put my Social Security card and birth certificate inside my wallet and leave the apartment.

Jess had already added my name to hers when we were married and I was off to do the same: to have the U.S. Government officially add my wife's last name of Bair to my last name Flannery, and henceforth be recognized as Sean Bair-Flannery.

The Chicago Social Security Office is next to one the greatest bars in the world—The Green Mill Cocktail Lounge—which, to me, is a further sign that the United States Government also wants me to take my wife's name. I go into the Green Mill, have some beers, then leave for the Social Security Office expecting to have a new name in less than an hour. When Jess changed her name at the same location, she said it was faster than getting a new license plate. "Hell," I think, "maybe I will even return to the Green Mill once I'm done and make a big show of opening a second tab under a new legal name?"

Once at the Social Security Office, I receive a number from a security guard. He is sitting behind a podium that is covered in paper signs. These signs were clearly made by him on the office's inkjet printer, and most of them are warning you not to use your cell phone.

I find a seat in the waiting area and start chewing a piece of gum; I don't want my breath to smell of beer.

Jess and I were married in Columbus, Ohio—her hometown—and when we went to the courthouse (in Ohio) for our marriage certificate, the clerks made us raise our right hands, then asked us their first question: "Do you swear you are not cousins and you are not presently drunk?"

After you swear you are neither inebriated nor cousins, the clerk congratulates you and moves on to the rest of the questions. In other words: Ohio gets so many marriage requests from people that are wasted or related that they hold off on the congratulations until they verify that detail.

So, I'm chewing gum, hoping Chicago isn't so concerned about booze in these matters when the quietness of the lobby is shattered with screams of:

"NO FOOD! SIR! SIR! NO FOOD! NO FOOD IN HERE, SIR!"

I look around and realize the security guard is screaming at me. While yelling, he is pointing down to his handmade signs; buried near the bottom this totem pole of cell phone warnings is a single warning about no food: a sign with a chicken leg and a line crossed through it.

"NO FOOD!" he keeps yelling.

"It's gum," I counter.

"GUM *COUNTS*!" he hollers back. "I JUST

AIN'T GOT NO ROOM FOR A GUM SIGN!"
I nod my head to signal I understand. My number is called. I walk to the guard, place my gum in the garbage for him to see. He nods approvingly and I walk to the counter that has called me.

"What can I help you with today?" asks the clerk.

"Hi, I was just married a few weeks ago and I'd like to add my wife's name to my own name."

"You wanna do what?" The lady behind the counter reacts with a mixture of wonderment but also visible apprehension that she cannot help.

"I have the marriage license and my driver's license," I tell her, "isn't that all you need?"

"Not for a man," she replies.

(*This was fifteen years ago, before Illinois supported gay marriage and at a time when many government documents and processes were dated in their sexism. A female friend of mine bought a condominium earlier that same year and her title in the mortgage documents was "spinster." I had to look that word up; it means, "An old unmarried woman beyond the usual age of marriage." She was thirty-five.*)

Another clerk joins the conversation, adding, "For women, yes, they come in with a marriage license and ID and we give them a new name; because they do it so often we have to make the process easy, but for a man...It's like a court case: you have to see a judge, take out an ad in the newspaper announcing the change, give people time to object to the name change. It's a whole process."

"What about men who marry into rich families," I ask, "like when a guy marries a Rockefeller or a Hearst? They always add that name."

"Sir, look outside"

I do so. There is a man, with a peg leg, throwing up into a garbage can. One of his hands is gripping the garbage can for support. The other hand is raised high in the air, holding aloft a forty-ounce bottle of St. Ides—almost like an Olympic torch—in order to protect it from being sullied by his own vomit.

"This is the Lawrence Avenue Social Security Office," she continues, "we don't get too many 'Rockefellers' up here."

"I see."

"Wait!" my original clerk pipes up. She has an idea: "The State of Illinois does allow you to change your name on a 'sex change.' We could use that."

She turns to me, and warming to the idea, explains,
"What we do is: we turn you into a woman! Got it? Fill out that paperwork; turn you into a woman and, when we do, you get to pick a woman's name. Then, we submit that, OK? So you are, legally, a woman for a minute or two in Illinois. Then we change you back to a man! And when we change you back to a man, you add your wife's name!"

There is a pause. I make sure I understand the plan:

"So, I'm gonna be a woman for a few minutes?"

"Just in the state of Illinois!" the other clerk adds.

"And only on paper!" says the first.

"OK, so I will be a woman for a few minutes. Then you are going to turn me back into a man and I can add my wife's name?"

"Yes, that's right," the first clerk responds.

As I repeat the plan, she, for the first time, seems to grasp the gravity and peculiarity of it.

"So...I mean," she attempts, "I think that's the only way we can do it, Is...is that what you want to do?"

"Ma'am," I respond confidently, "that's *exactly* how I want to solve this problem."

There is a bit of cheer from the clerks helping me and they begin assembling documents. At this point, a bald man rises from behind cabinet files, and inquires sternly, "What is going on over there?"

He had clearly worked at the Social Security Office long enough to know people are not supposed to cheer here; the U.S. government does not suggest solutions that taxpayers enjoy hearing.

"He wants to add his wife's name to his own," my clerk responds. "We are going to change him into a woman."

"On paper!" the other clerk assures.

"Then change him back to a man," my clerk adds, "and add his wife's name when he turns back to a man."

The middle-aged man has reached the counter while they explain the process. He looks at the array of forms and quietly shakes his head "NO" back and forth for what seemed like five straight minutes.

"I got an easier way," he finally adds, "we can use the female form. We will just say he's opted not to specify his gender."

"You can do that?" the clerks ask.

"Yeah, I'll add a 10-56 supervisor's endorsement form too. It will work, and we don't have to change him to a woman."

"What if I want to be a woman?" I ask, "ya know...for a few minutes."

At this point, the particularity of the solution has won me over and I begin to entertain the idea of being a woman for a few minutes. For example, the next time I see my buddies at some dive bar and they ask, "Do you think that joke would offend women?" I could answer, "As someone who was a woman for a few minutes, yes, I can assure you that it will."

The bald man exhales unamused, again shaking his head "NO" while speedily signing boxes within a triplicate form.

"Listen," he asks, as he annoyedly passes the form to me, "do you want to have your wife's name or not?"

"Yes," I say.

"Sign that, write the new name down and show her"—he motions to the clerk—"your documents."

He walks away. I sign everything and show the marriage certificate and driver's license. The clerks are happy to certify the new name though, according to Jessica, I rendered it incorrectly. I am, legally: "Sean Bair-Flannery." Jessica tells me that one's "maiden" name is supposed to be first and that by rights I should be "Sean Flannery-Bair," but I don't think that flows as well as "Sean Bair-Flannery." And therein lies the advantage to being the only man I know to take his wife's name: I can tell her with unshakable certainty (as men are wont to refute all points), "Actually babe, that's how *women* are supposed to do a married name. Not men. It's different for men."

The bald man mentions, as he is walking away, that I will get a new Social Security card within a few weeks.

I never received that card. Several times, I have had issues where my name was rejected on filings because they claimed my name on the form doesn't match what the Social Security Office has for me. That bald guy changed something, but I haven't quite figured out what exactly.

Jessica believes I was drunker than I realized and misspelled some part of my name and don't have any real idea what I'm currently called. But I know better. I spent enough time almost being a woman on paper to recognize a blowhard when I see him. That bald guy had no idea what he was doing! He probably turned me into a corporation or something with my wife's name. For all I know, those forms were for a hunting license.

My wife is a bit embarrassed that, as a matter of pure detail, she can't say that her husband knows his own name. But I learned an important lesson: always question the easy-to-explain solutions of a confident man. Is he really helping you? Does he really understand the problem? Or is he just trying to move along the line with the smallest paperwork?

I find myself reasserting all of this to Jess one morning, a few weeks after the whole situation occurred.

"Mmm-hmmm," Jess mutters, pretending to agree while she opens the mail.

"You don't believe that confident men can be a problem?" I challenge.

"Ha! Well I married one, so I'm well aware of their faults, for example"—she raises one the envelopes from the mail (I realize, upon closer inspection, that it's our bank statement)—"they might drink [here her voice changes noticeably] *sixty dollars worth* of beer at the Green Mill before going to a government office to change their name!"

"Your point?"

"I don't think the office manager was the problem. I think by that point you probably couldn't spell 'Sean' correctly."

"I've been awfully drunk in my life, but never enough to misspell 'Sean.'" I pause and think about it for a second, then add, "My middle name—Michael—does get tricky."

"What?" she asks, laughing.

"Well, as I think more about it, I might have put my own middle name as 'Michelle.'"

"What?"

"I do remember thinking 'Michael is trickier than it should be.' I wonder if I wrote Michelle?"

"Hahah!" Jess laughs, walking away, adding,

"I guess that just makes you twice the feminist, Sean Michelle Bair-Flannery."

Have A Nice Day Cafe
Cleveland, OH

In downtown Cleveland there's a nightlife district called The Flats. Bars line both sides of the river and every summer some kid would drown attempting to swim from a tavern on the east bank to one on the west bank. The river is narrow here—only about 150 feet across—so it seems like an easy swim. Drunks dive in regularly and some even make it to the other side only to discover it's a shipping lane with huge metal banks they can't climb out of.

As a young man, this taught me an important lesson: drunkenly diving into a river is a lot like declaring war. *You must have an exit strategy.*

I have swum in many different bodies of water: Oceans; bays; rivers; a cove or two; all drunk. Once, I even broke into a hotel by swimming under a gate. Each time I made sure to identify my eventual exit point before entering the water. Back when I was drinking real hard, I would catch myself locating each exit inside land-based bars before I ordered my first drink—*just in case.* Drinking is a bit like being a very poorly trained Jason Bourne: you might need to leave suddenly, and you may not know exactly who you are, so it's good to have your escape routes planned in advance.

Each time a young person drowned in The Flats, the Cleveland media would hyperventilate and wonder: "Does The Flats need to be fixed?" "Is this too dangerous a landscape for bars?" As though the notion of drinking by water was introduced by Cleveland, just a year or two before email was invented. Humans have been drinking near water since Mesopotamia. In the ancient world people were simultaneously so drunk and betrothed to the sea, it was generally assumed that at some point you'd probably wind up inside the belly of a whale for a few months. It was as common, back then, to wake up from a bender inside a cetacean's gastric tract as it is for us to come-to on a plane to Vegas.

Only in modern America would a town, upon learning of a drunk's death by drowning, debate relocating its entire nightlife district rather than admit drunk people are idiots who sometimes accidentally kill themselves. Plus: *Moving bars inland will not save any lives!* Any drownings you prevent will be offset by all the drunks now trying to cross electrified train tracks or falling off statues they've climbed. Believe me—and I always wished I could testify before City Councils as an expert witness in order to say as much—the kind of guy who wants to swim across the Cuyahoga River is going to find a way to kill himself in any landscape:

COUNCILWOMAN: "Can you provide an example of what you are talking about, Mr. Flannery?"

ME: "Sure, as just a for-instance, your proposed new location is next to a historic cemetery. That's easily five impalings a year from drunks trying to scale the fence. And you're not too far from the zoo. Never underestimate a drunk's desire to do footraces, particularly against animals!"

I began drinking in The Flats in the 1990s and assumed this was how the area always was: littered with bars on each side and the occasional river/beer-related death every five to ten years. It was only after I left Cleveland years later that I learned that period was an anomaly and that, prior to the 1980s, drownings were almost non-existent, and dropped off again after 2001. Cleveland officials are not sure why the numbers were so high during the period I was there, but, to me, it was obvious.

First, no one would have attempted to swim across that river prior to 1980. In 1880, the mayor of Cleveland, Rensselaer R. Herrick, called the river "an open sewer through the center of the city," and it didn't get any cleaner during the next century. It smelled terrible when I was growing up, and when people asked what "Cuyahoga" meant I always answered, "it's an ancient Native American phrase that translates to 'river of manure.'" It caught fire at least thirteen times, the worst infernos being in the 1950s and 1960s, making Cleveland a national joke but probably saving the lives of a few shit-faced iron workers who would have otherwise tried to doggy paddle home.

A drunk believes he can swim across any body of water if he sees a bar on the other end of it, *but*: light the river on fire and he starts having second thoughts. He wonders: "Even if I make it to the other side of this burning river, what if my wallet catches on fire and I can't buy a beer?"

Drunks started drowning in the Cuyahoga

River in the 1980s because it was finally clear enough to jump into. This is the dark side of The Clean Water Act of 1972. Yes, it saved whole ecosystems and sanitized our drinking water, but it also decontaminated city waterways enough to cause a huge spike in moron drownings.

But! The morons did stop drowning, at least in Cleveland, in 2002. Cleveland officials are not exactly sure why there are less drownings in The Flats, but they believe it is due to more police on patrol, better management of bars, and (again, I want to testify before City Council as an expert on drunks to tell them the real reason) *cell phones.*

Drunk people today want to swim across rivers just as much as they did in 1997; they just don't want to have to return for their phone. Over the last decade, smartphones have probably saved more drunks from drowning than life preservers. I despise smartphones—I hate them more than Republicans hated The Clean Water Act—but I do concede that this infernal device has at least one advantage: fewer drunks are drowning in industrial waterways.

> **People I'd Like to Have a Drink With:**
> *The Guy who Drunkenly Swam the Detroit River*
>
> In most disciplines, the more clever and well-crafted an idea is, the more fame it receives. Drinking stories are the opposite; their fame is proportional to how stupid the idea is. Make

a smart choice drinking, and you land safely at home and no one hears a word of it. Make a dumb choice drinking and you land in jail and the whole neighborhood hears of it. Make a wildly dumb choice drinking and you land in global news and the entire English-speaking world knows your name, like John Morillo of Windsor, Canada.

After a night of drinking, John Morillo, 47, swam across the Detroit River, from Canada to America, prompting, according to Fox News anyway, "an international rescue operation." Morillo unraveled the story to a reporter from the Windsor Star the next day:

"I was drinking, but I wasn't really drunk. The thing is, I've been telling people I'm going to swim across the river for years and they're like 'yah, yah, blah, blah, you can't make it.' So, I don't know, last night I just decided it was the time to go…If I'm going to be in the paper, I'd at least like them to say I actually made it, even though I got in trouble and everything. I gotta pay fines and stuff. But I don't want it to sound like I didn't make it, because then my buddies are going to say 'ha, ha, you didn't make it.' Because that was the whole thing, to show them I could do it."

Morillo's claim that he was not drunk is amazing. First of all, he jumped into The DETROIT RIVER! I have lived in Chicago and Cleveland, industrial cities that are bisected by a river, and I have seen people jump into them, but never sober. If you were to go up to a sober person in these cities and ask, "how much for you to jump into the river?" they would answer "Twenty Thousand Dollars!" It would set you back half a decade financially, to get a sober person to jump into The Chicago River. But a drunk person? They jump in like they are escaping a fire.

Secondly, and this is a "tell" that all drunks should drop when defending themselves: never unsolicitedly add that you were not drunk. Only drunks add, with no prompt, that they are sober. If you pick up a child from a daycare and the staff struggles to find the kid, they would never add "we are not drunk!" because, you would call the police due to how suspicious it sounds.

"When I got to the Renaissance Center", Morillo continued to the Windsor Star, explaining how he emerged on the American side, "I couldn't find a way to get up onto the platform. Then some guy said 'Hey there's a ladder over here.' I climbed up the ladder, then people were asking to take their pictures with me. There was one woman, she said she was from Windsor and she thought I was crazy. She was right."

While posing for pictures on the American side, a helicopter began circling above and Morillo, assuming it was looking for him, jumped back into the river to swim home:

"On the way back I kept diving underwater when the helicopters went over. I was trying to hide. But finally I got almost to the shore and the spotlight from the helicopter was right on me and I said 'Oh that's it.'"

For those people drinking at The Renaissance Center: talk about a man of mystery. A guy yells, "Hey how do I get out of this river?" from below—the *Detroit fucking River*, by the way—and you help steer him to ladder and he ascends and takes a few photos and makes small chat but then, when a helicopter arrives, he announces, "Whelp, I should leave" and dives back into the river, swimming to Canada. You have an answer, the rest of your life, when asked, "Who's the strangest person you have met at a bar?"

"EASY!" you will answer. "The guy we fished out of the Detroit River that an international task force was searching for!"

Morillo was charged with "being intoxicated in a public place" and was immediately barred from any city property along the waterfront, but that was thought to be only the beginning. As the Windsor Star told it:

"The harbour master told Morillo, he'll likely be fined for swimming in a shipping channel, which could run anywhere from $5,000 to $25,000. Authorities also stressed that swimming in the

Detroit River is 'extremely dangerous' because of the strong undertow in the shipping channel. It's also prohibited under Port Authority Operating Regulations. Harbour Master Peter Berry with the Windsor Port Authority couldn't be reached for comment but Morillo said: 'The harbour master was extremely mad at me. I don't know, maybe they pulled him out of bed or something.'"

Imagine how interesting it will be for future employers to interview Morillo:
"Have you ever been convicted of a crime, John?"
"Yes. Swimming In An International Shipping Lane."

I would hire him on the spot, though maybe that's one of the reasons why I don't run a business, but assuming your office isn't along the waterfront—in which case he can't legally enter the building—Morillo is the perfect addition to a small team: he's determined; a risk-taker; fun; great energy; and, as we learned when he reached The Renaissance Center, he collaborates well with others and, perhaps most importantly, he understands that in both business and drunk swimming, the most important question you will answer is, "what's my exit strategy?"

All quotes from Trevor Wilhelm's reporting, Windsor Star July 23rd 2013; some AP summaries from FOX News July 24th 2013

On this particular night, I was drinking in The Flats, along the river, but it was winter; way too late in the year for drunk swimmers. But this is still a story about exit strategies. We were leaving some nameless bar, heading to a place called HAVE A NICE DAY CAFÉ. I had no business continuing to the next bar. I was owl-eyed drunk.

I started drinking about seven hours previously when my buddy, a successful accountant, asked if I wanted to meet them and their coworkers for happy hour. Happy hour, they pointed out, "was on the company's dime; you will drink for free!" I had plans for later in the evening that I did not want to miss, but I thought: how drunk can I get with accountants?

What a miscalculation! Accountants drink like high beam steel workers that just saw a coworker die. There are the only people I have met who drink like they want a blackout that moves in two directions: one that eliminates both past and future memories. The first two accountants I met at the happy hour were drinking in Cleveland because they were "stuck here" after drunkenly boarding the wrong plane in Houston and flying half way across the world in the wrong direction.

"I was pretty fucking sure this ain't Spokane," one of them explained, "when there was no mountains on arrival!"

They both laughed uproariously and shot tequila. I joined them. After another hour or three of drinking, we were best friends and we all insisted none of us move to another bar without the others.

"I'm meeting friends at Have A Nice Day Café," I said, sharing my own plans.

"Well, we're with you!" the Texans pledged.

"Perfect! Follow me," I announced and, after closing tabs, we all left together. As we moved past the first set of heavy doors in the bar's vestibule—before we got to the main exit doors and hit the real weather—I turned to the Texans and cautioned them, "This is going to nip a bit more than home".

It was five degrees outside. I later learned that Houston's coldest recorded temperature, from January of 1930, was five degrees. Meaning these drunk accountants who walked five blocks with us to Have A Nice Day Café are probably the only Houstonians alive who can describe what it felt like on Houston's coldest night; a sensation they learned bar hopping in Cleveland.

We reached the bar and there was a huge line to enter. My buddy who had invited me to happy hour turned and asked, "What do you think?"

"This could be a problem for Space City", I say, pointing to the Houston people, only to see they had left us and were now talking to the bouncer.

They waved us forward and we got right in.

"What happened?" we asked.

"I paid the guy $200 to have us jump to the front of the line. I'm not waiting in that cold!!"

My buddy and I laughed so hard that, for a moment, it was louder than the DJ.

"We're in Cleveland, you idiot!" my buddy

yelled back. "You could have bought us to the front of line with a twenty!"

"I had to get my car out of tow-lot yesterday and it cost less than getting into this bar," I added, laughing, "let me at least buy you all a round of beers after spending that to get us inside."

I walked to the bar and noticed my other friends—the ones I planned to meet here—already at the bar, ordering drinks.

"Hey!" they yelled, noticing me too, "you made it!"

"Of course!"

"Let's do shots!" one yelled.

"Aaah," I hesitated, "I don't think I can do shots. I'm pretty far in the bag."

"Come on!" they screamed back in that whine men use when disappointed at a bar.

I used to think men whine when you refuse shots because they felt you were boring—that you were not participating in the group outing—but, as I've spent more time in bars, I've concluded that dudes are pushy about joining them for shots because that's the only way they know how to express friendship. It's not that you are being boring; it's that you've taken away their only method for affirming emotional importance.

This is also why men tell their friends—when they are super drunk—"You know I'd take a bullet for you, right?" Men are so afraid to affirm each other that, rather than say, "I enjoy hanging out with you because you're a nice dude," it is easier to imagine the guy's attempted murder and you intervening with your own chest, to take that bullet, and sharing that death-fantasy is a less weird way to announce we are friends.

"Come on Flannery, I'd take a bullet for you!"

"I know you would. But I'd rather you take a shot for me."

"Come on!"

"OK, but," I bargained, "it has to be an easy shot!"

They ordered shots, we all put them down the hatch, and they started laughing uproariously. It was Bacardi 151.

I was going to vomit.

I turned from the bar and started running. I *had* to vomit. Always a river man, I knew my exit strategy. The bathrooms were too far away. I sprinted to the main doors, where we entered, not five minutes ago. The doors were heavy, so I brace to open them shoulder-first, running at top speed, but security had already noticed me and opened the doors for me (happy to see me leave), so, all that energy I was going to use to bust open the doors, propelled me head first through the doorway. I flew out into the Cleveland night. I am not going to claim that the distance I traveled is greater than what you see in Olympic long jumps. But, what I would say is: if you told Olympic long jumpers to leap into concrete, I'm not sure they would have reached my distance.

I crashed, head-first into a giant concrete block on the opposite end of the sidewalk. I hit it like a bird that didn't see a window. My body crumpled to the sidewalk where I vomited.

The concrete I flew into was part of a new beautification project, where potted trees and flowers were destined to one day live, but, at that current moment, it was barren and unfinished. There was a sign on it, just above the spot where I was presently quietly vomiting and bleeding:

"Your tax dollars at work! Coming soon: A NEW CLEVELAND."

There was still a huge line to enter the bar and, in what was a great summary of how alcohol works, not a single person got out of line after witnessing me crash into the concrete and crack my head open. People were waiting in freezing-cold weather, wondering if this place would be worth the wait—if they would meet the right people there—and saw a guy shoot out of the bar like he was ejected from a cannon, straight into a rock wall, and said to themselves, "Yep, this looks like exactly the right place".

That was my last memory: being surprised no one left the line. Then things got dark.

I woke up on the floor of a kitchen. There were a couple pots around me and this weird ash-like substance. I stood and recognized the apartment: it was my buddy's, the one who invited me to drink with the accountants the day before. I didn't hear anyone stirring—it was early—and I needed to leave. I debated about knocking on the bedroom door to announce I was leaving but it occurred to me: I was probably a very high maintenance house guest the previous night. Better to let my host sleep in, I thought, and left a note instead.

I went into the bathroom to look myself over before leaving. I had a huge black-and-purple welt on my forehead with dried blood around it. But at least my suit looked mostly free of both wrinkles and blood. "Thank God," I sighed, "I'm late for a job interview."

I stopped at a pharmacy and covered the worst of my wound in giant bandages then arrived at the office location about ten seconds before the interview was scheduled to begin. The first five people who met me at the company said, "Jesus, are you sure you are OK?" and "Do you want to reschedule this?" which is not what you want to hear as the first words in an interview.

I was pessimistic about getting this job back when I was planning to interview without a massive head wound, so, at this point, it felt like both parties were only going through the motions. So I started providing each group with a separate explanation for the cut on my forehead, just to crack myself up. I told the secretary I was in a car crash; the recruiter heard I hit my head on a low ceiling helping my friend move; and the network administrator was told about how I was fixing a computer and I forgot to disconnect the power supply, shocking me, which in turn bolted me upright, causing me to smack my head on the desk (which, actually, *did* really happen to me once).

But, by the end of the interview, I was so convinced I wouldn't get the job, I told the new business director that a bird dropped a rock on me during a nature walk. He found this story spurious, but I told him it was more common than people believed and that even Plato had died that way.

"Are you serious?" he asked. "Plato?"

"Yeah, I mean I'm a philosophy major." I explained. "It's one of the first things you are taught."

"I never knew that!"

Now, I should make it clear: Plato did *not* die that way. But this was before Google and smart phones and it was much easier to be a liar back then, particularly about the ancient world. People were swallowed by whales back then! Who wouldn't believe that a bird killed a person or two? Particularly some philosopher that seemed to spend most his life outdoors?

I got that job.

The note I left for my buddy back at the apartment where I had awoke on the kitchen floor, said:

"Thanks for hosting me! Sorry I got so drunk. Hope I didn't ruin your evening. Would thank you in person, but I have to run- late for a job interview. Wish me luck!"

The company that hired me closed three days after I started work. That did not flabbergast me. A company eager to hire a guy who was bleeding from the head in his job interview might have additional, strategic problems.

"You're really calm about this," one of the other new hires said to me, after noticing me simply shrug my shoulders and begin walking to the door after hearing the news.

"Gotta have exit strategies in this town," I answered, as I walked out.

77 North
Cleveland, OH

One of the forgotten features of old cars is how *quiet* they were. Not the engine, perhaps, but the interior. The dashboard of the modern car blares, flashes, and otherwise emits constant visual and audio warnings and updates; your every movement is monitored and evaluated by the car. The car is constantly of the opinion that you are a sloppy and dangerous driver. An old car is the opposite: no complaints. You can drive an old car off a bridge and you won't hear a single alert or alarm; you get to die in peace, with only the wafts of wind against the window as your best signal that you are not on Earth anymore and, likely, will never rejoin it, alive. I should know: I drove my old car off a bridge at seventy miles an hour.

It was the most peace and quiet I've ever had.

I was driving two friends to an early-season Indians (as Cleveland's baseball team was known then) game in April, which is a time of year when cold weather cities like Cleveland have started their baseball season but still have snow. My friends and I debated about driving all the way to the stadium and paying for parking, or wondered if instead we should drive to the train station—The Rapid (RTA)—park for free and take the train into the stadium? Eventually we felt there wasn't enough time to park and transfer to the train—mainly because had I left work later than expected—so, a drive to the stadium it was, and quickly.

Cleveland fans were warned that weather would be terrible at this game—a blizzard was expected—but, as my friends and I departed, it was but a drizzling, spitting rain and we laughed about how our weather forecasters were always so histrionic. We were about halfway there when I noticed that not a single car had passed us; what's more, we seemed to be the fastest car on the highway! This was NOT how it usually went. I drove a 1987 stick-shift Chevy Cavalier where one door was attached with chicken wire. I rarely passed highway traffic in that junker. It started shaking like a NASA vessel reentering the atmosphere every time I entered the fast lane to overtake someone. This was weird; this was rare.

"We are making great time!" my buddy exclaimed as we zipped by all the other cars in the slow lane.

"Yeah," I agreed, "it's pretty easy to make good time when everyone else is driving like an asshole, right?"

And, with that, we hit a patch of ice and I immediately lost control of the car.

When you drive in engulfing snow—something Clevelanders are accustomed to, as the city averages nearly five feet of snow a year—drivers tend to switch to the slow lane and follow the tire path of the leader, like elephants plodding trunk to tail. Clevelanders drive well in the snow due to a combination of heavy annual accumulation and the fact that our municipal services make no effort to plow or remedy the situation. The city's policy on plowing and salting seems to be: "Well, you made the decision to live in Cleveland, didn't you?"

Our ability to drive in bad weather has created a genre of Cleveland "justice porn," where we enthusiastically laugh, to the point of ecstasy, while watching videos of warmer cities reacting to minor dustings of snow. A few years ago the city of Atlanta shut down all of its highways, activated the National Guard, and shuttered all non-essential government buildings due to what the city's meteorologists called "Snowpocalypse." Drivers abandoned their cars on active highways as panicked citizens hoarded food and supplies.

One inch of snow had fallen.

There's a certain type of Midwesterner who cannot eat spicy foods. We are terrible dancers and we apologize four times per sentence; we probably seem bland and unadventurous to most of the country. But we will drive in anything. I was once at a wake that took place during a series of terrible storms, including several tornadoes. I overheard one of my uncles say, "Oh, yeah, I saw the tornado. It wasn't too far from me, right over at Pearl Road, but it was hovering above the turnpike and I wasn't about to pay those damn tolls anyway, so, no big deal for me."

When Clevelanders saw the footage of Atlanta closing its entire city and requesting a standing army due to an inch of snow, we achieved metropolitan karma: finally, we were laughing at a major city as joyously and patronizingly as they normally laughed at us, at Cleveland.

But at this time, on our way to Opening Day in bad weather, I was young and I was about to hit snow for the first time. I was only seventeen—funtionally, an Atlantan—driving headlong and happy into a blizzard, until I hit the right amount of ice and lost control of the car.

As the car skidded off the patch of ice, it initially snaked back-and-forth, mostly within our lane, but had soon built enough momentum that it suddenly banked hard right. We darted out of our lane, between two barely moving cars to the right of us and with no deceleration, flew off a bridge.

We went from happily passing all traffic on the road, rhapsodic in the "great time" we were making, to flying in the air.

"Huh," I remember thinking, as we floated away, "I didn't even know there was a bridge here. Also: Wow! What a view!"

Cleveland's first nickname was The Forest City, which was taken from Alexis De Tocqueville's 1830 work "Democracy in America," which in turn referred to how leafy and verdant the town was, while still being a bustling, emerging port. About 100 years later, this vine-covered marsh was the fifth biggest city in America, and busy erecting huge skyscrapers. As we dropped to our deaths, and I noticed the tree-covered hills leading into downtown with its glistening towers, I said (in what, I thought might be my last words), "This city is prettier than people realize."

There was a second or two of nice silence. The slide off the highway happened so fast, that my passengers were muted by total confusion. Plus, back then, there was no in-car GPS to complain about the sudden route change. No irksome "Recalculating... RECALCULATING!" So, I enjoyed the scenery for a few seconds hearing only the hum of the engine and the occasional plop of a new snowflake landing on the window, peacefully floating to my death, while taking two additional lives with me.

When I recall this incident, I oddly spend less time thinking about how things felt inside the car and more time wondering how it looked to the other drivers. For the last ten miles, we were flying past all other traffic; whizzing by scared, careful people, plodding along in the slow lane, white-knuckled on the steering wheel, probably complaining that their wipers weren't working well enough to even see. Then suddenly, a flash of blue—a car with a street value of $800 driven by a idiot—jets past them, recklessly launching itself into a blizzard. And what does every careful driver say, when passed by that kind of person?

"God, I hope he gets into an accident."

I like that, no matter how much gender politics evolve and change in this country, Americans can always agree: we assume "He/Him" is the correct pronoun for asshole drivers. And that, additionally, it is okay to wish for "him" to crash. It is human nature; you want to catch up with that reckless idiot after he slides into a ditch along the side of the road or crashes into a semi. You want it so badly, you will trade the stability of your own trip for it: "God, please put that jackass in an accident; I will gladly sit in the extra two hours of traffic it will cause! I need to see HIM suffer consequences!" Outside of war, humans make no wishes more despicable than what we desire upon other drivers. I believe it is for this reason that genies hide in the desert, because, if discovered in a city, the genie knows you would waste your first two wishes on killing other drivers.

I find myself yelling abhorrent things when stuck in unusually bad traffic: "There had better be a dead body up there!" as though a human life must be sacrificed to the gods of commerce in order to justify all the time lost in this gridlock. Often, it's the first time you've spoken to God in months, maybe years: "Lord, I'm sorry I haven't prayed to you in a while—probably not since I asked for that horse to finish in the top three last year—and I know I haven't been perfect, but I have a proposal: I will become a better, more-caring and understanding person if you could kindly just kill the driver of that black BMW for me. Thank you. Amen."

So when I retell this episode, I think first of those other drivers on 77 North, who begged a Higher Power for me to get in an accident, then watched me fly off a bridge disappearing into the sky. For the first time in their lives, a prayer was immediately and decisively answered and they were left with the guilt that the one prayer God decides to act upon instantly—as though responding to a text message—is the one where they asked for three people to die.

"Oh wow," I imagine them saying, in shocked self-recrimination, "I...wow...I just...Lord, I didn't mean for you to *erase* him. I mostly just wanted his insurance rates to go up a little bit; maybe be really delayed for work; not be tossed to a fiery death!"

Meanwhile inside my car, people might be surprised to learn, everything was quiet. People say time slows down when you're about to die, but that's not technically true: it's not so much that time slows down before death. It's more that it's the first time you realize how many separate thoughts your brain can have at once when it wants to. When you're in a calamitous situation, like, say, driving yourself and two friends off the edge of a precipice, you process more unique thoughts in a fall of a few seconds than you compile in the average month. I pondered everything from childhood memories, to arcane baseball statistics, to financial misgivings like, "I should have checked 'yes' when asked if I wanted to deposit two percent of my paycheck for a life insurance policy."

If humans really use just ten percent of their brain, as the old saw goes, then at the moment of death the active ten percent of the brain—the module that's supposedly been doing all the thinking since birth—must knock on the door of the other ninety percent and yell, "OK it's now or never if you want to clock in!" Because in that moment you progress mentally from a person who can't balance a plate to a juggler spinning an entire dinner set, a chainsaw, and a live bobcat all at the same time. If I operated at that level consistently, I would own kingdoms. Maybe that's how Alexander the Great and Attila the Hun dominated the world? They were the smartest humans on Earth because their mind believed it was dying half a dozen times per day, giving them moments of purest clarity. The domain of what your brain oversees in those moments is vast, beyond the memories and calculations and predictions, your brain is also observing a bafflingly complete picture of what's around you. When we left the bridge, it was so quiet and my brain—faced with the very real prospect of imminent oblivion—was now so nimble and perceptive I was able to notice a giant delivery truck for Little Caesar's on the highway beneath us and I remember thinking, "Do they still give you a second pizza for free?"

Then we landed heavily, mud and dirt spraying everywhere. We bounced a few times, and began sliding down a ravine.

"My God," I thought, "we survived! We are alive!"

As it turned out the bridge we had driven off was actually an extension of the existing bridge, designed to meet with what would be a new, raised on-ramp. It was under construction and did not have guardrails installed yet. What looked like it would be a plummet of several hundred feet, was a drop of but a few feet, to a steep ridge that we were now sledding down.

We *were* alive!

I slammed the breaks, but the car barely responded; we continued to skate down the hill, swerving left and right. My passengers, who finally

137

realized they were alive, began to scream. When you hear people scream from real fear—not the stuff you hear on roller coasters or when watching horror movies, but real, honest-to-goodness fear—it is a sound you can not ignore. One of the reasons we evolved so successfully as a species is that when we hear a real human scream, our brain will not allow us to concentrate on anything other than helping that person.

They screamed so ear-splittingly that I felt they required an update. So I turned fully around to face them, and stated, calmly:

"I have lost control of the vehicle."

"*What?*" they scream-asked.

"I. Have. Lost. Control. Of. The. Vehicle," I repeated, more deliberately this time.

"NO. FUCKING. SHIT!" came the reply.

My passengers seemed to "get" that I did not intend to drive my car off a bridge and toboggan it down a ridge. It was, in retrospect, a pretty redundant update.

"How are we holding up, back there?" I asked, thinking a new question would break the tension and silence.

"Look ahead, you fucking moron!" was said back to me.

I turned around and noticed that we were descending rapidly and heading directly towards a separate, active highway.

"Out of the frying pan, into the frog pot," I announced and grabbed the wheel.

"Buckle up!" I screamed, as though we were in a damaged helicopter spinning toward the ground. During this entire tumble, I had my foot pressed down hard upon the brake pedal, to no avail, so I yanked up the emergency break, hoping that might add some resistance. Then I did what any driver should do before landing on a crowded highway after careening down a grassy incline: I put my blinker on.

As though, five months later, I would find myself in the office of an insurance lawyer and, when they bemoaned the fact that we appeared to be liable for a huge amount of damage, I could counter, "Oh, no. No, we have nothing to worry about. Did I not share this before? I had my blinker on."

"Mr. Flannery," he'd explain, "you landed on two vehicles."

"No one is denying where I landed. But that was a valid merge, clearly signaled and everything. The law is pretty clear here, I feel."

At the bottom of the hill we were slaloming down, there was a small gully that curved up to meet the berm of the highway we were approaching. We hit the end of the hill, still gliding at a pretty good clip, so the other side of that small gully acted as a ramp, and launched us into the air.

It was in *that* instant—soaring, about to land on another interstate highway—that I was certain we would die. And it is nothing like how they describe it in movies. In movies, they say your whole life flashes before your eyes and, because of that, you have important, final epiphanies: you realize you haven't traveled enough or been honest enough with people; maybe there was an unrequited love who you never shared your feelings with; or there was a family member you abandoned due to the small, silly grudge. And because of these flashbacks and the emotional insights from them, people die with powerful last words like,

"I never stopped loving you."

or:

"I've never been to Paris!"

But that's not what really happens. All you really think about when you are going to die suddenly and unexpectedly is about the clothes you are wearing. In that final second of life—when your brain is finally entrusted with its full range of computational powers—ninety percent of your closing thoughts are on what embarrassing item you may have left in plain view in your bedroom or what unflattering outfit you'll have on when they pull you lifeless from the wreckage.

This was particularly true for me, T-minus three feet from impact, because I was wearing my work uniform. Where did I work back then? Lady Footlocker.

That's right. I was about to die, dressed as a referee.

Furthermore I remembered: I was wearing women's size 12 shoes (my employee discount made it significantly cheaper for me to purchase women's tennis shoes) and I wondered, if this accident is bad enough, are the cops going to release a bulletin stating,

"If you hear of a sporting event that's waiting on a very tardy, very tall female referee, well, she killed herself by driving off a highway."

This thinking is an amazing insight into the human mind's real power: its ability to give you fifty thousand ways to doubt yourself. Perhaps that's how we dominated the planet. The Cro-Magnons and Neanderthals probably had the happiest, most self-encouraging brains in the world: "Hey, that's a great, near-spear you built!" or "Even if you can't start a fire, everyone values you!" Whereas even the first humans had our brain: "What are you doing idiot? If you don't build a functional fish net in front of all these people, your life is over! People will think you are stupid, because you *are* stupid."

And, as you are about to die, your brain's odd, neurotic focus on what you are wearing or what you forgot to do at home, completes its final purpose; it makes death awkward by choosing last words that baffle everyone.

I was no different.

Just before we landed, I raised the whistle from my referee's costume, and told my passengers,

"This whistle doesn't even work."

Yep. That's what I selected as final words: that my close friends, people I've loved since childhood, should know the whistle around my neck is a fake. That is the info they should take to their grave; not that I have always had fun with them or that I regret killing them but that, should it ever matter, they cannot count on using the article currently dangling from my neck to call for a foul.

We hit the other highway. The other cars all scattered, like mice after a cat jumps out of a bush. It was the closest I have seen in real life to what a racing video game looks like when a new player suddenly enters mid-match. We bounced a few times and, now on pavement, I was able to slow down the car and regain control; we merged easily into traffic.

For the next few seconds, I sat in what felt like the longest silence of my life, as everyone in the car absorbed the fact that they had survived. As we sat, dumbfounded, the other cars on the highway started to pass us and each driver stared unblinking into our car as they did so. There seemed to be a lot of judgment in their stares. I waved to them; the standard showing of gratitude when another driver provides room for you to merge onto the highway; even (and especially) if that merge was airborne.

I should probably describe my car at this point: it was a 1987 Chevy Cavalier with several large dents and holes but, most prominently, a giant image of the Cleveland Indians mascot—"Chief Wahoo"—was hand-painted over the hood and "GO TRIBE!" was written (messily) along the car's two doors. I painted that car, with friends, after we watched the Indians win a game in the bottom of the ninth with a three-run homer and we were convinced they would win the World Series that year. Therefore, we reasoned, our group needed an appropriately decorated car for reaching the games (we were wrong then and have been wrong since; Cleveland has not won a World Series since 1948).

So these other people were watching not just a car slide down a ridge towards them, but one that looks like a Cleveland General Lee with a referee behind the wheel:
"Jesus in Heaven, WHAT is that car doing? Is that Chief Wahoo? Holy…They are going to land on us…Is that a fucking *ref*?"

Some of them might still think about that accident, particularly those drivers who were on the bridge above who never saw the resolution.

One of the numbers I am most curious about is: how many people are out there, walking this Earth, who think they witnessed my death? People who have either had or will have conversations with their children years after the relevant incident, that go:

"Mom, have you ever seen a car crash?"

"Oh, yeah, I saw a bad one. I saw the world's biggest Cleveland Indians fan drive a car off a bridge to his death."

I'd like to believe that, at least for this incident, the number of people who thought they watched my death fell a bit each month. My car was (surprisingly) not damaged in the fall off that bridge so I continued to drive it around Cleveland for two more years and, it being a memorable vehicle, I hope there were a few times someone from the accident passed me, exclaiming inside their vehicle:

"Holy Shit! I thought that guy was dead!"

"What? What are you talking about?"

"That dude, up ahead! It's a long story, but just give that guy with Chief Wahoo a *lot* of space. Trust me."

I don't know if you have ever nearly killed half a dozen people, but there is an awkwardness after everyone survives, a kind of—almost mousy—silence where none of the survivors know who should break the tension and speak first.

It was I who broke the tension:

"Well, it's not how I would have drawn it on a map, but...this is going to be a quicker route."

I think when I said that, I could hear a "click" in my head which was the other ninety percent of my brain going back to bed, slamming the door shut and saying, "He's *your* problem again."

My passengers were now yelling, rather vocally, at me. I put the whistle in my mouth and blew as hard as possible.

Nothing.

"See?" I told them to utter confusion and accelerated into traffic, determined to make the first pitch.

We arrived before the first pitch. But, we learned, that was because the first pitch was in Detroit. I had read the schedule wrong, and the Indians were out of town.

Web Clout Solutions
Cleveland, OH

I used to enjoy interviewing for jobs that I wasn't qualified for. "What's the worst that can happen?" I asked myself. "You don't get the job?" As it turns out, the worst that can happen is that you get the job. Then you show up Monday, meet everyone, and have no idea what to do.

During college I interviewed for a job as a network administrator. I was not and never have been a network administrator.

The firm was called Web Clout Solutions and I was interviewing with Doug, the owner and founder. He was personable, with a great sense of humor. He seemed to be an obvious eccentric, moving erratically between topics and changing voices weirdly. I very much enjoyed talking with him. We mostly discussed how to deal with customers and what we wanted out of life. Doug had a lot of buddies who were very high up in Cleveland manufacturing—steel plants and foundries and whatnot—and he had created this company to sell IT services to (essentially) his buddies.

The interview was going well, and then Doug asked Troy—the guy I would be replacing since he, Troy, was being promoted—to join the meeting.

"Troy's going to ask you some technical questions, if you don't mind," Doug explained. "You'd be working directly under him."

"Sounds great," I answered energetically.

Troy entered, and this was his opening line: "How would you install a DHCP server for a company with over two hundred employees in five office locations?"

"Five offices?" I asked. Now, I should point out that, as I was asking Troy to confirm the number of offices, I had never heard of a DHCP server before and I had no idea what it does.

"Correct. Five offices," Troy replied, "because, as you know, that will impact the design, right?"

"Sure will," I responded, confidently.

I couldn't admit that I didn't understand the opening question, so I began building a response that would let me avoid it.

"What do you run here?" I asked.

Troy looked around, puzzled. We were surrounded by several computers, all clearly running Windows '95 which, at this point in time, was what about 90 percent of the companies in the world were running.

"We run Windows," he replied.

"Damn it!" I bemoaned. "I only know how to do it on UNIX."

Doug, the owner, nearly flipped out of his chair with excitement. "What? You know how to do it on UNIX?"

"As sure as the sun rises," I answered.

I had never used UNIX.

In fact, I had never heard of it until that very morning when it was mentioned in an NPR segment on the growth of the internet. I was hoping that the good people at Web Clout Solutions would be equally unfamiliar with UNIX and, due to that unfamiliarity, would allow me to move on to the next question or, maybe, they would decide my "UNIX" skill set did not match with their position and I could exit the interview with some dignity.

Unfortunately, I had only served to pique Doug's interest. "How many years of UNIX experience do you have?" he inquired.

I looked at the ceiling and asked, "Well let's see…how old am I?" and I started a fake laugh, as if I had been using the platform my whole life (which I later discovered, to my amazement, was chronologically possible: UNIX was invented in the early 1970s at AT&T Labs).

Troy, however, was a little more skeptical than Doug.

"Why would you apply for a Windows Networking position if you only know UNIX?" he wondered.

"I'll have to level with you Troy," I said, "I'm not a details man."

Doug waved it all away.

"Frankly, this could be for the better!" he enthused. "Troy, I haven't even had a chance to discuss this with you yet, but I was talking to Denny at Great Lakes Steelworks this morning and he wants us to start doing some UNIX mainframe support! I told him 'sure thing'!"

"We don't have any UNIX expertise," Troy reminded Doug. Doug merely pointed to me and I smiled, "You do now."

"Hmm, I don't know," Troy worried aloud, "I don't have enough expertise on UNIX to vet a candidate. We could have him take a test?"

"Great idea!" Doug hollered eagerly. "I know it seems impersonal, Sean, but since we know so little about UNIX, would you mind taking a test? We have a skill-set software package and I'm sure we could find a UNIX test in there. Could you do it right now?"

I grimaced, glanced at my watch, and then began shaking my head in frustration, as though the watch had told me bad news:

"I got a ride picking me up in three minutes."

"I'm sorry?"

"I don't think I could take a test right now," I explained, "my roommate drove me here and he starts his job at the Beachwood Mall in fifteen minutes."

This was also a lie. My car—a 1987 Chevy Cavalier with no hubcaps and Chief Wahoo spray-painted on the hood—was sitting in their parking lot at that very moment.

"You gave yourself ten minutes for this job interview?" asked Troy.

"Well, I must have lost track of time," I conceded. "Again: I am not a details man."

Doug once again, waved it all off. "You know what? No problem. We'll bring you back next week and do the test, then? OK? I'll have my secretary schedule it." He looked at both of us expectantly, to see if we agreed.

Troy looked nonplussed, while I beamed my acceptance.

"Perfect!" I said, shaking both of their hands, "I look forward to that call and the test!"

They walked me to the door, where I saw a car driving by slowly. I decided to pretend this was my friend coming to pick me up. I began waving wildly, and when it continued past I started running after it, yelling back to Doug and Troy, "Gotta run! He warned me he wouldn't wait!"

I picked up my car from their parking lot about an hour later, sneaking into the lot from the nearby woods so no one would see me. I sped out of the lot and assumed, based on how suspiciously I had acted during the interview, I would never hear from them again, and would certainly never have to take that test. But early Monday morning my dad told me I had a call and it seemed important.

"Sean?" said a somewhat familiar voice.

"Yes?"

"It's Doug from Web Clout. Remember how I told you about that company we were gonna start doing UNIX support on? They have an emergency with their mainframe. I told them we could fix it. Would you be willing to go on-site today and take a look? You'd be paid for it of course."

At this point, I realized Doug loved bluffing employers even more than I did.

"So you'd be hiring me? You're offering me the job?"

"Not quite yet," Doug explained. "I think more discussions need to happen on that. Troy def had some questions after that job interview. For today, you would be a contractor. We can W-9 you for today. Or, if we do hire you and you accept, we could add today's hours to your first week. We can work that all out later, but you would certainly be paid for today, regardless of what happens."

"I don't know, that sounds kind of like a tax headache."

"Tell ya what: You come up and fix this problem, I'll also buy ya as many beers as you can drink afterwards."

"I'm walking to my car."

I got into my car and, once on the highway, it hit me that I was driving to a factory to fix a UNIX problem, and it would be the first time I have ever used—or indeed, seen—UNIX.

Luckily I did have the foresight to go to the library the day before and, on the off chance Web Clout did call me back about taking a test, I read every UNIX book they had. So I felt, as long as this mainframe wasn't in charge of pouring liquid steel or releasing pressure, I could probably fake enough commands to look like I had seen UNIX before and not break anything too important.

A voice in my head piped up: "What if the program is in charge of pouring molten alloys?"

"Well, we will melt that bridge when we get to it," I answered.

I parked about a mile away from the factory's address and took the bus the remainder of the way down, as I did not want Doug and Troy to see me arrive in the broken-down Chief Wahoo Chevy Cavalier that had spent two unexplained hours in their parking lot the previous week.

Doug and Troy greeted me in the lobby and introduced me to the factory manager. She explained that they had bought a dozen or so new printers and they were unable to connect them to the office mainframe, and they needed them for printing shipping manifests.

"OK, so is your office mainframe stand-alone?" I asked. "Like, if something happens to it, your whole factory won't explode, right?"

"What?" she blurted.

"It only runs the office, correct?"

"Yes."

"And it's backed up? If anything happens?"

"Yeah, we pay someone for that, a different company," she explained. Then added, worriedly, "Why? This shouldn't be a major thing, right?"

"You'd be surprised," I answered.

I found a terminal and got started by running a few pointless commands on the mainframe—with Doug and Troy and this manager standing right behind me—just to prove I at least knew how to log in and type.

After a few commands, I swiveled around in my chair and announced: "OK, I can fix it."

This was a lie. I did not know how to fix it.

But, as luck had it, I had read about this exact problem over the weekend in one of the UNIX books I had crammed. So I knew what was causing the issue and, though I did not know how to rectify it, I sort of understood how a competent person might. But, as there were no competent people on hand at that moment, I decided to act like I was one.

"The issue is that the kernel doesn't currently support enough printers," I told them. "We have to at least change the config and, potentially, upgrade the kernel."

"O…kay?" replied the factory manager, who seemed to be simultaneously reassured and unnerved by my tech-speak.

"My first question would be: Do any employees use this mainframe?"

"Of course!" she replied.

"OK, are they working on it actively?" I inquired. "Could they afford to lose some time while we reconfigure it and reboot it? And, God forbid—I mean, I am good, but—if something goes wrong and we have to keep it off-line for a few hours while we restore? Can they take the afternoon off if things go bad?"

"Of course not! Our whole office runs on this thing."

"Gotcha," I said, adding in a chair-swivel for effect, "well, that's the problem. It sounds like it needs to be solved during off-hours though. Sounds like I can't do anything right now."

The office manager was disappointed, and also a little suspicious of my explanation, but ultimately agreed to my plan and thanked us for our time.

So, Doug, Troy, and I went to lunch and started

drinking beers. Around the fourth round, Doug got a call from the factory manager. Her UNIX consultant had arrived early and looked at the problem, and she wanted to share with us that he had agreed with my diagnosis and was particularly impressed that I talked them out of doing anything during business hours; he was also appreciative that I had asked a lot of questions about what else was connected to the system and if backups existed. Now of course what I was actually doing was stalling for time so as not to reveal my incompetence, but my desperate tap-dancing had been mistaken for probity and caution.   A legitimate expert, it turns out, behaves much in the same way as a person who learned the skill two hours previously; the expert has seen some stuff and is aware of how many things can go wrong, so they approach each problem just as hesitantly as a novice/idiot does.

Doug high-fived me and said it all went perfectly, adding, "They want to work with us because we can offer the same services, but get there quicker!" More beers arrived.

I woke up the next day in the top bunk of my younger brothers' bed. I'm not positive how I got home the previous night, but know for a fact I did not drink and drive because I had a voicemail telling me that my car was in a tow lot in west Cleveland. A heavy layer of snow had blanketed the city in the days previous, and it turns out that when I parked a mile away from the factory (so they would not see my Chief Wahoo car), what I had thought was a perfectly legal, wide-open spot, was in fact an alley that had not been plowed. I had blocked people in four apartment buildings from entering or exiting, and the City of Cleveland probably towed me before I had my first beer at lunch.

This sort of thing happened all the time: My car was always being towed or booted, either due to tickets or because I didn't pay attention to where I was parking; or maybe I did pay attention, but then I got drunk and had to leave it overnight in a restricted parking zone. When I talk to friends who have quit drinking, they always talk about the money they save by not buying beer or rounds at the bar and I always think: Well, what about how much you save in tow fees and missed flights?

Under-discussed in the cost of alcohol is how many fees you pay as a drunk. I'm convinced it approaches or surpasses the cost of the actual booze. You forget and lose credit cards and cell phones. You are never on time; rental cars and tuxedos are returned late. You break and stain things. My brothers and I were staying in a motel for a wedding in rural Ohio once when I ran into the dresser at 4 a.m. I then puked all over my bed since I couldn't make it to the bathroom. I broke three ribs when I hit the dresser.

The motel charged us for a "biological discharge cleanup" on the sheets and damage to the drywall because I ran into that particular piece of furniture so hard, the corners smashed into the wall. When we checked out, I was tempted to deny the drywall fee and claim the damage was already there, but then realized

I was in a sling and visibly injured. My claim of innocence was probably not hugely credible.

Instead I actually took the time to read the fee amount: $25. My God I thought, I was ready to tip them four times that, just to deal with the problem. The lesson being: if you ever need to raise hell in a hotel room, do it Troy, Ohio.

Two days after the factory visit, Doug called me to offer me the job. "We don't even need to do a UNIX test," he said.

"Doug, I really appreciate that and you have a great company," I replied, "but, I'm sorry, I accepted a different job yesterday." This was true; I had been interviewing at a few places and a place that paid more than Web Clout (and required fewer hours) had offered me a job, so it was a no-brainer.

"Would you reconsider if I increased the money?" he asked.

"I don't think so, Doug. They offered a lot more, to be honest. It's a much bigger company and, if we are being real honest with each other Doug: I think you can find someone that will be a better match."

"OK, sorry to hear that Sean."

There was a long pause, then Doug broke the silence:

"Sean, seeing, as we're being honest, can I ask you one last question?"

"Of course."

"Do you drive a Chevy Cavalier with Chief Wahoo on it?"

Guy's Party Center
Kenmore, OH

I attended the wrong wedding. Twice.

Whenever a comedy booker asks me to supply a bio for promotional purposes, that's all I send: "Sean Flannery attended the wrong wedding. Twice."

It sums everything up.

The Second Time

It was around 2002 or so and I was back in Ohio for my buddy Tom's wedding. The wedding was at one of those large complexes where multiple weddings occur at the same time, each in its own ballroom. The ceremony was in the afternoon, so I met a friend for drinks beforehand and then left for the venue.

It was a massive white building; I entered and went directly to the information desk.

"Can you point me towards Tom and Jodi's wedding?" I asked.

"Well sir," came the reply, "traditionally, a wedding is identified by the bride's last name."

The attendant was clearly trying to make me feel small and uncouth, but what this haut monde functionary didn't know was I'd already been thrown out of a wing joint a mere thirty minutes prior.

The place where I had met my buddy for drinks was a chicken place called "SCORCHERS" and somehow we had got on a run that lead to us chasing tequila shots with the bar's hot sauce instead of lime; and although though we did not vomit, it still went poorly enough for the manager to suggest we leave "before the lunch rush" started.

"Worry not," I answered, "I'm on my way to a wedding anyhow!"

So the last person I spoke to tried to throw me out of a bar inside a strip-mall, meaning I was well past any feelings of shame. I looked at this concierge and replied, calmly:

"Come on buddy, do I look like a 'last name' kind of friend? I don't do his taxes. I'm his drinking buddy."

There was a fifteen second sigh from the booth. You'd think I asked him to fix a clogged toilet.

I still had no answer, so I started pointing at different sets of doors with raised eyebrows, establishing that I was willing to find the wedding myself, which I was pretty sure he did not want. I walked away from the desk, further into the venue—I think I might have even started skipping—and began happily pointing at doors like a contestant on a game show trying to decide which one contained the best prize.

"The point is made, sir," the attendant finally conceded, "you are, I suspect, looking for the 'Bednar-Flory' wedding. It's in The Oak Ballroom, which is past the fountain, then follow the hallway to your left; second-to-last door."

"Thank you, my good Marquis!" I yelled back, happily adopting/mocking his stilted language as I skipped past the fountain and headed—visibly and clearly—down the wrong hallway.

As I did so, it occurred to me that this might be the first time I really absorbed the bride's last name. I had always assumed—rightly or wrongly—that she was Italian (because my buddy, the groom was) but thinking about it in the moment, "Bednar" sounded almost French to me. I began wondering what a French reception would be like. I started thinking about French desserts, and whether the bar would only serve red wine instead of beer. And, as these thoughts rolled around in my brain, it occurred to me that I might not have been paying *perfect* attention to the concierge's directions.

But then I reached The Garden Room. Thank God! The exact room the attendant mentioned! I had reached the right place albeit through a totally different, but-not-longer route than was suggested. I burst through the door quickly, ecstatic that I found a shortcut that no one on staff was aware of.

It was a small ballroom with garden murals and a bar near one end. I didn't see a single, familiar face; however, as the wedding party was not present, and every person I knew was going to be in the wedding party, I thought nothing of it. I walked to the bar and learned that the main wedding group was busy still taking photos, so I ordered a gin and tonic. I met a few people at the bar and we made small talk. Another round of gin and tonics were ordered, and I began to worry: if cocktails were happening this fast, I should probably be proactive and put my card and gift to the couple with the pile of presents before I became too drunk.

"How do you know the couple?" someone asked me, as the G&T's were being distributed.

"Oh, I have a funny story about that!" I said. "But, first, excuse me: I want to put my card in the gift box."

The gifts were displayed prominently to one side of the wedding party's (currently empty) table. I inserted my card and was heading back to my new friends at the bar when the wedding party entered.

That was when I realized I was at the wrong wedding. I didn't recognize a single person. The bride and groom were the two most unfamiliar people I have ever seen in my life.

This was not the first time I'd done this.

The First Time

The first time was worse. The first time I flew to the wrong *state* for a wedding.

(At least the second time I was in the right state! Hell, I was even in the right venue; just the wrong room.)

People ask me how it's possible that I flew into the wrong state for a wedding, and I always counter with: "How have you *not*?" Our minds have been rotted by the internet; take Twitter for example, where the whole concept is you can't communicate thoughts more complicated than a sentence, and then—after becoming used to that level of writing—we suddenly get a wedding invitation, which reads like a 12th century armistice.

As far as I can remember, my mailboxes have been filled with mass-produced credit card offers for me and the previous resident, then, one day, a hand-written epistle—as though delivered by a crow—arrives. I might partially recognize the sender, but it always takes me a moment to decode; "Mister Theodore Paynter?" Could that be my buddy, Cowboy Ted? Then I open the invitation and, yep, it's Cowboy Ted inviting me to his wedding in language I barely understand:

"Mr. Percival Montgomery Dakota and Mrs. June Rosemary Dakota request the honor of your presence at the wedding of the daughter Amelia Suzanne Dakota on the seventh day of the month of August in the year of our Lord 2022."

How does *anyone* get the details correct? These invitations read like Beowulf. I usually find myself just sighing and saying: "Fuck it! I'll buy a ticket to Cleveland and figure out the rest after I land."

And that plan worked pretty well, the first few years out of college. I would fly to Cleveland, unaware of the details of the wedding, crash with family, then call friends who I knew were also invited to the wedding and get more concrete details. One time, I did fly in a week too early, but it was no problem: I called work, told them I had appendicitis, stayed in Cleveland for a week, and went to the wedding.

Now, admittedly, the plan becomes harder to salvage when you get the date right but the state wrong; there's less wiggle room.

In this particular instance, it was a Saturday morning, about an hour before the event. I knew fewer people at this wedding, but I was very good friends with the bride's cousin, so I called her, to get more details:

"Hi. Where's the wedding at?"

"The Good Shepherd," she replied.

"The Good Shepherd?" I repeated. "I've never heard of that! And I know every church in this town! I thought the wedding was downtown?"

"It *is* downtown," the cousin replied, "right by the river."

"What the hell are you talking about?" I snapped back, baffled. "There's no river in downtown Akron!"

"Sean, the wedding is in Louisville, Kentucky."

At this point I did recall that on the back page of the wedding invitation there was a map of Ohio and Kentucky, with a route detailed on it and I remember thinking, "Ha, those hillbillies from Kentucky are so unsophisticated they need a map on how to get one state north!" I even took some pride in having a wonderful, natural sense of directions as I booked a flight to the wrong state.

"Louisville? That could be a problem for me," I answered eventually.

The cousin expressed her confusion as to how and why I was in our hometown of Akron—two weeks after I had moved to Chicago—when the wedding was in Kentucky. My mistake was so great, she struggled to grasp the scope of it; she thought she was mishearing the details.

"I think," I confessed, "that I may not have taken in all the details of the wedding invitation as well as I could have."

"What are you going to do, Sean?" the cousin gasped. "It starts in two hours; you can't possibly make the ceremony."

"Let me talk to my date and get a plan going here."

"You brought a *date*?" She started to laugh; a loud, boisterous laugh—a cackling journey that went on for at least a minute—before she left me with an extended, "Goooood luck!"

The Second Time

Back at Tom's wedding—or, that is to say, back in The Garden Room for the wedding of two total strangers—I realized I needed to find the correct room, but I also needed my card.

"Where was that gift box again?" I thought, while scanning the room. Suddenly I remembered: "Oh, yeah, it's located right next to the bride and groom," who were now seated with all eyes on them. I noticed a woman dressed in a pantsuit, ordering staff about; she was clearly the wedding planner, so I approached decorously, thinking it would be more appropriate if she fetched my gift rather than me rifling through the well wishes.

"Hi, beautiful wedding," I started.

"It is!" she responded, adding, "Doesn't she look

gorgeous?"

"I've never seen her look more radiant. Are you the wedding planner?"

"I am!"

"Well, you have done an amazing job! Everyone's been raving about how great the entire day has been!"

"Thank you!"

"I was wondering if I could ask a favor of you? Due to an error: I am at the wrong wedding."

"I'm sorry?"

"This is not the wedding I should be at. And...I was wondering if you could fetch my card out of the gift box?"

"But...well," she stammered, "even if I opened the gift box...how would I know which card is yours?"

"I think the easiest way to identify it is: it will be the card with the wrong names on it."

The Oak Ballroom
(Still the Second Time)

I had now located Tom's wedding in The Oak Ballroom. I had too much pride to ask the concierge to repeat his directions, so I walked in on two more incorrect weddings before finding familiar faces. I had my card too; the wedding planner was not thrilled about opening the gift box, but I convinced her that the retrieval was only going to get messier if we waited ("Given the open bar and all."). I also made damn sure that when I did walk into those two additional, incorrect weddings, that I took a good look at the bride and groom before putting anything into the gift box.

You should know, the worst part of flying to the wrong state for a wedding is the greetings you receive at every future wedding you attend. Have you seen those videos where a soldier comes home from deployment sooner than expected and surprises loved ones at some event? Everyone goes crazy upon seeing them back home in the flesh. That is also how I am greeted at weddings except, unlike the solider arrivals, everyone is being deeply ironic. They are feigning happiness and surprise that I am attending the correct event.

This occasion was no different. As I entered The Oak Ballroom, I saw Joe, the cousin of the groom, and one of my good friends at the bar. Joe flung his arms in the air derisively, like he just saw someone kick a ninety-yard field goal.

"OOOAAAH! Look at this! He made it, all! Sean Flannery flies to the CORRECT state for a wedding!"

I shared his laugh and we hugged. Joe ordered us two drinks and, as the bartender fixed them, I confided:

"Actually, I was at the wrong wedding inside this venue."

"No way!" Joe started laughing. "For how long?"

"Two gin and tonics."

"Oh, that's not too bad," he answered.

I like to measure time in drinks. Studies have

shown people are terrible at measuring time when the available stimuli are unfamiliar: a prisoner locked in a room with nothing to look at will believe themselves to have been in there for days when it was actually just hours and, conversely, a person busy with many interactions—a waitress, say—will think what was only an hour of time was actually their entire shift. But gin and tonics always go down at the same rate. It's a more accurate, more objective gauge of time, like the half-life of radioactive material.

Four gin and tonics later, dinner was served. As is the custom, the bar was shut down while the guests ate. Some people (well, some drunks) were annoyed with the cessation of liquor service, but I used it as an opportunity to return to the other weddings I was at previously, since I figured. "Hey, they're probably well past dinner and the drinks will be flowing."

I walked back to The Garden Room and ordered a gin and tonic. I saw a few of the people from earlier and we started chatting again. "How do we know you again?" they asked, clearly struggling to remember how I connected to their event, to the loving couple that was just married. Mark Twain once said, "If you tell the truth, you don't have to remember anything" and I think there is a related corollary: "If drunk enough, you don't know how to lie."

"I'm supposed to be attending a wedding three auditoriums down but the bar is closed," I answered, "and I was here earlier because I didn't know the names of the correct wedding party."

They loved that answer and, after a long

hard laugh, they agreed with me about how wildly outmoded the language of wedding invitations are. We hit it off so well that I invited them to join us after the reception: "We are going to Brubaker's in the Valley! Huge group! It's gonna be a blast!"

Much later, say ten more gin and tonics or so, I was at Brubaker's with Tom's cousins and friends after the reception. I told Joe about how I stopped into that other wedding again and invited them to join us, and how I was disappointed they didn't meet us because they seemed like fun.

"What Brubaker's did you send them to?" Tom asked.

"The Valley, of course," I replied

"Sean! We're at Brubaker's *downtown!*"

"Well," I answered, chewing on the mix-up, "that's what they get for listening to an asshole who walked into the wrong wedding."

Allstate
Medina, OH

I once interviewed at the wrong company. It was one of my better interviews.

There are two ways to talk someone at the wrong company into interviewing you:

a) be so charming they feel they must talk to you further even though they have no idea who you are; or

b) be so uninformed—so incapable of providing any of your details—they cannot be sure if perhaps someone somewhere in this organization did actually schedule an interview with you.

I fell into the latter category.

I like to arrive at interviews with as few details as possible. In fact, I usually only write down the street address and the time of day; that's it. I don't write down the name of the company, nor the person interviewing me or even the position I'm being considered for. I go to a job interview armed with only a time and an intersection, the same way one would go to pay off a ransom demand.

Believe it or not, there *is* a plan behind that strategy. And, yes, my strategy is an overcorrection to a terrible weakness of mine: I am terrible with names but, worse even, is that I still loudly gamble that I might have the right name when greeting people.

If I see a person who's name I think is Kevin, I will confidently walk up and say, "Kevin! Great to see you again!" and he will usually reply with, "Actually it's

Bill." Ninety percent of my introductions are countered with the word "Actually," which is not the mark of a smooth conversationalist: "Actually I'm Allison."; "Actually I'm married to Joel, not 'Sven.'"; "Actually we have met, but you were very drunk," and so on.

I am a high risk/low reward greeter and it has caused problems with countless job interviews because I was making so many errors on names.

Then it hit me: if I never learn the name in the first place, I can not get it wrong!

Thus, I purposefully omitted names from the details of upcoming job interviews. I only wrote addresses down, then walked into whichever building I found at that address. Usually, there was someone waiting for me in the lobby. That person would see me—a young kid in a suit holding a manila folder—entering around the time of our agreed appointment and would yell "Sean? Hey, it's Jamie! We talked on the phone!" But the "plan" falls apart when you walk into the wrong building.

I had arrived inside a small, shady parking lot with many small offices around it and began to realize my usual procedure was kind of flawed when it came to strip malls.

But I noticed one office in the mall had an "Allstate" sign and I *had* scheduled an interview with them for a quasi IT/actuarial position; where I would help create risk algorithms for their mainframes. Allstate must be the right business, I thought.

I walked into the Allstate office and lingered for just a bit, hoping someone from would walk through the office doors and greet me, but the person behind the information desk noticed me before any of that could happen:

"Can I help you?" she asked.

"Yes, hi. My name is Sean Flannery," I replied, "I have an interview at 11 a.m."

"Oh, really? Hmm, who is it with?"

"I'm not sure. I'm embarrassed to confess I left my day planner at a coffee house."

This was, of course, a lie. I didn't have a day planner; plus, I don't think I had ever even been inside a coffee house at that point in my life.

"Hmm, OK, nobody mentioned a job interview today," the receptionist said.

"It would be an IT position if that helps."

"And you don't remember who you talked to?"

"Well, Luke from Digital Solutions set up the interview."

"OK. Well, if it's in IT, it must be with Dave."

"That sounds right," I assured her.

She called Dave. As she was dialing, I started to realize that this particular building seemed smaller than I was expecting, given that the job was supposed to be with corporate Allstate. This looked more like some regional office. While the receptionist called Dave, I walked around the lobby, admiring the view of the forest behind the parking lot. Then I heard the inner doors open and Dave came out, apologizing profusely.

He explained that corporate HR had been setting up the interviews for him and there had been a lot of confusion and somehow this particular interview wasn't on his calendar, but he had a free hour before lunch and he felt we could do it in that time.

"Sure," I responded, and he took me back to his office where I was given a technical quiz.

The quiz was mostly made up of questions on network administration which surprised me since I was expecting this to be more of a software/math role, but I answered each one solidly and we moved on to more personal questions which were also going well until he asked, "What's your greatest weakness as an employee?"

"Probably the same thing as my greatest strength," I answered, "I am not a details man."

"How is not being a details man a strength in network administration?" he pressed.

"Well, Dave, I look at details a bit like speed bumps. Why do speed bumps exist Dave?"

"To slow people down."

"Exactly! But who do they slow down Dave? Who do they really affect?"

"People who drive too fast."

"Exactly! Idiots! Speed bumps, just like details, are for idiots, Dave."

Dave took a moment. I think he was trying to figure out if he was more troubled by how little that analogy made sense, or how troubling it would be as an ethos if it did make sense. I sat back confidently in my chair and crossed my right foot over my left leg. That's when I noticed the pair of shoes I was wearing did not match; that is, a different type of shoe on each foot. It also bears mentioning, at this point, I was incredibly hung over.

I like to interview while hungover. I believe you should always interview for a job in the same state you will be working it in. Most candidates will put their best clothes on, and give their most careful, eloquent responses during a job interview; but they probably won't work that way once they're hired.

When I interview, I like to give you an honest representation of the kind of employee you're going to have the Monday after a holiday weekend: bags under the eyes; lots of "Whoa, you need to give me a minute on that question"-type responses.

The interviewer, Dave, squinted at me. I think he had just noticed my mismatched footwear, and asked, "Well, in my experience, details are very important in IT, particularly in networking."

I burst out in a loud, fake laugh and started my response by calling him by the wrong name, "Bob, I don't think anyone here is saying details are not important! I'm just saying, if you're already heading to the right destination via your instincts, aren't details slowing you down?"

"So, you're saying," he said, his tone changing to one of disbelief, "you're an instinctive network administrator?"

He had now mentioned network administration about five times so I was pretty sure I was interviewing at the wrong place.

I decided to go for broke and be fully honest with him on the off chance he was looking for a

jackass, "Phil, I am *recklessly* instinctive."
He showed me the door.

> ## Questionable Decisions I Have Made In Job Interviews:
>
> ***1. Told the interviewer that aliens landed in my yard***
>
> I was interviewing with a phone company for a job developing software. For the technical quiz, they directed me into a room where a senior engineer had written a bunch of data on a whiteboard. That engineer introduced himself and asked me if a "heap sort" would be good in this case. I didn't know what "heap sort" meant—I was woefully unqualified for this job—but I did notice this senior consultant wore large, tinted glasses and had a rat-tail hairstyle, which, I estimated, meant he probably believed in UFOs.
> "Can't we just ask the green men upstairs?" I joked, rather than commit to an incorrect answer on the 'heap sort' question.
> "What?" the engineer asks back excitedly.
> "Look, I'm happy to get back to your question," I explained, "but isn't it so odd that we are here talking about sorting strategies, when there's a race (I change my voice to a whisper) 'up

there' that has already solved this!" I pointed to the sky while saying "up there."

The engineer gave me the hardest, most accepting handshake I have ever received and proceeded to talk about aliens uninterrupted for sixty minutes, until the office manager walked in and asked, "How did he do?"

"PERFECT!" my man answered. I got that job. They flew me out to Dallas the next Monday to start.

I was fired three weeks later after losing the company car. I never learned what a heap sort is.

2. Showed off my legs

In college I was interviewing for a retail job and the manager read my resume and said, "I don't know. This position? And you're majoring in philosophy? I think you'll get bored. You might be too smart for the job."

I had noticed, just prior to the interview, that my socks didn't match and I somehow thought my mismatched socks would demonstrate I wasn't intellectually overqualified to be a cashier at a Linens 'N Things. So, wanting the job, I raised my legs above the desk, let my pants fall down enough to show the socks (along with a good part of my calves), and asked, "How smart does *this* look?"

I got the job.

What I discovered later was: I was in fact wearing a matching pair of socks. Due to the lighting and my colorblindness, I just *thought* they were different. So, when urged to honestly assess my intelligence, I put my legs up in the air and asked how smart that looked. And the manager, sitting before a philosophy major with his legs in the air, spread eagle, concluded: "There is enough 'off' about this guy for him to be happy at this place."

3. Claimed I was from the future

My senior year of college I was offered a generous job at a big consulting firm but I did not see myself fitting in at a consulting firm so I asked, "When do you need an answer by?"

"I think we need a commitment by the end of the week, or we'd have to move on," they answered.

"No problem," I reply, suggesting that I would spend the next three days deeply pondering this offer. Instead, I scheduled a rush of job interviews to see if I could find a "cooler" place to work that might approximate the same money. This is a plan that might make sense in theory, but the way it unfolded in practice was: I interviewed like a total asshole with everyone who took my call.

I made moonshot attempts at unheard of salary demands. I told one company that if they ever contacted me after work hours, I would immediately expect to have the following two days off.

Another company estimated that I would sometimes spend three hours a day driving to clients and I responded:

"Well, I think I speak for any self-respecting candidate, when I say—good people—you are hiring me a professional driver for said trips or we can end this interview right now."

"What? You think we are going to hire a professional driver for a $25K engineer?"

I did a loud fake laugh and answered, "I say! If you think you are getting me for only $25K, maybe we do need to end this interview!"

I was an outright jackass.

I did interviews hungover, drunk, in silly suits. I wore a purple ascot to one. I figured: I was never going to find a better salary than what this consulting firm was offering, but maybe I'd find a place that was totally comfortable with jack asses and that would be the better overall fit.

Plus, the power dynamics of a job interview always bothered me. You are wearing a suit; they are dressed in a tee shirt they received at a softball tournament. You arrive early; they explain why they are ten minutes late. You talk about how you want the job; they talk about how they want you to do the job then a bunch of extra unpaid stuff. So, if I am being honest, it was very freeing to do a job interview with a better offer in my pocket because I did not have to mollycoddle that power dynamic.

One of the final interviews was for managing the computer systems at an Akron company that printed and sold novelty tee shirts. The owner was interviewing me. He was rude, uninquisitive, cheap and prone to bragging; atrocious features in a boss, but I thought the work might be so easy I should listen.

He looked at my resume and his first question was, "Philosophy major? What's that?"

"You mean, how did I get into computers from a philosophy major?" I asked. It was pretty common for the first question in my interviews to be about the uncommonness of a philosophy major working in IT, so I assumed that was the real thrust of his question.

"No," he clarified, "'*philosophy*.' What's 'philosophy'?"

"You've never heard of 'philosophy'?"

"I was a business major." (This last was said condescendingly.)

At this point, I realized I would be working for a person so incurious, he was able to graduate college and start a business without ever learning what "philosophy" was, the discipline that started education itself; so I knew full well I will never work here.

"Philosophy is the study of *physical computers*," I answered.

"You mean like printers and monitors?" He was now interested.

"No, it's the study of computers as physiological systems: putting computers inside biology. *Cyborgs*."

"Really?" He was now *very* interested.

"Yeah, it's the next wave. It's mostly theoretical right now, but it's coming. In about four years; my prediction: when a customer walks through your doors, you won't know if it's a human or not."

"My God..." he gasped, staring off into the distance for a moment, before adding, "...that sounds really complicated...why do you want to work *here*?

"They're all gonna need shirts right?"

I was offered that job.

I never called the owner back to even decline it, but my hope is that he walked around for a few days telling everyone, he was waiting for a guy "that builds cyborgs" to come run the computers at his tee shirt store.

After Phil, or Dave or Kendrick or whatever I called the Allstate employee who interviewed me finally showed me the door, I walked out to the parking lot and sat down in my car, noticing that I had parked in front of his office. I saw him looking out the window, so I gave a wave—no hard feelings on my end I suppose—before I pulled out, turned and drove off.

When I got home, I walked around the car and saw my passenger side for the first time. The entire side was covered in dry car wax; it looked like I drove through a giant, uncooked cake. I had washed the car the previous day and I must have become distracted and only taken the wax off one side of the vehicle.

I started laughing as loud as an alarm. I realized that it was the side of the car that would have been facing Dave as I drove off. His last visual of me, as he still processes the odd frankness of me saying "I am not a details man," would be seeing me oblivious to the fact that one whole side of my car was slathered in dried car wax.

My dad, who had been working in the yard, noticed me laughing. He came over, and quickly spotted something out of place.

"Are you wearing two separate pairs of shoes?" he asked me.

"I am, Dad."

"Where are you coming from?"

"A job interview."

"Do you think you got it?"

"Dad, even if I did, I don't think I could find the place again."

Janet's Boss's House
Somewhere in Cleveland, OH

I was in the emergency room of Akron General Hospital, waiting for a doctor after they had just taken X-rays on my chest, back, and both legs. I was part of what the ER staff probably calls "the last call injuries." Between the hours of midnight and 4 a.m. there isn't a bar in your city that has more drunks inside it than the ER. When I entered, around 3 a.m., it was like entering Grand Central Station but in a world where every passenger is drunk and doesn't know what train to board. Actually, it was more like a giant monster had attacked a Jimmy Buffett concert and this was the hospital they rushed all victims to.

A guy across the aisle from was in one of those two-person donkey costumes, but with the second person missing, so the ass-end of the costume was dangling on the floor. The front end of the donkey was standing above a man who was passed out on the floor; this passed-out body must have formally been the ass-end of the costume. From what I could gather, the guy on the floor concussed himself in "a major karaoke mishap."

The guy in the front-end of the costume explained that he could not see too well so, when they decided to sing karaoke together, the front-end accidentally backed the ass-end off the edge of the stage, causing the rear-end to fall off violently, ripping open the donkey costume and concussing the ass-end.

The worst part of injuring yourself in a donkey

costume in August is that you feel the need to explain why you are in a donkey costume. Every time a doctor or nurse entered and asked what the problem was, this guy began with, "Well first let me explain why we are in a donkey costume..."

(They were both SMU grads, by the way.) I once read that the Center for Disease Control and Prevention—America's foremost scientists in the fields of public health, safety, and pathology—estimate that the consumption of alcohol costs the U.S. economy $225 billion in lost wages due to workers not being able to perform well because of injuries or hangovers. I believe every penny of that is correct based on what I saw inside that ER that night. We are probably losing a couple million dollars in damaged, two-person donkey costumes alone.

> **A Shot of Science:**
> *The Real Costs of The Hangover*
>
> A 2010 study on the economic effects of excessive drinking by the CDC concluded that the U.S. economy loses about $250 billion a year in economic productivity due to drinking. Egypt's GDP that same year was $218 billion, meaning our hangovers, if they were to become a country, would be richer than fucking Egypt.
>
> America loses money due to injuries and hospitalizations from drinking but, by far, the

biggest slice of that $250 billion loss comes from workers permanently exiting the economy due to boozing; that is to say, deaths. About 90,000 Americans die each year from excessive drinking; drinking kills more people than the flu or diabetes in a normal year.

    I once calculated that, if the entire U.S. economy loses $250 billion a year due to drinking, then Chicago (where I live) probably loses around $8 billion per annum. When I share that with fellow Chicagoans, they usually answer with something like "I can believe it," but I don't think they appreciate how massive that number is.

    Take forest fires for example. In 2017 America had one of the worst forest fire years in history; I recall reading the news that year and, each day, seeing that a giant swath of a new state out west was on fire. In that year, the U.S. lost $2.4 billion to forest fires, meaning that Chicago, by itself, drinks so much that its effect on the economy is like five western states being on fire for three straight years.

    The CDC further added that, of that $250 billion, seventy percent of those costs ($175 billion), are due to the effects of binge drinking, which I one hundred percent believe. Most of us head to the bar with a plan to only have two drinks and, I can assure you, the people who are fucking up the U.S. economy to the tune of a quarter trillion bucks are NOT the people who stick to two drinks. No, it's the people—and I am often one of them—that failed to stick to not only two drinks but two bars; that are at tavern number three at last call on a Tuesday night, proposing that everyone head to a 4 a.m. spot. If you have ever proposed a plan and most of the group reacts with "Don't you have to work tomorrow?" you are in that group running up that $250 billion deficit.

The productivity costs of alcohol are so huge, that in the same study the CDC estimated that in order for the U.S. economy to recover that fiscal damage, every alcoholic drink should have an additional $2.05 surtax; that's every drink, not every six- or twelve-pack. The CDC proposed that a dozen beers should incur about $25 dollars in taxes alone.

Thank God we live in a country that doesn't listen to science.

Everyone in that emergency room seemed to have a shocking, obvious injury—burns and fractures and wide, bleeding cuts—yet no one could remember how they hurt themselves. There was a constant murmur of phrases like, "We are still trying to piece it together," or "I'm not sure what happened," or, my favorite, "Honestly, doc, I think I may have been given a bad beer."

Nobody blamed their injuries on alcohol. They each went out of their way to blame their injuries on everything but the volume of booze they consumed. One guy said he fell down two flights of stairs because the stairs weren't built correctly. A woman with alcohol poisoning contended, "I think it was drinking in the hot sun that got me. As a doctor you know this, but the sun is your worst enemy."

I suppose, to a degree, I was like them. When a doctor finally reached me, he was holding a packet of X-rays and asked, "So what exactly happened?"

"Well, Doc," I answered, "I guess the easiest way to explain it is: I just really like Huey Lewis and The News."

Huey Lewis and The News have always been one of my favorite bands, but at the time of this story—the late 1990s—they had fallen somewhat from their 1980s-level fame. I was fresh out of college, working as a network engineer in Cleveland, when my buddy Eric, a childhood friend who was now in med school, returned home for the summer. Eric was studying to become a pharmacist, and when he and I were making plans for the weekend, he mentioned a pharmacy convention he knew of that had an open bar and had Huey Lewis and The News booked as the entertainment.

"What?" I gasped. "I love Huey Lewis and The News! We gotta go!"

"I don't know," Eric demurred, "it's not open to the public. It's invite-only. I can probably get a lanyard for myself, but how would we get you in?"

"The convention is run out of a hotel, right?" I suggested. "We'll go to happy hour there—everyone will be wearing the lanyards—and we will find some old guy that doesn't want to attend the concert. Old guys don't stay up for concerts. I'll ask to borrow his lanyard and attend as him!"

We went to happy hour and got unexpectedly drunk. "Unexpectedly drunk" is a common phrase among my friends. We talk about drinking the way a sailor talks about weather, like it's out of our hands:

"I had no intention of staying out late," I will explain to my wife, "but the bar was selling Manhattans for only $4. They might as well have kidnapped me!"

Eric and I got drunk at the hotel happy hour, and, better yet, got hold of a lanyard. The plan was working! We met Bob Doppell, an old guy out of New Jersey who was attending the conference, and who let me borrow his credentials. I went to the Huey Lewis and The News show as:

BOB DOPPELL
Vice President of Operations
BOLD MEDICAL SOLUTIONS
Morristown, New Jersey

We went to the show and it was open bar and it was great. We spent a lot of time near the bar and I was pretty good about introducing myself as "Bob," remembering my fake credentials. However, each person I met was curious about the strategy behind "Bold Medical Solutions."

"What makes it so bold?" they would ask, and I probably should have avoided the question, but I thought to myself:

"God dammit, I'm *Bob Doppell*. I'm the Vice President of this company! I probably built it by hand and Bob Doppell didn't get where he was by evading questions at an open bar, so I'm gonna do what Bob Doppell would do and answer this question and hit it out of the park!"

Which led to me answering such questions with, "Well, for example, we're the first company to ask, maybe cancer isn't the problem? Maybe human beings are the problem?"

Eric gave me a look as if to say, "You're really going to go with that?" I kind of shrugged at him, indicating that I couldn't think of anything better. But then the person I was talking to would chew on my response for a moment and come back with, "That's really interesting; that's really different."

And that's when I realized: these assholes were more drunk than us!

From that point forward I stopped even thinking about my responses. I had a different, ludicrous answer for each person I talked to. I told one guy I was trying to cure hangovers in mice. I told another drunk salesman that I was the person who had come up with the term "Broken Branch Syndrome."

"What's that?" he asked.

"You know that feeling you get, when you are about to fall asleep and then suddenly your body jolts up because you feel like you are falling out of a tree? Yep, I named that."

(I later looked it up and there is a real name for that sensation—a hypnagogic jerk—and, though I realize that in my guise as Bob Doppell, I was a fake medical expert, I nonetheless consider "broken branch syndrome" a significant improvement on the existing nomenclature and worthy of publication in whatever sleep journal does the most cursory credential checks.)

We kept drinking and Huey Lewis and The News kept playing and it was a great time. As the show wound down, I saw Eric talking to some of the other convention-goers and nodding his head. He returned to me with a woman, Janet, who invited us to an after-party.

As Janet began explaining how to get to the house, I stopped her with, "I think we will be fine with just the address thank you," which was a bold interruption given that according to my cover story I lived in New Jersey and we were currently in Cleveland.

Thing is: I've always hated listening to driving directions.

To me, finding a destination is like listening to a song; you need to be quiet and let the beat guide you. Directions are a distraction; you become so busy reciting and re-verifying your memories of the directions—"Did they say 'right' here?"; "Was it the first light or the second?"—that you miss the song. It becomes an obsession. I like to be laid back and let the road—the music—lead me.

I got lost *a lot*. This time, we were missing, driving around aimless, for almost ninety minutes; an achievement when you consider the house was only ten minutes away from the venue. Nevertheless, we reached what we thought was the after hours party, but it was so quiet that we were worried that either we had the wrong house or the right house and everyone had left.

The house seemed asleep; in fact, the entire neighborhood seemed to be resting. It was in a peaceful, beautiful section of Cleveland; hilly with old houses and the river off in the distance. We were wondering if we should leave when a couple came out onto the porch to smoke, spotted us and asked, "Who's there?" I yelled back "It's Eric and Bob!" They laughed about how long it took us to get there and invited us up.

It was a huge Victorian house and we met people on the first floor, in a large, open living room. Eric knew some of them and they were most assuredly not like the drunks at the convention; this seemed to be the "A" team. They clearly understood the science behind pharmacy and didn't seem to be as obnoxiously drunk as the previous crowd, so probably wouldn't accept my claims about innovating in the field of cancer unchallenged. I started to think, "I might be out of my league here," and resolved to avoid talking about work.

I walked into a separate, empty room, and that's when I noticed the view: a huge, curved bay window, with the Cleveland skyline, alight above a gleaming river.

"It's beautiful," I said to myself.

A thought occurred to me. I raised my voice and asked, loudly, "WHO WANTS TO GO UP TO THE ROOF?" I ran back to the living room where the other guests were, my arms bouncing wildly, letting them know I was about to propose the best plan:

"Who wants to go up to the roof?" I demanded, again.

"Uhh, I don't think it's that kind of roof, Bob," someone replied.

"Yeah, um, technically this is our boss's house, Bob," Janet interjected, concerned, "and he's not here and...I just don't think we should do anything stupid."

"Well you know what," I countered, "when I said I was gonna start my own company a lot of people told me *that* was a stupid idea."

Eric was gesturing "NO," at me by slowly but emphatically shaking his head back and forth. Everyone else was staring at me blankly.

"Sometimes in life—just like pharmacy—a lot of stupid ideas become smart," I intoned solemnly, before yelling: "Now, who's with me? Let's find that roof!"

I led a charge up the stairs, expecting the entire party to follow but I only heard the next song come on the radio: Matthew Sweet's "Girlfriend."

I charged straight to the top, the third floor. As there was no obvious attic or drop-down ladder to reach the roof, I opened a window and put my torso out to get a sense for how hazardous the climb would be. The roof had a dizzyingly steep angle with slick tiles; it would be like walking down a greased playground slide. "Damnit," I thought, "I can't lead these drunks onto this roof; they'll probably kill themselves!"

I quickly returned to the stairs and descended to the second floor. When we arrived, I had noticed there was a portico between the first and second floor and realized I could probably get on it from one of the second story windows. I opened one of them and, sure enough, it was just a few feet down to the portico. I easily descended to it; it was as flat as a pier and perfect for viewing the skyline. I started thinking about how wrong that guy who said "It's not that kind of roof," was gonna be when he got up here and saw this perfect platform.

I began to explore the portico more fully, trying to discover the best vistas of the skyline; the ones with the fewest trees blocking one's sight, and as I was doing so, I started to think about how we would fit everyone up here. You can't invite fifteen people to a roof, then look like a moron with no plan when they arrive.

Eric told me later that by this point, everyone inside had moved to the large bay window, the one I had been gesturing to earlier, and they were reassuring each other that there is no way "Bob" could actually get onto the roof; that he would be fine. Janet turned to Eric and asked, "You don't think he's going to do something stupid do you? Like is he going to fall and accidentally kill himself?"

"Listen," Eric reassured her, "Bob drinks a lot, yes, but he's got the Golden Touch. In life and in business."

And with that, the assembled party guests saw me free-fall into the concrete. Gathered around this giant bay window, they watched my body pencil-dive straight into the concrete walkway, like a vacationer jumping into a lake.

To an outsider, it probably looked as if I was trying to kill myself but wasn't a good enough athlete to flip my body around to land head first.

Days later I asked Eric what it was like in that room when they saw me hit the ground.

"It was the most disgusting sound I've ever heard," he said.

"Oh, wow, you actually heard my bones break?" I asked, amazed.

"No," Eric answered, "it was the sound of ten people thinking they saw a man die. Gasping, screaming. Janet yelled that her boss was going to fire her! It was like being in a box of fear."

Still screaming, the guests rushed out of the house, and ran down the stairs to the footpath where I had landed. I was moving a bit and grimacing in a kind of muffled pain, so they could see that I was not dead. Not yet at least.

I had walked straight off the roof, not paying

attention to my precise position in three-dimensional space. That is to say, I did not slip; I did not lose my balance; I walked straight into the night sky, thinking I had a solid step of roof under me. I don't know if you've ever done this in your house but it was a bit like when you are descending the stairs and you think you are at the last step, and you put your foot down—expecting it to land firmly on the floor—but there's nothing but air? You missed a step. It was like that, except I was not one, six inch step above the floor; I was two stories above.

    Another way of looking at falling off a roof is: you have exited a house at the speed raptors fly at. Which is to say: it's discombobulating. It takes several seconds to piece together what happened. One moment—often, the last instant you remember—you are strolling upon a perfectly nice roof; the next you are rolling on the ground, in pain, with strangers above you screaming and wailing.

What's more, the people crowded above me, as I twisted in pain, could not have appeared any stranger: each of them looked unfamiliar and, more confusingly to me (in that, bewildering instant), everyone was calling me Bob.

    "Bob? Bob? Are you OK?" asked one.

    "Bob? Do you know where you are, Bob?" pleaded another.

    I was so flustered by the fall that for a brief moment I forgot I was "Bob Doppell." For a second I was just Sean Flannery, about to die on a sidewalk. But their questions eventually placed me back at the party and I remembered: these people don't know me as Sean. They think I'm Bob Doppell, successful healthcare executive. And that caused a deep dread within me, because I was certain I would die from my injuries within the next few minutes, and, when that happened, these morons would call Bob Doppell's wife.

They will call his wife and, for two days, until the *real* Bob Doppell flies back home to New Jersey, she will believe her husband of thirty years is dead. Moreover, she will think he died like a jackass:

[*RING RING*]
"Hello?"
"Hello. Is the wife of Bob Doppell?"
"Yes...is everything alright?"
"I'm afraid I have some bad news ma'am...Bob is dead."
"Oh my God! What was it? A heart attack? Stroke?"
"No ma'am, he walked off a building after drinking about 82 beers."

I decided my last act on Earth cannot be to sow this confusion. I sat up as best I could, raised my finger to indicate I was about to impart important, final words, and I commanded:

"I don't care what happens next: no one talks to my wife about this!"

"What?" came a concerned and puzzled voice. "What do you mean, Bob?"

"Do *not*," I intoned, "under any circumstances... call my wife!"

I relaxed back onto the ground, exhaled deeply—as if I had completed a great and significant task—then closed my eyes, I suppose, to die.

"Bob?"

"Bob?"

"Bob? Are you OK? Can you hear us?"

At this point I realized I was not drifting off to a better place or getting loopy. I was just laying on concrete with a pretty consistent pain. I began to think that perhaps I was not dying.

"Should we call an ambulance?" someone wondered.

"Should we notify someone at the convention?" asked another.

I reopened my eyes, now fairly confident I was not about to expire. I stared up into the sky, to the anxious faces circled above me and confessed,

"Guys, I gotta level with you: I don't really know that much about healthcare."

Eric stopped me from unburdening myself further, interrupting me with, "OK, I think we should get Bob to the hospital!"

Someone whispered to Eric, "I think he has a concussion." The circle of faces all nodded in agreement: the Vice President of Bold Medical Solutions was on the ground, claiming he knows nothing about healthcare, and rambling orders about not contacting his wife. Clearly this man was not himself.

"Let's get you checked out, Bob," Eric suggested,

and told everyone to go inside.

"Bob's gonna be OK," he assured everyone, "I'll take him to the hospital."

"Are you sure?" someone asked.

"Yeah, no problem. I've got him. Go enjoy the rest of the party."

It's clear to me now that Eric wanted to get us away from these people before they figured out that I was not Bob Doppell; that I was, instead, some drunk who snuck into a free concert, fooled his peers with elaborate, cocksure lies, and then walked off a building. If they discovered all that about me, then they would also discover the truth that worried Eric even more: that Eric hangs out with idiots.

"Yep, we are good everyone," I told the crowd and they began to withdraw, signaling they were ready to return to the party. Then I shook my car keys to show that we were leaving soon, and motioned for Eric to walk with me to the car.

"Bob!" someone objected. "You can't drive!"

"Oh, I'm fine. Don't worry about me," I answered.

"Bob!" came the reply. "You. Fell. Off. A. Roof!"

Another effect of falling off a roof is that you cannot win any arguments for the next few hours. In fact, people won't even listen to your ideas for at least a few days. Each time I proposed a different plan, a whole crowd of people would dismiss me, out of hand, with: "You Just Fell Off A Roof!"

"Really everyone," I told them, "I appreciate the concern, but I feel fine."

This time they all chanted, back at me, in unison: "YOU FELL OFF A ROOF, BOB!" It's the closest I'll come to interacting with a Greek chorus in real life.

"Don't worry; I'm driving him home," Eric assured them, and pushed me into the passenger's seat. "Bob's not driving!" he insisted. Back then—when I was drinking harder—most nights ended with me being thrown into a car the same way Reagan was pushed into a limo after he was shot: a collection of men cramming me into a vehicle for my own protection.

At the time, I drove a 1987 Chevy Cavalier with over 200,000 miles on it that had "GO TRIBE!" daubed on both sides, with a huge image of "Chief Wahoo" on the front hood; all spray-painted by hand, by me. It also had zero hubcaps and the passenger-side door did not work, so Eric had to stuff me into the passenger seat from the driver's side, which caused the entire car to shake as I tried to maneuver around the gear stick,

"Wait? You drive a stick shift?" Eric asked after seeing me get stuck.

"Yeah," I replied, "and we are parked on a hill. Want me to at least get us out of this parking spot?"

"No. I got it," Eric said.

He started the car. The party-goers were still outside watching us, and got to hear the most annoying, ear-stabbing noise as Eric struggled to get the shifter into reverse. Eventually—after several seconds of it sounding like he was killing alley cats inside the vehicle—Eric got the car into reverse. With the car now humming quietly, Eric looked up and informed the assembled party guests: "Good to go!"

He hit the gas. We screamed backwards at full speed—like we were shot from one of those catapults the Navy uses to launch jets on aircraft carriers—and smashed into the car behind us. The guests began forming a semicircle, moving closer, concerned. I remember thinking that the nicely-dressed group gathered together on that wide, green lawn sort of looked like they were attending a polo game.

"Is everything OK?" someone asked.

"Yeah, they gave us a stick shift!" I answered back with a "can-you-believe-this-mix-up" shrug. I was still pretending like I was from New Jersey and, I suppose, driving a ten-year-old rental car with no functional doors. Eric was furiously attempting to get the car in first gear so we could leave.

"Got it!" he yelled as the stick moved into first.

"Don't do anything we wouldn't do!" I joked back at the polo attendees and Eric peeled out like we are cops leaving to save the mayor. He clipped the car ahead of us with my side mirror, but we were not slowing down for anything.

This is what we used to call "an embassy evacuation"; when we needed to leave a party hastily—at all costs—with every person in our group. An embassy evacuation was ordered after one of us did something —ruined a carpet or an appliance or a marriage—at a party and it was obvious that, once word of this update traveled, we would never be allowed back.

Eric accelerated over the hill; one could hear a

knocking noise as we disappeared, which was my side mirror scraping against the door as it dangled from the window. That is the last anyone at that party ever saw or heard from us.

There is a sort of freedom after a successful embassy evacuation, when you know you are never going to need to deal with those people again in your life. Usually, when something goes wrong at a party, you fret about the fallout: to whom do you need to apologize? Can we replace that vase? Do I still have a job? But, after an embassy evacuation, none of those things matter; that might as well have happened on Mars. You feel nothing but the joy of a clean escape.

Of course, in this case, there was some residual guilt that I might have irrevocably altered the professional reputation of Bob Doppell. That people in the pharmaceutical industry may have gossiped:

"Have you ever heard of this Bob Doppell, guy? He's supposed to be a legend: supposedly he's been in the industry thirty years, but he looks as young as you and can out-drink people half his age."

"Oh, I have not only *heard* of Bob Doppell, I've *met* him. I was in Cleveland for a convention. He had about 130 beers—easy—walked off a three story building, then told us not to tell his wife about it. Then, and this is the kicker: he and his buddy got into what was a clearly stolen car and drove off."

We were now close to Eric's apartment. He turned to ask if I was sure I was OK.

"Yeah," I answered.

In reality I had broken my back in three places and shattered my heel.

"I mean, don't get me wrong," I continued, "I'm not at my best right now and there's a general soreness but, overall, yeah, I think I handled that landing pretty well."

"Really?" Eric countered. "It looked pretty bad to me. I thought you were dead".

"I know, I know. Me too; me too," I conceded. "Wanna know what's even crazier? As I was falling—time kind of slowed down, y'know?—and I was calm about dying because, in my head, I was hearing '*The Power of Love*'!"

We both started laughing. And the laugh grew. Eric was laughing so loudly and violently—slapping his thigh and bending over—that he lost control of the car, causing it to jump over the curb and hit a tree. The car stopped instantaneously. Luckily (well, I don't know if that's quite the right word), Eric managed to puncture all four tires when vaulting the curb so we hit the tree slowly, what with the car no longer having functional wheels below it.

"Ugggh," I exhaled.

"Sorry dude," Eric apologized, before asking, "what do you want to do?"

"Eric, in the last four minutes I have walked off a roof and been in a car accident with a tree."

"So…," he pressed, "…*what* are you saying?"

"I think you should decide what we do next."

"Taco Bell?"

"Perfect," I answered.

We left the car exactly where it had stopped, against a tree on the lawn of a public library. Eric helped me walk to Taco Bell. By this point—and I'm not sure if it was because the adrenaline from when I walked off the roof was leaving me or if I had aggravated my injuries in the car accident three minutes after that, but—I was really struggling to walk.

We reached Taco Bell and they refused to serve us because we were not in a vehicle. Only the drive-through window was open and they insisted we could not walk through the drive-through lane, which I found ridiculous:

"You need to be in a car, sirs," they insisted.

"What?" I blurted. "We are the only customers in this line that are not actively drinking and driving!"

"Sirs, that's the rule, for safety."

"OK," Eric responded—he was an undergrad English major—"if we are doing plural formality, can we agree on 'gentlemen' instead of 'sirs'?"

"Yeah," I added, "we're not your commanding officers, we just want a burrito."

"I'm sorry sirs...I mean gentlemen," they relented, "I can't serve you if you're not in a car."

Luckily the car behind us in line heard the problem and invited us to order from their back seat. I will say this for Cleveland: it has its share of problems, but the drunks there look out for each other.

We ate our food, walked a block back to Eric's apartment and I went to sleep on the couch, but not before yelling, "Wake me up early so we can pick up my car before that library opens!"

I slept for about an hour before being awoken by a throbbing pain in my back. I initially assumed it was because I had slept in an odd position, so I straightened out, lay motionless on my back and expected to drift back off; but the pain only got worse. After about a half hour or so, I started to suspect that something was wrong with my body. That, maybe, walking off a building might have negatively affected me.

I woke Eric, told him I thought I needed to go to the hospital and that we should call my folks (even if it meant waking them up) and ask for a ride. Enter, my parents.

My mom and dad have been awakened by early morning phone calls several times—they have six kids—and it's never a positive call. It was usually one of us breaking an arm or leg or getting arrested; and every time my parents arrived they had two distinct roles: my mom would worry if everyone was OK, safe and accounted for; and my dad would just wonder if we did anything he could be sued for.

My dad raised six kids and, as far as he is concerned, this had merely created six different opportunities for him to "lose the house" in a lawsuit. That is how my dad ends every conversation or argument: that a stranger is going to take away his house in court. He might have originally been asked if the car needs gas or how The Electoral College works, but regardless of the initial topic, his reasoning will eventually reach a place where one of his kids will make a mistake serious enough for him to lose his house.

Better yet, these mistakes are usually innocent: a

simple matter of failing to shovel snow off the sidewalk or leaving a bike in someone's driveway; my dad believes somehow these can lead to someone seizing your property in retribution. According to my dad, that's how the American legal system works: one of your kids makes a trifling error, a stranger sues you over it, and that stranger is given your house. Same business day; no questions asked.

My folks drove me to the hospital. It was a forty-minute drive and they both talked for exactly forty minutes: my mom asking, over and over again if I was sure I was OK and my dad thinking aloud about all the people who could potentially sue him for leaving a car on the yard of a library.

My dad dropped me and my mom off at the ER so he could get back to the other kids. Before leaving he told me, "Sean, the next time you walk off a roof: don't move, because if you stay there, you can sue the homeowner."

Which I love because it is the oddest, most-paranoid way to give someone medical advice that is actually, in a round-about-way, correct.

The doctor had the results of the X-rays: my back was broken in three places and my left heel was more or less shattered. The breaks in my back were what's known as "compression fractures": the three lowest vertebrae were squeezed into a smaller area from the force of the fall. Essentially, I walked off the roof and was drunk enough to not realize I was falling so I kept walking in the air, not bending or adjusting for impact in any way. It was as if the house threw an anchor off its own roof and it landed dead on the concrete.

The doctor was mystified to the point of wondering if he had been given the wrong X-rays.

"I have never seen a compression fracture in this many vertebrae from a fall in anyone under the age of seventy," he said, adding, "I think we have the wrong X-rays. Because, for these to be correct, it would mean you made no effort to adjust. What. So. Ever."

"Does that sound like how you landed?" my mom asked, hoping to clarify if we indeed had the right scans.

"My landing," I answered to my mom and the doctor, "was not"—here I paused the find just the right word—"*skillful*,' so, yeah, I think we are probably looking at the right evidence."

The doctor was so disquieted by this that he brought in another surgeon and, after some kibitzing, that second surgeon abruptly left and reentered with a small group of residents.

The new doctor began explaining the uniqueness of my injury:

"Compression fractures from falls are very rare in young people because their reactions are usually good enough to better brace for impact, but this young man... He has several; caused by walking off a roof. We gather that he did not realize he was falling and he continued his walking motion in the air. He basically walked his way into the ground at falling speed."

"Like Daffy Duck?" one of his residents asked.

203

"Yes," replied the surgeon, "like Daffy Duck. Exactly."

"That said", the doctor continued, "walking off that way, 'Daffy Duck'-style as we are saying; being drunk—I'm assuming you were drunk Mr. Flannery?— probably saved your life."

"What?" I asked.

"The human body accelerates fast enough that a fall like yours, over ten feet?" he explained, "that's 1,500 to 2,000 some odd pounds of force on impact! Which is why, every fall above ten feet is lethal if you hit your head on impact. It's too much force for your skull and brain to absorb. But, by being drunk and landing like you did, you protected your head."

Another doctor, fearing I didn't 'get' the point, added, "Quite! If you realized you were falling, you would have bent your knees, which may have changed your center of gravity and that might have caused you to land differently, potentially hitting your head on the concrete. That would have been assuredly lethal."

"So", I asked, just to confirm I was understanding correctly, "being drunk saved my life?"

"In a way, yes," came the reply.

"*But*, doctor" a nurse interjected, "isn't it possible that a sober person may not have been on the roof?"

Shot of Science:
Are Drunks Invincible?

In 2012, The University of Illinois at Chicago (UIC) released a study that proved drunk people are better at surviving accidents than sober people and I remember laughing, "No shit, nerds; have you never attended a party with a pool and a second floor?"

The study did, however, present an interesting case on *how* drunks survive all this nonsense, and it's nothing like we are usually told. We tend to think that drunks survive accidents because they don't see the catastrophe coming and are loose and flexible; that they somehow bend their way out of the problem.

This is false.

Drunk people are hurt just as bad, if not worse, in the initial injury. The UIC study analyzed almost 200,000 trauma records from 1995 to 2009 and concluded that drunks were usually admitted with equivalent or worse injuries, when compared to sober people in comparable accidents. But, despite the damage being equal, drunk patients were fifty percent more likely to survive. A few years later, a comparable study by UCLA estimated the effect might be even higher (65 percent more likely). You see, drunks do not have some zen or Gumby-like ability to avoid injuries; instead, they get to the hospital and seem to forget to die.

Both the UIC and UCLA study landed on the same reason why drunks survive so much better: drunks are terrible at correctly estimating how hurt they are. What often kills you in a bad accident is not the injury as much as your body's own defense mechanisms: adrenaline is released by your body; your heart rate increases; massive inflammation happens; and it all combines to worsen blood loss to the point that you do not survive long enough for proper medical attention. Drunk people, by comparison, have no idea they have been injured, and can therefore survive much longer after the initial injury because they lose fluids at a much slower rate.

Let's say you are walking along a river and, for reasons that will not be understood until later, a harpoon enters your chest. If you are sober, you immediately panic. You scream for people to dial 911. Your heart is racing like never before, as you loudly bemoan the improbability of dying from a harpoon. Your panic increases further, as you wonder which people to call, to share your final dying words, and will you be able to drop the harpoon fixation long enough to share a meaningful last exchange? Or is it just going to be a bunch of incoherent whaling complaints? Then it goes dark. You have no pulse when the ambulance arrives due to blood loss. You are pronounced dead upon arrival.

Now, say the same thing happens and you are drunk. You don't even realize you have a harpoon in your chest until you reach the next bar and the harpoon prevents you from fitting through the doorway. "Look at this! Look at this!" you scream to your friends already inside the bar, laughing, "I look like a good damn foosball figurine! Ha!! I got this rod sticking out of me!" Someone yells, "That's a fucking harpoon, buddy!" and the bouncer says you may NOT enter with a harpoon sticking out of your chest and multiple people are calling an ambulance for you. The ambulance has to convince you to accept a ride. You live for another forty years and the harpoon is mounted on the wall of your apartment. You decline to press charges against the equally drunk and inattentive boaters who launched it at you because "the story is so epic."

That is a kind of chose-your-own-adventure example of why drunk people survive similar accidents so much better: they don't know they have been injured and, on that account, they can 'wait' longer for medical attention.

In each of these studies, the scientists belabored the point that though their conclusions show drunk people survive injuries better, they are not suggesting you should drink more; as, factored over multiple years, additional drinking leads to more injuries and diseases and would reduce, not increase, your long term safety.

I have reached a different conclusion.

The entire point of drinking is to forget reality—to mute the forever, background panic of your mind—which, as we just learned, not only helps us survive bad injuries but, I would also argue, life. Life is a harpoon to the chest that just bleeds slower. Society is nearly unbearable: your commute to work somehow gets longer each year; cooking recipes switch between ounces and cups, like you understand the conversion; your neighbors hate you if you don't cut your grass weekly. And that's when things are going well! Imagine adding sickness, injustice, calamities? Who wants to deal with any of that sober?

Which is why I concluded that these studies show I need to be drinking more. One, if the situation goes wrong tonight, I will probably survive. Two, while this means I might be signing up for fewer years overall, I'm pretty convinced they are better years. Maybe that's the real reason we survive the injuries? Maybe the researchers got it wrong? Maybe the reason the sober die more often is, staring at the aseptic light of the ambulance, bleeding badly, they begin asking important questions and decide, "I can't do another day of people talking about their favorite air fryer recipes; I'm going to quit fighting."

Whereas us drunks, we look up in the same situation and think, "I gotta find out why that girl with one arm slapped the dude in a captain's hat!" and we fight to live another day.

Ripley's Believe It Or Not Wax Museum
Niagara Falls, Ontario, Canada

It was hour two of sitting in a Ford Taurus with no keys in my high school parking lot, in twenty-degree weather. My body heat had warmed up the car so much that moisture collected on the interior windows, only to quickly turn to ice; a sheet of frost so thick I could not see out of the vehicle. I was in an igloo (which happened to have leather seats), freezing, and I started to think: "We may have planned this attempt to skip school too hastily."

We were seniors in high school and had arrived earlier that morning and, while meeting in the commons, decided on an impromptu plan to skip the second half of school and go to a nearby horse track. Me and my buddies did this often in high school: skipped half days to go betting; skipped whole days to go on road trips. The previous year (our junior year) we executed our grandest plan—we painted our masterpiece—by skipping school and leaving the country. We drove to Canada and back to Akron, Ohio, unnoticed. And the problem with painting a masterpiece that young is you start to believe that everything you doodle is an act of flawless genius. You get cocky, and the next thing you know you are spending a full day in a frozen car, stuck in the parking lot of the school you were trying to escape.

The plan we had devised that morning was simple, but it was impromptu and had definite risk vectors. My buddy Tyson and I, both frustrated with school, decided we would forge notes from our parents, each claiming that we were visiting a nearby college that day—you were allowed six days off to visit a college—and we would be leaving after our first few classes. To avoid suspicion, our exact departures and colleges would be different.

"I'll write the notes," I told Tyson.

Every time we skipped school I would forge a note from our respective parents. We did it so regularly that we started intercepting legitimate notes from them—donations to the school; offers to help with bingo—and I would forge a facsimile of the legitimate note so the school would never see what their real handwriting looked like.

"No, I got this one," Tyson replied.

"I think we should stick with the traditional plan," I insisted.

"No, this is a simple one. I got it," he said and left for home room.

I turned my note into the principal's office first, as my note had me departing first.

"I'm going to visit the Cleveland Institute of Art today," I told the secretary, "it's my dream college. Leaving after second period with my folks. Here's the note."

"Hmm, OK, all right. Leave it here," the secretary replied.

And I left.

A few minutes later a buddy of mine—who was delivering mail for the office—found me and said, "Hey man, I overheard them saying they think that note is suspicious and they're going to call your parents!"

Working quickly, I called up Kinney Shoes (the store where I worked), got a hold of my twenty-year-old manager and asked if she would call the school's office, claiming to be my mom, and tell them I have her go-ahead to visit The Cleveland Art Institute.

"Is this illegal?" she asked.

"I don't know," I answered, "but, if you do this for me, I'll promise to dye all the shoes for the next two wedding parties!" (Color-matched bridal footwear was a big thing at the time, and everyone at the store hated dealing with it.)

"Will they believe I'm your mom? I have kind of a high-pitched voice."

"I go to an all-guys, Catholic high school. Most of us don't know two women in life we aren't related to. There's no way they will suspect you're not my mom."

She made the call. I would learn later from my mail buddy that this assuaged the staff's fears, but at that moment I was busy looking for Tyson to warn him to expect similar pushback. I found him as he was entering his next period and barely had time to explain the situation:

"Tys! They were super suspicious of my note! They were going to call my parents. I had my manager call as my mom...Hopefully that works...I wonder if we should stage a fake call as your dad?"

"Oh, don't worry, they are not going to question my note," Tyson answered and confidently walked into his class.

People I'd Like to Have a Drink With:
Jeremy J. Van Ert

When men tour breweries and we see huge fermentation tanks or giant casks for aging liquor, we always do the same joke: "I'd love to fall into that and drink my way out!"
Jeremy J. Van Ert did what we always claimed we "wanted" to do.

Jeremy arrived at the Kwik Trip gas station in Marshfield, Wisconsin at 11:50 p.m. and entered the walk-in beer freezer. Kwik Trip closed at midnight, so the cashier locked everything down, including the walk-in freezer, which contained Jeremy. Jeremy saw the cashier locking the freezer and, at this point, most people would have said something. Maybe because they were a bit claustrophobic, or maybe because they realized that frostbite would set in in less than two hours, or perhaps just because they had places to be and didn't want to spend all night in an unlit beer freezer; most people would have yelled or screamed or generally kicked up a fuss. Not Jeremy J, Van Ert. Sensing the opportunity of a lifetime, he quietly watched the doors shut and proceeded to drink as much inventory as possible until the next morning, when another employee re-opened the store and unlocked the freezer.

This story could only happen in Wisconsin.

Yes, there are other states where citizens can handle freezing temperatures and, yes, there are a few states where the average customer is willing to be barricaded into a liquor cabinet for a night, but only a Wisconsinite can handle the Venn intersection of: "I think I can survive this cold, long enough to drink all this beer."

Don't believe me? A 2019 report by 24/7 Wall Street entitled "The Drunkest (and Driest) Cities in America," reviewed drinking data on U.S. cities and concluded that twelve of the top twenty hardest-drinking cities in America were located in Wisconsin! And, if that were not enough, let's hear let's hear from the Marshfield Police Chief, Rick Gramza, who responded to this incident:

"We've dealt with people who intentionally hide and get locked inside places with the purpose of committing a crime, but we never had somebody accidentally locked in a place and not make any attempt to be rescued or get out because they're satisfied with the circumstances. He just decided to run it out for the night. It had everything that he needed."

–(*interviewed by Rachel Siegel, Washington Post, October 27, 2017.*)

The next morning, at 6 a.m., a Kwik Trip employee re-opened the store and the moment the freezer was unlocked, Van Ert "made a beeline from the beer cooler to the door without any attempt to pay for what he had consumed or broken" (Chief Gramza's words) and drove home. The store reported that Van Ert consumed one 18-ounce Icehouse beer and three 23.5-ounce cans of Four Loko, and knocked over and broke three thirty-packs of Busch Beer on his way out, and it's not clear how much of that Van Ert also drank. Personally: I don't think a man like Van Ert ruins a lot of beer by accident.

Van Ert was charged with retail theft and it's kind of amazing to me that he got off so lightly because there is no way Jeremy J. didn't urinate in that freezer. To begin with, he clearly entered that Kwik Trip already buzzed. No one—I don't care how hard you drink—decides to spend all night in a beer freezer that quickly unless they have already enjoyed at least a few cocktails. Then you add that he drank about ninety combined ounces of Four Loko and Icehouse, and sat or paced in the same room for six hours? He definitely relieved himself in that freezer.

As I think about this, Van Ert must have knocked over all that Busch intentionally, to flood the place in cheap, amber beer in order to hide the fact he pissed all over the floor. Right? And if that's the case, then he's a criminal mastermind— the Hans Gruber of Marshfield Wisconsin—who, when his original, hasty plan to drink free beer went wrong, consciously spilled the cheapest beer in the freezer so he's not additionally charged as a sex offender or health code violator; or whatever else they add when you whip out your dick and urinate inside a public beer freezer.

Cynics will point out that Van Ert's retail theft charge (which, perhaps unsurprisingly, also triggered a parole violation) will surely cost more him more than if he simply paid for one 18-ounce Icehouse beer and three cans of Four Lokos, but—and perhaps this is why you become a cynic—such people do not see the brilliance of Van Ert's plan. Yes, that ended up being the most expensive can of Four Loko he will ever chug, but, for a mere ticket, Jeremy J. Van Ert has one of the greatest drinking stories on Earth; an astonishing tale in which he is equal parts Harry Houdini, Yukon Cornelius, and Keith Richards. Plus, unlike a lot of great tales, it can be easily inserted into just about any party conversation:

"Better grab a coat before we go outside, Jeremy, it's cold."

"Oh, I think I'll be fine: I've had colder nights."

Tyson was two hours late. My note said I would be leaving at 10:30 a.m. It was now 12:30 p.m. and I had been inside a frozen Mercury Topaz for two hours, watching the ice stretch across the vehicle. At that point I made a vow: I would not go back into the school to admit the plan failed. I'd rather them discover my frozen body inside my buddy's car, like a dead Everest hiker, than return to Chemistry 301.

Twenty minutes later, as I was relaxed, prepared to die solemnly, Tyson busted through the door. He had no coat on and was holding a giant piece of wood with "HALL PASS" etched into it.

"That's not good," I thought. That doesn't look like a man who's ready to leave campus.

"Well, they got me, dude," he began.

"What do you mean?"

"They found out my note was fake. In fact, it was pretty bad."

"What happened?"

"Well, you know, if we are being honest, I'm a better student than you, Sean."

"That' s very true."

"So the colleges I'm looking at, they are far away and—no disrespect—but I thought it wouldn't sound realistic that I was visiting colleges around here, like you are."

"No disrespect taken."

"So, I went in a different direction."

"Ok, what did your note say?"

"I said one of my close friends was murdered

earlier this week and I needed to attend his funeral."

"What?"

"I thought, they'd feel so guilty, they wouldn't ask any follow up questions."

"Do you know how infrequently teenagers get murdered in Copley Ohio? It would have been a huge story that everyone would know about!"

"Well, it gets worse."

"How does it get worse than that?"

"The principal called me into his office and said the note looked suspicious, and I didn't know this at the time but they had already called my parents on it."

"Oh boy," I interrupted.

"Yeah, and they told my parents to stay on the line. So, my parents were silently listening on speaker phone when the principal called me in and, again, he said it looked a little suspicious and they were wondering who was murdered so I panicked and said, 'Ya know what: the kid never meant that much to me. Why don't I just skip the funeral?' And I stood up to go back to class and the principal—he knew he had me trapped in a lie—so he questioned back, 'The kid did not mean anything to you?' And I said, 'People wear a lot of masks in life.' And, with that, I heard my dad scream, 'Christ, TYSON!' from the office phone."

We both exhaled, knowing he was in a lot of trouble.

"Well, I have to get back to Greek History in two minutes," Tyson concluded, pointing to the hall pass as he exited the car but, before shutting the door he dipped his head back into the automotive iceberg and said, "Oh, and they know about Canada."

"How do they know about Canada?" I asked.

"They were able to piece it together after my debacle. Like I said: it was bad."

"You didn't tell them that we had a Canadian friend that died?" I quipped, and he shut the door, laughing.

The next day the principal called us into the office and said, "I don't have the leeway to discipline you for that Canada stunt last year," which we found hilarious because this was a Catholic school. He could have forced us to drive the school's tractor to Manitoba as punishment—they were allowed to do pretty much whatever they want—but, separately, it was made clear that any time we missed classes in the future our parents would get a confirmation call and that ended our sport of skipping school.

I often tell this story—about being stuck in a car in freezing weather while my buddy lied about a funeral—and when the part about the Canada trip comes up people always say, "Wait…you flicked school and left the country? And you've never told me that story?"

And I would always respond, a bit ashamed: "It's not that great of a story."

It's a good *memory*, to be sure. One of the greatest days of my life. I laughed so hard that day I lost my voice, but it's not a good *story*. And it's not a good story because it was the most well-planned event in any of our lives. We plotted that day for months and executed it with practiced precision. Competency, even on very impressive missions, doesn't make for a good "story."

Look at NASA: The Apollo 11 mission proved we could reach the moon; Apollo 12 proved we could explore more of the moon; but ask any American to name an Apollo mission and they will say "13." The one where mishaps nearly killed everyone.

Our best-planned missions in high school often resulted in our least interesting stories. They had a kind of understated craftsmanship to them—quietly successful, like a baseball player that only hits singles—but they did not have the exciting twists and turns of a great story. The only exception might have been our friendship-long attempt to make, purchase, or swindle fake IDs for buying beer. That effort was both meticulously planned and disastrous.

Our first attempts to get beer underage were indelicate: we would wait outside the most white trash gas stations in town and ask any guy who drove a car with a bird, wolf, or flaming-arrow painted on the hood if they would buy us beer:

"Hey man, you getting beer?" we'd inquire.

"Hell yeah!" would come the inevitable reply; inevitable from anyone with some type of stylized carnivore emblazoned on their vehicle.

"We forgot our IDs. Yep, all five of us. If we gave you this twenty dollar bill, could you buy us a case of beer?"

There are two ages when kids are indisputably hilarious: when they are toddlers—they stumble into walls constantly; never wear pants; claim they are going to marry the family dog—and when they are in their late teens, talking to adults, and believing they don't sound like total shitheads.

Back then a case of cheap beer was about three dollars, which made our proposal sound even more ludicrous: we were paying for Busch Light like it had a street value above cocaine, and we were all wearing ties outside a gas station in an effort to make ourselves look older.

The main reason teenagers in this phase are so hilarious is because adults do nothing to correct their behavior. No one tells them: "Kid, people don't fly to Copley, Ohio 'for business'" or that "Five grown men don't split a case of beer." When five grown men enter a liquor store together—and I contend that the correct plural noun for five men in a liquor store is an "escalation"—they buy enough booze to submerge a basement because, each time they hesitate about needing one more bottle someone in the escalation says, "Just buy it; we can always finish it tomorrow if we don't get to it tonight." But that never works, for the same reason you can't go on vacation and just leave a week's supply of food out for the dog; it all disappears in the first eight hours, and your house gets destroyed in the process.

No, these adults never provided practical feedback. Instead, each stranger listened to our pitch, visibly held back laughter—almost convulsing, like a heron fighting back a fish trying to swim up its neck—and answered, "Oh, sorry honey, no, I can't tonight."

Then they would presumably drive to their

friend's party with their beer and enter the party laughing hysterically: "Wait till you hear what happened to me at the gas station! Ha. Five teenagers—in *ties*, mind you— tell me they've left their wallets back at "corporate!" At corporate! They didn't provide any more information on the company or their line of work! Then these five, corporate professionals asked me to buy one case of Busch Light—for five grown men to share—at three times its normal price! Hahaha! I asked if they were under twenty-one, just as a joke to see how stupid it could get."

"What did they do?"

"They did this fake, dad laugh—'OOOH HOO HOO!'—then said, 'You flatter us, ma'am.' *Ma'am*! 'I'm twenty-two years old!'"

Even on the rare occasion that the plan worked, we received no instructive feedback, so our gambit was destined to never improve. We would approach customers for about an hour, explaining our situation as business people without wallets, but each declined to help. Until, eventually, a guy (it was always a guy) usually covered in white paint would say, "Yeah, I got ya."

And we would hand him a twenty and he would emerge with an impossible amount of beer, go directly to his car, load it in—"Is he stealing it from us?" we'd wonder—but then he would roll over to us, hand us just one of the cases through his window, saying:

"Thanks! Don't do anything too stupid with that!" He would then peel out, keeping both the extra beer and the change. This last part was always unspoken and uncontested.

We rapidly learned this plan was not sustainable. A few of us got arrested, plus we couldn't afford to keep paying for beers at a price that wouldn't be fair inside Yankee Stadium, so we vowed to develop a more sophisticated scheme: "Let's eliminate the middleman and buy our own fake ID!"

We heard a tee shirt shop at The Arcade, an old art deco mall in Cleveland that was semi-abandoned at the time, would print fake IDs. We went there and, like all failing malls at the time, there were seven tee-shirt shops, but we eventually found the one that did print fake IDs. The place and the conversation were amazing, in its dubious flirtations with what is and what is not legal:

"We are looking to buy fake IDs," I told the guy behind the counter, in as clandestine a tone as I could manage.

"No one can sell fake IDs, kids. I'd get arrested tomorrow if I sold you a fake ID," came the prompt reply.   There was then a slight pause, just enough for him to see if our look of disappointment is genuine enough or not. "But, what we *do* sell here," he continued, "is novelty tourism photos and those can be very specific."

"What do you mean by that?" we asked.

"Well, ya know how when you go to the Grand Canyon and, for a memory, maybe you stand behind one of those wooden cowboy cutouts, where you stick your head out onto the body of a cowboy and someone takes a photo for ten dollars? Well, we do something similar but, instead of sticking your head out of a cowboy cutout, the state of Montana's official ID background, with random personal information, is behind you!...Ya know, for the memories!"

We contemplated this for a second, then asked: "Do you have any, um, '*memories*' that you have done for other customers that we can see, just to see how much we would, ah, 'remember' this event?"

The owner showed us a few examples and, to our untrained eyes, they looked exactly like out-of-state licenses. In fact, they looked perfect.

"Great. Let's get Ohio ones."

"I don't do Ohio," the owner said. "Makes it harder to argue it's a tourism venture."

"Makes perfect sense," we said in reply to something that actually made no sense.

"OK, then, I guess…Pennsylvania?" I proposed.

"Yeah and maybe, Indiana?" another friend suggests.

"And Michigan?" came a third.

"Gentleman," the store owner interjected, "may I suggest that all five of you get Wyoming."

"Wyoming?"

"See, Wyoming is the last state in the union to not use holograms. You likely did not notice when viewing the 'memories' I made for other people, but I am not capable of printing holograms. So, while I could print memories from Pennsylvania or Indiana and Michigan, they would lack the aforementioned holograms and, depending on who you are sharing these memories with—say it's someone who looks at a lot of different 'memories' each night, as say his job at, oh I don't know, a bar?—that kind of person might notice the missing holograms."

"On our memories?"

"Yes, on your memories."

"I don't know," I replied, speculating out loud, "I think five guys entering a bar in Cleveland, all from Wyoming, is more suspicious than missing holograms. I mean, if we go to dive bars, they just want to see something passable, but five guys from the least-populated state in the US entering together...I mean, it's like we are daring them."

"But," the owner interjected, "this memory is indistinguishable from an official Wyoming license. No technology on earth could differentiate it!"

"What would we say?" I asked the group.

"We could say we are all at Case Western, like we got some group scholarship?" someone suggested.

"We could say we are on the hockey team? We could look like hockey players," another offered.

"Say you're in town for the rodeo!" the owner pitched in.

"I don't know," I demurred, "as I said before, it's the least-populated state in the U.S. so, to have five Wyomingian...Wyoman..."

"Wyomingite," corrected the owner.

"To have five *Wyomingites* walking into the same bar in Cleveland? Statistically, it's like having five Oscar winners walk in. It's just as unlikely."

"Well, Sean," my buddy Tyson replied, "let's hope bouncers don't know as much about geography or statistics as you do."

We plunked down the cash for five Wyoming "memories."

The first time we used them as a group, we were all arrested.

And so we decided that these half measures—strangers at a gas station, out-of-state 'memories'—were not sufficient for a group of truly dedicated under-age drinkers such as these. We decided we must have real IDs; we decided to trick the state of Ohio into giving us real licenses.

Our idea was very bold, but also very simple: We would pay a twenty-one-year-old who matched our general physical description to give us their birth certificate and social security card for a few hours; then we use those documents to get a new license with our photo on it. Straightforward enough, but very risky. It was a bit like lion taming; a simple enough concept, but there were lots of ways it could go wrong.

Back then, one did not walk out of the DMV with your new license. You received it about a week later in the mail. We had researched our plan a bit and been informed by someone—I can't even remember who told us this—that the reason for the delay was because every new photograph was sent down to Columbus where a human compared the new photo to your last picture to prevent fraud; if the pictures looked too different, they would not issue the license and begin legal proceedings against every party involved.

Looking back at it, this claim is laughable: that a staff of—what, a dozen people?—was looking at every new license (in the seventh most populous state in the union) and asking themselves, "Can a person really lose this much weight or change their hair that much in five years?"

Nevertheless we, being teenagers, found the whole scenario highly credible. So much so that we decided to test the integrity of the system: we wanted to see just how different someone could look between licenses and still receive a new one. We had a buddy who was twenty-one and we asked if he'd be willing to get a new license looking very different; so different, in fact—that if the state of Ohio was really scrutinizing these pictures—there is no way he would receive the new license.

"Can I get in trouble?" he asked.

"I don't see how. At the end of the day, you're just choosing a radically different new look for yourself."

You may ask: How do teenagers with no experience in cosmetics, makeovers, or general aesthetics make a man look vastly different for his photograph? Well, we bought a werewolf costume. We used the costume paint to make his skin look considerably darker then glued the beard on him and dyed his hair. My buddy also borrowed his grandmother's impossibly large eyeglasses, each lens shaped like a giant hexagon. Our test subject looked absolutely nothing like himself as he went off to apply for his replacement ID.

He received his new license a week later. We had to pay him an extra $150 because he failed his eye exam due to being disoriented by the strong prescription on the glasses: his license had a vision restriction on it for a whole year. But overall, we had proved our plan would work.

Later that week we were at a Bob Evans, eating breakfast, and one of the waitresses called me by the wrong name and asked why I was eating "out here"; only after squinting at me a bit closer did she realize she had mistaken me for someone else.

"I'm sorry," she explained, "it's just that you look exactly like one of our cooks!"

"Is he twenty-one?" my friend asked instantly. "And if so, could we talk to him?"

And that is how we met the person that would rent his social security card and birth certificate to me, to get what we were now calling "a misrepresentative ID," rather than a fake ID, since it was a genuine Ohio state ID; it just had the wrong driver on it.

The plan was an abysmal failure and we were very lucky to not get arrested.

I entered the DMV with the cook's papers, explained I needed a license and sat down for my picture and, as I was preparing to smile with all the jubilation of a person about to finalize a Mission Impossible-esque heist, they asked me, "And, Geoff," — that was the name of the cook—"can you tell me your mother's maiden name?"

I wish they had taken the photo of me right as I was reacting to that question. Even more I wish there was some way for me to get a copy of that picture, because I don't think anyone—not in vaudeville, in silent movies, in opera—made a face more visibly and comically aghast as I did when they when asked me to verify the name of my misappropriated grandmother.

"You mean, the name my mom had before marriage," I asked.

"Yes."

Panicked, I scanned my eyes around the office and noticed that behind the person asking this question was a billboard detailing the fees for each DMV service. A license renewal was listed as seven dollars.

"WHOA!," I exclaimed. "Hold on. Is this seven dollars?"

"What? Yes, a license replacement is seven dollars."

"I thought it would be free, ya know, off my taxes!" (I knew enough about impersonating adults to bring up that you pay taxes and expect that that entitles you to a vast array of unrealistic benefits.)

"Of course there's a fee."

"Well, because I don't have a license, I didn't even bring my wallet; didn't see a point. I need to go get my wallet."

"All right, well, that should not take long. I will just keep all your papers right here."

Something inside me sank as I realized I was now going to have to pay that cook at Bob Evans a lot more money now that I'd lost his identity papers at a DMV in Fairlawn, Ohio. And potentially implicated him in a federal crime. But I managed to conceal my alarm and responded, with relative calm, "Given that I don't have a wallet, I appreciate you keeping the papers here."

I rose from my chair and headed out of the DMV. I had to pay that cook at Bob Evans $300.

"What am I going to do?!" he screamed at me, justifiably.

"Just go to the DMV and follow through with the plan," I explained. "Say you need a new license; they have your papers; you look enough like me, they won't notice you are a different person."

He did so and it worked. The DMV clerk even joked with him (thinking he was me), "I thought you were trying to scam us. Sorry."

"I appreciate you being so careful," he replied, in an artificial voice, "think of what would happen to me, if it was a scammer! My identity gone? No thank you. Good to see my tax dollars at work here!"

But those were our bad plans. Great stories, bad plans. The Canada trip was a good plan.

We left Akron Ohio around 6 a.m. We told our parents we were developing film at school—in those old-fashioned dark rooms with the red light and vats full of chemicals—for a study we did about local wildlife and the dark room was only available in the morning. I don't think our school even had a dark room.

We reached Niagara Falls around noon.

One of my friends used his dad's car phone to call the school, and we each took turns pretending to be each other's father, saying our son would not be attending today, giving various excuse as to why. But, as we entered eastern Pennsylvania, he remembered that his dad's plan only worked in Ohio, so we had to do the last two calls quickly:

"Hello?! Hello!" I barked into the phone, in my best "somebody's dad" voice, "this is Doctor Phil Addemack, father of John Addemack. John is not feeling himself today and will be staying at home. Very good. Very good. Thank you. Now, well, due to an unusual set of circumstances, my dear friend Harley Kastner—successful lawyer—is seated next to me and requires the phone..."

John Addemack grabbed the phone. "Yes? Yes? Good, I have you? This is Harley Kastner, known lawyer. My son Jeff is also not feeling well and will not be..."

About four hours later, we reached the border. We had heard various reports on what you had to bring so we had our social security cards and birth certificates with us in plastic bags (which was also a funny addition to our early morning plans: "Mom, I am using the school's dark room at 6 a.m. so you will not see me today...also, can I have my birth certificate?").

As we approached the border security guard, we reminded each other, "Be cool, be cool; we have our documents if needed."

We were surprised by how empty it looked. We were arriving at an odd time, in the late morning, and the weather was atrocious- bitterly cold with whipping winds. We were the only car.

The guard asked, "U.S. citizens?"

"Yes."

"How long are you staying?"

"How long does it take to do a U-turn?" our driver laughed. We explained that we were only entering the country to win a bet and will immediately turn around.

Today, that answer would probably get you shot, or at least bitten by a Doberman. But, back in the 1990s, it resulted in hilarity; the guard waved us forward, laughing, "That's the perfect damn reason to visit!" He further offered to take a photo for us to prove we won our bet.

We have a photo of the four of us, outside our car at the border, taken by a border guard.

As we walked back to the car to leave, the guard asked, "How are you doing on time?"

"Pretty good," answered our driver.

"If you think you have thirty minutes," the guard suggested, "I recommend the Ripley's Believe or Not Wax Museum. It's one of Canada's great sites."

— — — — — — —

EDITOR'S NOTE: *Astute readers may have noticed that while this chapter is called "Ripley's Believe It Or Not," the titular attraction shows up exactly once in the entire story, in the very last line. The Editor dutifully brought this up to the Author, who merely shrugged and ordered another Negroni.*

The Birds Nest
Akron, OH

When I worked at Comp USA, customers would become infuriated if we were out of stock on a cable they needed or if they felt the prices were too high on cables. They would swear at us and say the entire store—me included—was run by idiots.

I think they wanted me to become angry or upset, but I always remained calm and would reply, "Honestly I don't even know why you buy cables here, when Cabling Solutions has such better options and prices."

"Really?" they would ask, and I would give them directions to Cabling Solutions. This was before mobile phones with GPS and Google, so I gave very specific directions.

Now, in actual fact, there was no such thing as Cabling Solutions. Instead, I was giving them directions to The Birds Nest, a strip club in a bad part of town.

One day I walked by the cabling aisle and overheard a colleague directing a customer—who seemed perfectly nice—toward Cabling Solutions in order to find the cord she needed. I took the employee aside:

"Why are you sending her to Cabling Solutions?" I asked.

"We don't have her cable," they responded.

"OK, but...Cabling Solutions doesn't exist. I made it up."

"What? You send people there all the time!"

"I send *assholes* there! It's a strip club off Kenmore Boulevard. We can't send that lady there."

"Well, I assumed it was real...I mean, you seemed like one of the more knowledgeable employees...so..."

"I don't even own a computer, man."

"So, you're...like...just a *jackass*?"

Most of the people who know me would probably say that exchange pretty well sums up what it's like to maintain a friendship with me.

That Comp USA closed. The Birds Nest closed a few weeks later and I'd like to think that's related: that I sent enough assholes to "Cabling Solutions" to keep that strip club afloat.

Ultimately, I suppose both businesses were killed by the internet. And what's even more sad than all the businesses that the internet has killed, is that the internet has also made it really hard to send assholes away with bad directions.

SLAMMABLEDICKCAVES.COM
The Internet

In 2014, The Chicago Reader, my city's finest alternative newspaper, interviewed me for their "Best Of" issue and I assumed, naturally, that I would be named Best Stand-up Comic in Chicago. I was not. I was named Best *Drunk* in the city.

Your wife is never thrilled when a newspaper names you the best drunk in town, but, when you are named the best drunk in Chicago—a city of almost three million people known for getting blind drunk at baseball games and partying so hard on St Patrick's Day, it dyes the river green—she will be particularly bothered.

> ### How Did They Do That?
> *Dyeing the Chicago River Green*
>
> Chicago has been dyeing its river green for St Patrick's Day for half a century and you would think a project of that size—changing the physical makeup of a river that moves two billion gallons of water a day situated next to America's third largest city—would be a careful, well-planned operation. And if you thought that, then, well, you're not from Chicago.
>
> Chicago's official slogan should be "I know a guy" because everything in this city gets done by buddies from the neighborhood. And the tradi-

tion of dyeing the river is no different: It was a spur-of-the-moment idea from Steve Bailey, the head of the plumbers' union, president of the Chicago St. Patrick's Day Parade Commission, and (probably more importantly than either of those titles) neighborhood buddies with Mayor Richard J. Daley.

In 1961 the city of Chicago started to identify and punish polluters of the Chicago River. They employed plumbers to insert green dye at various locations that would help identify which pipes or businesses were illegally dumping into the river. One day, one of the plumbers returned to union headquarters covered in green from the colorant, and Bailey noticed the brilliant emerald hue. Being in charge of the city's annual St. Pat's parade, he started to dream up the idea to use the dye on the entire river.

The following is a description, from Bailey's assistant, of how they 'planned' the entire operation that afternoon, after Bailey saw the plumber with the green stain, and is a fascinating insight of how fast-and-loose the city of Chicago was with its water supply:

"When the plumber left and we were alone... he said, "Why couldn't we dye the whole river for St. Patrick's Day?"
"I'm serious. Who would know about this?"

Reaching for a straw I answered, Capt. Manley, the port director. He is the only one I know who answers questions about the Chicago River.

In a second he was on the phone to Capt. Manley.

Bill Barry, first deputy port director, happened to be in Manley's office when the call came in and related the following conversation.

"Say John," said Bailey, "I've been wondering whether we could dye the river green for St. Patrick's Day. What do you think?"

"It might work," said Manley, after a moment's hesitation. "Just a minute."

Manley turned to Barry and put the question to him.

"Gee, Cap, I don't know," said Barry. "If the Fire Department can shoot colored water into the air from its boats, I don't see why we couldn't try it."

Manley went back to the phone and told Bailey he was sure it could be done.

(–from "The Man Who Dyed the River Green: Stephen M. Bailey" by Dan Lydon, then-assistant to Stephen M Bailey.)

That story is amazing. As a narrative, it might be more fascinating and chilling than the creation of the atomic bomb. The fact that, in 1961, you could just call a harbormaster, reach the assistant, and say:

"Yeah, hi, I want to dick around with your river. Change the color for a few days. Throw a parade."

And not only is the call taken seriously, you get a tentative "yes" in under one minute.

And better than their planning was their execution! Bailey and his plumbing buddies procured a green fluorescent dye from the same company that provides dye for Navy rescue operations. When a sailor or pilot falls into the ocean, they break a dye packet which spreads a bright green patch across several acres, making it easier to spot and recover them. In those situations, only a few ounces of dye are needed to cover a fairly sizable area.

Bailey and his plumbers bought several hundred pounds. The river stayed green for a week.

Better yet was Bailey's response when some Chicagoans started to worry that the green coloring might never dissipate. He resolutely gave the following statement:

"The Chicago River will dye the Illinois, which will dye the Mississippi, which will dye the Gulf of Mexico, which will send green dye up the Gulf Stream across the North Atlantic into the Irish Sea; a sea of green surrounding the land will appear as a greeting to all Irishmen of the

Emerald Isle from the men of Erin in Chicagoland, USA."

Not only does Chicago let a few hard-drinking, Irish plumbers screw around with the river, but, when concerns are raised that they might not have thought this through, and the media ask for a response, their reply is: "Guys, we are *fucking legends* for doing this!"

By 1964, the third year of the tradition, they learned that only twenty-five pounds of dye were needed to make the river green for about twenty-four hours and no more. For the first decade or so they continued to use a chemical dye but, in the 1970s they moved to an organic dye to minimize environmental impact and, today, they use around forty pounds of an environmentally-friendly organic dye.

Other cities have tried to copy Chicago's tradition and dye their own respective rivers green for St. Patrick's Day, but, luckily for Chicago (in terms of bragging rights), the plan is always vetoed by the relevant state's environmental protection agency. Most recently, Saginaw, Michigan (the Saginaw River) and Fort Lauderdale, Florida (the New River) both attempted to copy the stunt and both were denied since the cities could not prove there would be no environmental impact from it. One of the reasons why they cannot prove this is: The only city in the

> world that actually does it (Chicago) has never attempted to show it has no effect. We've always just assumed our river is already so polluted that no amount of annual discoloration could possibly make it worse.
> And our experts agree! Asked to evaluate the risk of dyeing the river, Margaret Frisbie, the executive director of the Friends of the Chicago River advocacy group said:
> "The environmental impact of the dye is minimal compared with sources of pollution such as bacteria from sewage-treatment plants."
> Only in Chicago could an environmental engineer seek to allay fears about the possible damage to the city's main river from a festive makeover by reminding the populace that it's already full of shit.

A night or so after I was named "Best Drunk" my wife and I left a bar at last call and grabbed a cab. To me, a cab ride home after last call is the closest most Americans will be get to a safari trip, where you stare from the safety of your vehicle at creatures and skirmishes not normally found in civilization: Men headbutting each other at full speed like rhinos competing for pasture; women in high heels walking drunk, like a newborn giraffe finding its legs.

"God," Jessica said after taking it all in. "I can't

believe I'm married to the worst drunk in this city."

"*Best* drunk," I corrected her.

"Ugh, is there a difference? Also, by the way, have you Googled yourself since you won this major award?"

I had not Googled myself. Upon arriving home that night, I did just that and discovered that when you Googled "Sean Flannery" the search engine would suggest, helpfully: "Did you mean, 'Sean Flannery DRUNK'?".

The fact that Google, the modern world's broker of knowledge—today's library of Alexandria—felt the need to clarify the inquiry in this manner is unfortunate testament to the brilliance of the search engine; the fact they would recommend rephrasing that question the same way you would at a party:

"Do you know where Sean Flannery is?"

"You mean Sean Flannery, the drunk one, right?"

"Shit," I said, upon seeing these results. I had just started a job search for the first time in years and this was probably not going to help my chances.

"Well," I mused aloud. "Maybe the people interviewing me won't Google me?"

"For a technology job?" Jessica asked sarcastically.

"God, I hate Google," I said, and turned off the computer and went to bed.

A few years before Google identified me only as "Sean Flannery the drunk," my buddy

Mike texted me that he was at one of my favorite bars, Wrigleyville North, and was looking to start a bender because his wife had left him. This is a matter you encounter often in Chicago, not so much friends getting divorced, but people proposing a bender, like it's a nature walk or architecture tour:

"Are you doing anything tomorrow? No? Come join me for seven Rob Roys before lunch!"

I joined Mike and we drank. He was initially bemoaning the fact that his marriage fell apart, but soon, he began to complain that, because he and his now ex-wife had been together since high school, he had no idea how to talk to women anymore.

"I've been out of the game too long. I wouldn't even know how to sound cool," he explained. "The dialogue has changed, right?"

"Um, I don't think so," I countered. "Not too much."

"Come on! It's different! What do you young guys call chicks?" he asked (Mike is five years younger than me).

"I think it's all pretty much the same terms from when we were growin' up, man," I replied. "Chicks. Girls. Ladies?"

"No!" he insisted. "What's the new term? There's gotta be one! You're hiding it from me!"

I assured him I was not hiding any "terms" but he grabbed me by the lapels—he was so drunk he was finding it impossible to believe his friend might be being honest—and then he suddenly said something so loud, so unexpected, and vulgar, it was like a meteorite fell from space, crashed through the roof of the bar, and knocked me to the floor:

"Let me guess," he spat, "'Slammable Dick Caves!'"

"*What?!*"

"You young guys! You call women Slammable Dick Caves, right?!"

He seemed to be suggesting it seriously; that he thought the phrase "slammable dick caves"—which, beyond its contentious and generally objectionable tone, is an awkward, bulky mouthful—had replaced the common terms of "chick" or "lady" during his seven years of marriage.

I fell over laughing. The phrase seemed so crazy, so unexpected, and so silly, I thought that, maybe, it could actually catch on? I was so drunk I began to think that "slammable dick caves" could conceivably become part of the American lingo, so I took out my phone and credit card and, while thinking, thank God I'm not as drunk as this guy, I registered the domain name "SlammableDickCaves.com" on the internet.

Not only did I register it, I expressed amazement that it was still available.

"You're not gonna believe this!" I told Mike after clicking about on my phone for a second or two. "It's what, 2007? And Slammable Dick Caves DOT COM is still available!" I emphasized the "dot com" loudly, to show we were getting the internet's best real estate; none of that .info or .org stuff for us!

"Are you serious?" Mike questioned in wonderment.

"I know!" I responded. "You'd think some entrepreneur would have gobbled it up by now, right? We're gonna make some serious dough off this!"

I have no recollection of what happened that night after registering SlammableDickCaves.com. To be perfectly honest, I didn't even recall buying SlammableDickCaves.com the next morning; I left for a trip to New York with Jessica, thinking nothing of it.

Three years later, almost to the day, I was in Ohio marrying Jessica. Jessica and I said our vows, had the best night of our lives, then spend a week in San Francisco and the Napa Valley for our honeymoon.

We returned to Chicago and entered our apartment on that great high that all newlyweds have when passing through their home's doorway for the first time as a married couple. After reminiscing a bit on the wedding and laughing, I went and made some coffee while Jessica picked up all the mail we had missed that was lying on the floor.

I heard the sound of letters being opened in the other room, then Jessica's voice, tinged with confusion: "Sean, what is this?"

More folding and opening sounds, then:

"$300 for SlammableDickCaves.com?!"

It was a bill for registering and retaining the domain name SlammableDickCaves.com. And, once she said it, all the attached memories flooded back; the entire blackout unrolled in my mind and I recalled buying the domain with Mike as though it happened just minutes before. It was like when you choose to restore a file from the recycle bin.

I recalled that not only had I purchased SlammableDickCaves.com, but had also drunkenly clicked "YES" to auto-renew the purchase in three years' time. Evidently, I had felt there was no way my business with SlammableDickCaves.com could be completed in fewer than 36 months. Of all the gods in the pantheon, I know that Cupid has the best sense of humor because what was I doing on that day exactly three years into the future, when SlammableDickCaves.com renewed itself on my credit card?

Marrying the love of my life.

"$300 for a website?" she exclaimed. "A website called, what? What? SLAMMABLE DICK CAVES DOT COM!?"

(Quick side note: Although she probably wasn't ready to admit it at the time, I could tell by the way Jessica over-pronounced the "dot com" that she was actually impressed that I had secured the most prestigious and official version of the domain name.)

"What the hell are you into?" she spluttered.

I entered the room and answered with confidence, "Ok, first of all, I'm not 'into it'. I *own* it."

"What??"

"You are not talking to some *customer* of SlammableDickCaves.com. I am the owner and operator."

I went on to explain the situation—Mike saying this farcical phrase and me drunkenly registering the domain—and Jessica laughed, but she did mention that we were low on money and should avoid such empty-headed purchases in the future. I agreed completely and went online and changed my account to ensure that SlammableDickCaves.com would not, once again, renew itself in three years.

"Well, you got three years to make it work now," I murmured while making the change.

"Who are you talking to?" Jessica asked.

I paused.

"SlammableDickCaves.com, I guess."

And, with that SlammableDickCaves.com receded into a dark storage room in the back of my brain and, again, I more or less forgot all about it.

A few years later myself and Jessica were expecting our first baby so I had to return to work. My trade at the time was software development with a specialty in identity and security applications.

I was contacted by a bank and interviewed with them. It went well; I mostly answered technical questions. A second interview was scheduled and I was told that due to their security regulations a background check would need to be performed, which I had no problem with.

I entered the second interview, expecting it to go just as smoothly as the first, but was soon struck by how many non-technical people were in the room, almost as if a trial were about to start. An older woman with a folder full of papers introduced herself as one the team leads, and said that, the background check having been completed, they now had a lot of questions.

"Mr. Flannery, on the application and résumé that you submitted to us…have you listed all your professions?" she asked. "That is to say, have you given a complete account of all the ways you make money?"

"I think so, yes," I replied.

"Really…*everything*?"

"I don't know if I listed anything past ten years ago. My high school jobs didn't seem relevant, but, within the last ten years, yes. Well, I do perform stand-up comedy at night, but it's not a lot of money and I did mention that in the interview."

There was a pause while she collected herself.

"All right, let me just come out and ask it: Mr. Flannery, are you a pornographer?"

"What?!" I responded, shocked. "No! Of course not!"

My mind began to race. What could have prompted them to ask such a ludicrous question?

All of a sudden it hit me, and I asked:

"Wait, is this about SlammableDickCaves.com?"

When I hear friends talking about job interviews, they are usually uncertain of how it went, whether the employer considered them the right fit or not. I, on the other hand, marvel at the notion of leaving an interview with this kind of doubt. My interviews are like watching a long-jump skier landing: everyone in the building knows instantly if it went well or was a horrifying disaster.

"Do you expect a callback from them, Sean?"

"Well, they are a bank that asked me if I am a pornographer so…No, Eddie. I don't think I will ever hear from them again."

A year or so after that, I got a call from a telemarketer.

There's something called "internet squatting" which is a swindle where people look for domains that have been registered for multiple years and wait for them to expire; they then immediately buy them with the intent of selling them back to the original owner at a huge premium. Many domains expire accidentally; perhaps the owner wished to keep it longer but didn't realize the lease was ending or maybe they changed their contact or billing info and the domain couldn't be processed automatically. In those cases, the original owners, who created the domain, now have to spend a huge amount of money to get their site back from these internet squatters.

"Mr. SEEEN Flannery?" the telemarketer/squatter asked.

One of the nice things about having a Gaelic spelling of your name is that telemarketers immediately identify themselves:

"Hello. Is SEEN Flannery there?"

"This is Seen, yes."

"OK, may I call you Seen?"

"I prefer to go by Seen, yes."

"Well, you have allowed your internet domain to lapse and, Seen, I'm afraid it's been purchased by another firm. But, for a small fee, I can buy it back and return it to your ownership, Seen."

I have owned a few domains over the years and

I had no idea which domain he was referring to and, honestly, I thought it might be one that I actually I cared about retaining.

"Thanks. I own, or have owned, a few domains. Can you tell me which domain it is? To see if I still want it."

"Of course, Seen. Because, Seen, I don't want you to lose the great business opportunity you had going at...oh...hmm..."

At this point it became obvious to me this call must be about SlammableDickCaves.com and this guy hadn't looked at the domain in question until this exact moment.

"What business opportunity am I missing?"

"Well, it's...I'm sorry. Just...someone here is talking about...It's your cave domain, Seen. It expired."

"My cave domain? Could you give me the full name, so there is no confusion."

There was a pause.

"Slammable...Dick...Caves...Dot. Com"

"Slammable Dick Caves Dot Com?" I confirmed.

"Yes, Mr. Seen! Mr. Seen! I bring terrible news: SlammableDickCaves.com is in the hands of your competitors!"

Technology Corner!

According to a survey released in 2018, 40 percent of Americans admit to purchasing goods online while drunk, and the total annual sales for those drunk purchases is estimated to exceed thirty billion dollars. To put that number in perspective, McDonald's had about twenty-eight billion in sales the same year, meaning our drunk shopping is so unrestrained it exceeds the world-wide sales figures for what is often considered to be the most well-marketed company in business history.

Well before the internet, scientists knew that we spend more money when hammered- not that we need a doctor from Oslo to tell us that, yeah, we don't seem to make our most judicious financial decisions on Friday night.
We spend more when drunk to a combination of social and mental changes.

Socially, we like the happiness rush of buying things for ourselves or others. We also use displays of money to impress people—to establish social dominance—and, as you get more drunk, your need to make people happy or impress them increases, resulting in you spending more money.

Mentally, our brain slows down as we become drunk to the point where we cannot correctly tabulate how much money we are spending. This is why you often start your night with a promise like, "just one, maybe two drinks! I'm broke," then, three hours later, you have put your credit card down at the bar and are ordering drinks for people like you are a Walmart heir. We do not realize that we can not afford this.

But, thirty years ago, the worst damage a drunk could do to their fiscal wellbeing was an exorbitant amount of drinks and food. Then the internet happened and now drunks are buying a grill or an above-ground-pool or a sword. Previously, the kind of places that sold things like that they were closed by 9 p.m. and would not do business with you until the morning. Imagine how rich you would need to be to purchase a battle ax at 2 a.m. twenty years ago. You would need to be sufficiently powerful to wake up a small business owner, assuring them they do NOT want to miss a sale from you, and they travel to the store to unlock and light it, just for your single purchase. But, with the Internet, countless businesses say, "Yes! We would love the opportunity to sell you a battle ax at 2 a.m.! We are imminently ready to take your money!"

A price comparison website, Confused.com, published a report on drunk shopping in England (in 2014) that said one in five consumers admit they shop online when buzzed with the average drunk purchase coming to £142. The report detailed recent examples, which are amazing:

"One person bought ten lobster pots while drunk, while others snapped up...diving equipment, a folding ladder and a washing machine."

Going by that list it reads like Brits come home drunk and starving and start believing that, maybe, they could fetch a late snack from the ocean if they had the right equipment:

"Let's see, it's half past two in the morning, so the fish-and-chips shop is closed. But, now, the sea itself is only a three block walk, if I only had me a lobster pot and a ladder! I'd be eating like royalty!"

Yankee Stadium
New York, NY

Saturday night, I walked off a building, breaking my back and heel. Tuesday, I was fitted for crutches and a steel torso brace at a place coincidentally called Yankee Bionics; I say coincidentally because, Friday, I left for a previously scheduled road trip to watch the team that was then known as the Cleveland Indians play at Yankee Stadium.

I never mentioned to my friend—the person driving us to New York—that I had broken my back; in fact, I don't think we spoke at all during the week leading up to the trip. We merely assumed we would both be in the agreed-upon meeting place in time for the outing.

My friend pulled into the driveway, and I exited my apartment in crutches and a full metal torso brace.

"What happened?" she asked

"A non-trivial roof miscalculation," I answered, "but it looks worse than it is."

"What is 'it'?" she asked.

"A broken back—three places—and a shattered heel."

"Actually," she countered, "that's *exactly* what it looks like."

We started the drive, figuring on about a seven-hour drive to Manhattan. Like all Ohioans that had never left Cleveland, we did not account for traffic and assumed we would have no problems finding street parking in Manhattan.

This was my first exposure to the difference in scale between big cities and small cities. People from small cities do not tolerate, nor grasp, the entropies of big city traffic. When you encounter traffic in a small city, you eventually come to the cause of it: some accident, or lane consolidation, or disabled vehicle. You assume that you will see the reason for this traffic so much that, if the delay is significant enough, you might angrily yell, "People better be dead up there!"

You get no such resolution in a big city: you reach no lane closure nor the encouraging signs of dead people. It's causeless delay; slowness, stacked upon slowness.

In many ways, Chicago (where I live now) has the worst traffic in America. Statistically it ranks second to Boston. And certainly, people from LA and Houston claim to have more crowded highways, but what makes Chicago traffic so bad is that its drivers never seem to expect it. Ask any Chicago driver how long the drive will take and they answer "twenty minutes." They put no thought into traffic or distance; reflexively it's "twenty" for everything: a house across town, Soldier Field, the fucking airport. Thus, they drive with the anger and aggression of someone who left the house expecting to arrive on time. Chicago is nine million drivers on the road at the same moment, each convinced that if they could just get ahead of the one car in front of them, everything would be fine.

I did not own a car in Chicago when I first moved but I quickly understood how aggressive its drivers were one week in the mid '00s when a South-west flight slid off the runway at Midway airport. The plane went through a concrete embankment before stopping on the road outside—Cicero Avenue—an important multilane road. I was new to the city and remember them interviewing passengers on the plane, which went something like this:

"I have never been so scared in my life! Our plane slid right off the runway! Mud was going everywhere, then we went through a God-damned wall! And we ended up out on this road and all the cars…they were passing us and honking at us!"

The reporter then started blithely asking follow-up questions about the plane, completely ignoring the fact that the interviewee had just described one of the most terrifying and hilarious things I've heard in my life: Chicago drivers witnessed a jet plane crash into the road before them and were at best unbothered and at worst mildly irritated. How aggressive are these people, I wondered—nay, feared— that they are honking and passing a functioning 737 that just broke through a wall, like the Kool-Aid Man, with its engines on!? I cannot imagine the conversations in those cars:

CHICAGO DRIVER: Oh, now, what's this asshole trying to do?
[*Plane breaks through wall; engines deafeningly loud; blowing litter and debris everywhere*]
CHICAGO DRIVER: Are you serious, guy!
[*Chicago driver accelerates to claim the lane that a four engine jet airplane is sliding into*]

CHICAGO DRIVER'S WIFE: [*screams*] Honey, just stop!

CHICAGO DRIVER: I got da right of way! 'This moron doesn't even have a blinker on! [*holds down horn*] I said we would be there in twenty minutes and we will!

I was expecting New York drivers to be frighteningly aggressive, but I found them to be mannerly, though I think it stemmed more from abject nihilism than kindness. They would create room for you to merge on the highway; they maintained safe distances; outward signs of kindness. These were not drivers, like in Cleveland or Chicago, that were under the misapprehension they could reach their destination in twenty minutes. These were drivers that accepted: what does having one more Pontiac in front of me mean, if there are two million cars before us? The volume of traffic created a defeatedness that bordered upon kindness.

This was one of the things I mentioned to friends in Ohio upon returning: how nice everyone was.

"Really? I always heard New Yorkers were assholes!" my friends exclaimed.

"No, that's wrong," I answered. "They are assholes to *each other*." They have a kind of code where they speak to each other with frightening violence, but treat tourists with business-like kindness, sort of like how feuding armies agree not to kill civilians.

We spent the first night having a great time in Manhattan. The next day we woke up and soon left for Yankee Stadium (to see the Cleveland Indians play). As we were getting ready, someone pointed out that it was forecasted to be very hot; I said I'd heard the same and asked for my bag. Someone grabbed my large, overstuffed duffel bag and nearly threw it into the next room.

"Jesus!" they exclaimed. "What's in that? It weighs nothing!"

"Oh, just my stuff," I answered, unzipping it.

Dozens of impossibly long, white tube socks popped out like snakes from a gag jar.

Like everyone else, I had heard the temperature would be in the 90s that weekend and my metal torso brace was brutal in the sun; it was difficult to weather ten minutes in the heat in it, let alone a nine-inning baseball game. So, I went to a Big And Tall store and bought three packs of their longest white tube socks.

I took my shirt off and started tying the tube socks tightly around my belly.

"This is my summer cast," I explained.

We got into the stadium and the usher noticed my crutches and large cast and that it was 100 degrees and I was sweating like I had been poisoned.

"Buddy, you might want to think about the handicap section," the usher suggested.

"Ah, do I qualify?" I asked.

"Well, ya can't fucking walk, so, yeah, I'd say ya qualify."

He pointed to where our new seats would be

and they were in a section of the stadium that we could never normally afford. We happily relocated to that section.

"Sean! These seats are amazing!" someone gasped.

"I know!" I concurred. "They say that when I'm fifty, I'm going to regret walking off a building but, I gotta say, so far there's been almost no downside!"

Which was true: traveling with a big, painful injury is the best. People hold doors open for you, give up seats, help you carry beers back to the table; it restores your faith in America, that most people are genuinely kind. On each interaction, the person helping me with a door or a seat or a bag would ask, "What happened?"

"I'm a big Huey Lewis and The News fan and, well, one thing led to another. I fell off a building."

There would be a pause, while they absorbed all that, then a confident agreement: "Yeah, great band."

The Cleveland Indians went up big in the second inning and we were all cheering, and the Yankee fans around us were being really cool—almost laughing—about it. We took in more of the area around us and noticed that the women near us were uncommonly gorgeous; the entire section was full of bizarrely well-dressed beautiful women. Our buddy from Cleveland had told us the previous night that everyone in New York City dresses better than back home, but that had seemed like hyperbole until that moment. We also began to notice that these women were exceptionally well-informed about the players: cheering for utility players that would not normally get this level of support. It was after a few more innings and beers, that the penny dropped: we were seated next to the players' wives.

You are not aware of how psychopathic the average fan's cheering is until you sit next to someone with a human connection to one of the players. Standard cheers like "FUCK YOU, ya redneck moron! Go back to Oklahoma and FUCK A SHEEP!"; you know, all the usual things that us fans love to hear and say, sound a tad excessive when you scream it next to that player's wife; the other, loving half that is helping to raise a family with him. Suddenly it seems that these traditions might not be the healthiest way to engage another human.

We continued to root for the Indians, but the newfound knowledge of who our neighbors were caused us to be more conciliatory in our cheers. Plus, everyone began to introduce themselves to one another and it was in general a good time, despite the scorching heat. And perhaps due to the heat, or how much fun we are having, the cold beers began to go down ever more quickly and, by the third inning, we were out of money.

"No big deal," I announced, and began to unfasten my cast. I fiddled with some of the pockets inside it and raised it my mouth.

"What is he doing?" someone in our group asked

"We snuck vodka into his cast," my buddy

answered.

"It's 92 degrees! You are going to drink vodka that's been inside his cast all day long, in 92 degrees?"

I passed the cast to my buddy and we thought about the question for a moment.

"Well, the human body temperature is 98 degrees," I replied, eventually.

"Yeah, so technically we are cooling ourselves down," my buddy added as he took a swig.

It turns out that when you drink vodka warmed to about your body's temperature, its effects are doubled. Or at least that's how I defend losing the next ten hours of memories. My next conscious recollection jumps forward to me suddenly (or at least it seemed sudden) inside a bar on the Lower East side; it was late at night and we were with a new group of people, all unfamiliar to me. Drinking while you are within a blackout is the closest we earthlings can get to being teleported from a spaceship. You open your eyes and find yourself in a brand-new locale, even though you could have sworn that just a second earlier you were on what amounted to a different planet.

More damning, my last memory before the time-jump/teleportation was taking back my cast, raising it to have another sip of vodka and assuring the people next to us: "Don't worry we are the last people you need to worry about on this trip."

Then I lost ten hours.

This is standard for me. My final words before a blackout are always the most wrongly optimistic statement I've said that week. It's never anything like, "I'm worried I've been drinking too fast." No, it's always something ironically cheerful like, "I couldn't have a bad night in this city if I tried!" Then I wake up in a cemetery with a separated shoulder.

I think it's because our brains are highly thematic—they like a story with a climax—and wish to end on the right note. I imagine the neurons within the brain complaining about rising levels of booze—"We need to initiate blackout protocols!"—but there's an old grizzled neuron in the front, an old veteran who knows when to hold steady, yelling, "Not yet! Not yet!" It's around that point that you say something like "I DON'T THINK LONG ISLAND ICE TEAS EVEN AFFECT ME!" and that's when the hoary old cerebral commander yells, "NOW! Shut it all down NOW!"

Your brain wants you to remember that hubris. It wants you to recall that last, damning sentence. And it's equally as choosy about when it wakes you from a blackout.

You never come out of an active blackout in the middle of great sex or just after you have finished an amazing story, with everyone around you laughing. It's always at a new bar, in a totally different part of town, and you are settling the bill for seventeen people you don't recognize. Again the old weathered neuron in your brain sees you offering to pay your last week's salary in drinks for people you don't know and announces to the rest of the brain: "OK team, let's bring him out of the blackout to remember this! This is a keeper, for sure!"

Regaining sentience in an unfamiliar New York watering hole, I found myself not only buying a round of drinks but paying in cash, which was worrisome because my last previous memory was drinking out of a cast (in front of the Yankee wives, no less) precisely because I had no money on me. Yet now I somehow had $400 in readies on me. As scary as it is to suddenly come to penniless, it is far more frightening to retain your wits and discover you now have more money on you. I would rather find human blood on me.

"Thanks for the beers!" someone yelled after I settled the bill.

"My pleasure," I answered to whomever, while still trying to assemble where I am and how I got there.

"Can I reach over you and grab my beer?" I asked no one in particular, and proceeded to do just that and took a long sip.

This was the moment when New York got less friendly. In less than a minute I was thrown out the bar and yelled at for vomiting.

But I did not vomit.

What happened was, the thing that I had reached over and grabbed was not my drink, but rather, a candle. I was so drunk that I picked up, and sipped from, a lit candle. I don't know if you have ever reached a place where you were sufficiently smashed to mistake a warm, flaming illumination for your beer and raise it to your lips but, well, let me satisfy your curiosity as to what happens when you do that. When you take a long, confident sip from a burning candle you have two immediate and pressing issues. First is the hot wax scalding its way through your mouth, burning everything from the roof to the floor; and secondly and shortly thereafter as the wax reaches the back of your throat—much like lava meeting the ocean—it starts to cool and coagulate. Your new predicament is you have a soft but growing ball of wax stuck jammed against your epiglottis, very much creating the sensation that you are choking.

So you start spitting out the wax so as to not asphyxiate, and it's an ugly, loud combination of spit and wax and, in general, you do not look well. And this was precisely the state I was in when the bar's bouncers grabbed me and escorted me outside. It took three bouncers, not because they thought I was that dangerous, but because two were holding my crutches while the main big guy just hoisted me out. I should point out that I was still wearing my summer cast made entirely of cotton socks which was why, as the big guy started to carry me I heard him say, "This guy must have some weird health problems." I looked super fat but felt like a big blanket when he picked me up.

They deposited me outside, with a reprimand: "You're out of here! You just vomited in the bar!"

"False," I countered, "that was *not* vomit, sir! I've never vomited in a public house!" (When drunk I have a tendency to talk like a bad Shakespearean actor, in a doomed effort to sound more sober.)

"What?" They weren't buying it.

"That was a candle!" I explained. "I mistook a

candle for my draft! I was spitting not vomit, sir, but wax! Hot wax! Wax hotter than Icarus's melted wings, sirs!"

They found it so funny that a guy as visibly injured as I was, with a torso that felt like an alpaca's coat, demanded to be allowed back into the bar because he drank a candle (as though that's the level of sobriety you want in your establishment) that they allowed it. Again, New York is the nicest city in the world.

We were kicked out five minutes later when I mistook a stranger's red wine for my beer and tried to finish it.

The next day we woke up to find it even hotter. Nonetheless, we decided that before leaving the city, we would walk (for what seemed like three miles) to a make-shift memorial for John F. Kennedy, Jr. He had died a few days earlier in a plane crash, and my friends wanted to pay their respects.

We brought flowers, laid them down, and one of my friends opined:

"It really shows you how short life is; how it can be taken at any moment."

One by one the group agreed, something along the lines of, "Yep; you said it." When it was my turn, I merely exhaled wearily—I was so hot from walking on crutches in the heat while wearing a vest made of cotton footwear—and said, "Honestly, I think I've learned that lesson." I did a sign of the cross and headed into the nearest bar while the rest of them said longer goodbyes.

Inside the bar I ordered "your coldest drink." The bartender made me a chilled vodka martini and handed it to me. I started laughing.

"What's so funny?" he asked, "something wrong with the drink?"

"No, not at all, buddy" I explained, "it's just that yesterday I drank the most opposite version of this drink you can think of."

Keith Building
Cleveland, OH

In the spring of 2018, the most watched YouTube video in history (at that time), "Despacito," was deleted by hackers.

I'd like to think this hack was done by music snobs, another incident in the long tradition of hackers targeting bad music, which, I'd also like to think, *I* started.

In the late 1990s I worked at one of Cleveland's first internet service providers (ISPs), inside the Keith Building, an old skyscraper in the city's theater district. I worked in Level One Tech Support, meaning I answered phone calls from confused users and, as this was during the budding days of the internet, everyone was confused. People did not grasp even the most rudimentary, computing concepts. I would instruct a user to "Double-click on 'My Computer'" and about 25 percent of the time the customer would snap back: "How am I going to touch *your* computer?"

"No!" I would interject. I had dealt with this mix-up—where the user does not understand that 'My Computer' is an icon—often enough that I knew how to explain it: "When I say 'My Computer,' I am not referring to the machine I'm working on. Instead, I want you to look at *your* screen. On your screen there is an icon with the words 'MY [here I would pause] COMPUTER.' That's what you need to click on; the icon that says, 'My Computer.'"

"What's a click?"

When you work in tech support, there are two or three calls a day where you ask yourself: do I want to bite this off? Do I want to try and explain how a computer runs to someone who just revealed that they don't understand how metaphors and symbols work?

The answer often came down to how polite the customer was. If the user was clueless about computers but nice and willing to listen, I would work with them as long as needed to solve the problem. And if the customer was smart but an asshole, we could usually work quickly to figure out the problem. But if they were an asshole and clueless, that was a death blow and I would fake disappointment and say, "Actually, sir, I apologize, upon further investigation, I can't help you right now; the network perambulator is down."

Which was, of course, a lie. We were not having an outage and 'perambulator' is what the British called a baby carriage when it was first invented. I used the word as an excuse because "perambulator" sounded like the kind of device that an asshole considers essential to the internet.

There were about three of us working at any one time and we supported about 9,000 users in an office that was smaller than any apartment I ever lived in. My manager blasted FM radio while we worked, which we all enjoyed. It created a nice background noise, allowing us to better-focus on our call rather than what the tech two feet from us was saying.

One day I had started working around 11 a.m.

and the FM station we were listening to was having an "80s Flashback Lunch." The DJ came out of the song that was playing with:

"OOOOH! That's The Clash! With 'Rock The Casbah'! Their only single to reach the Top 40 chart, and you can see why. Great song! Their other stuff? Pretty iffy if you ask me."

"WHAT?" I screamed, and immediately hung up on my caller.

"Is there a problem, Sean?" my manager asked.

"Yeah! A huge one! Not sure if you were listening but this DJ just said 'London Calling' by the The Clash is 'iffy.'"

I continued to fly off the handle. I had to ask for a lunch break to process the nonsense this DJ was presiding over our city's radio waves—the supposed Rock 'N' Roll City—and that he thought "Rock The Casbah" was The Clash's only decent song.

After I returned from the lunch break, and after a fifth consecutive coworker approached me with some version of, "Why are you yelling?" I realized: this was up to me. I was the last sane man in Cleveland. "The '80s Flashback Lunch" was brainwashing these poor people.

The DJ of the Flashback Lunch kept boasting that you could email song requests to the station. Back then, email was so new it was discussed like having a new, in-ground pool. Owners would brag about it and insist you come by and use it: "Did you hear? We have an email address now! You must send us a message!"

This was before webmail with unlimited storage.

Internet plans back then, even for businesses, had a certain megabyte limit as to how much email could be stored, so email clients would have an option to "DELETE MAIL FROM REMOTE SERVER AFTER DOWNLOAD" to save space. Once you downloaded an email to your computer, the email would be deleted from your ISP's mail server so the message no longer counts against the storage limit on your plan. This meant that email programs had to pay close attention to which messages were fully downloaded versus which were still being transferred, otherwise they could delete a message from the server before you had a chance to read it.

I assumed this radio station used Macs, and thus would be running a program called Eudora to send and receive email. I *also* knew Eudora had a flaw in it where, if one sent a huge email to a Eudora user and that user wasn't patient enough to let the full message download, Eudora created a "temp lock" file that usually resulted in an infinite loop where the user could not download mail. Once the lock was created, most users would become stuck, unable to receive any email until they called their ISP, which would usually need to delete both the lock and the large message that kept causing the loop.

I asked my boss for another break, saying "I think I can finally let this go if I have a sandwich." My boss assented, and I went and sent a 70 MB email to the radio station.

When I came back to my desk, I heard the DJ return from a commercial break with, "Hey Cleveland, gonna have to ask you to hold off on those email requests. Looks like we are having a problem with our web server. You know how new all this stuff is!"

People think that growing old is terrible but there are many benefits; one of the greatest being: you learn to ignore both bad music and bad opinions about music. After a certain age, bad music is like an ambulance siren blaring off in the distance: You can hear it and know it's bad, but it's not intended for you so it goes in one ear and out the other. It's background noise. It won't change your mood.

But, in my youth these things enraged me to the point where (on reflection) I flirted with federal hacking crimes.

A few days later I noticed that they were back to taking email requests so I suppose someone fixed the issue. I always wondered if the IT person who corrected it read the email that I had sent which caused the lock.

The subject line was "LISTEN TO *THIS*, ASSHOLE!"

There was no message body to the email, just a 75 MB attachment named "PROOF.mp3" which was the album "London Calling" as a MP3.

I remember thinking, as I sent the email, "This might be illegal; not sure, but no judge in the world is going to convict me for defending The Clash. I'll just introduce 'Rudy Can't Fail' as Exhibit A and the case will be dismissed."

Hi-Tops
Chicago, IL

Early in our relationship, I was putting on a suit to attend a wedding with Jessica and she advised me, "Sean, you really shouldn't wear white socks with a dark suit."

"I haven't put my socks on yet," I said, "that's the color of my feet."

That's how pale I am. Unless you are close enough to make out the hair on my legs, you'd assume I am wearing a set of socks—that are so white and glowing—they have never before been worn.

Everyone loves the sun. It is responsible for life on Earth, and convertibles, and rompers, and frozen daiquiris. But when you are as pale as me and abhor the sun, you hate something that everyone else loves. It's a bit like hating Tom Hanks; people don't even believe you dislike it. You, a member of a club so lonely, people just assume that you are making it up.

The sun has been a lifelong adversary: my Lex Luthor; my *Joker*; except, in this universe, everyone loves the Joker and doesn't mind that he's a homicidal maniac. When you are as pale as me the sun emits two kinds of rays: the solar rays (the normal rays of energy we all know of) but also the rays of ridicule, which is the sun's ability to shine mortification down upon you. When I was young, my mom would pack sun hats that I found to be humiliating and, worse yet, she would never remember that she packed them until the exact moment when I found all my peers at the pool:

"Jeez, it's getting hot. And where is Sean? Oh, there

he is; he's making friends. That's great, he often struggles with that. You know, that reminds me: I have a giant, powder-blue sun bonnet I want him to wear."

My dad was even worse: He would talk about the sun like we owed it money and it was looking for us. "Do not underestimate what he's capable of!" he'd warn us, pointing to the sky, just before we ran out to the beach. It sounded less like he was talking about a star and more about a crazy, drunk neighbor. My brother Paul was once talking to girls at the zoo, when my dad came running down the stairs of the elephant exhibit, screaming:

"Paul! Paul! Get to shade! It's a blast furnace out here!"

"Do you know him?" the girls asked. Paul could not speak. He had been petrified by the rays of ridicule.

"Paul!, can you hear me?" My dad was waving his hands for attention while yelling, as though he saw a plane about to crash where Paul and the girls were standing.

"GET TO SHADE! The sun is out! It's PURE ENERGY!"

It was always amazing to me that Irish skin evolved in such a way that it could not even handle a summer in Cleveland, Ohio; not exactly the most Mediterranean of U.S. cities. The older family members who were born in Ireland tended to receive the most sun damage. They would arrive at weddings and be missing an ear or have a new, fake plastic nose where patches of skin cancer were removed and they would point at whatever part was missing and explain: "The sun got me."

"Got me," which is something you normally say after a sheriff tickets you for speeding, not losing a body part to melanoma.

Perhaps they were that fatalistic about it because they did nothing to avoid it. None of them used sunscreen and I believe that is because fearing or loving the sun is a lot like fearing or loving dogs: It's entirely based upon your childhood experiences. They grew up in Ireland, where the sun is docile and well-behaved, so they consider it approachable and cuddly; they do not fear it, nor appreciate the power and destruction it is capable of in other parts of the globe. I was bitten by the sun often enough as a kid to always fear it, no matter where I am on Earth. It was a giant, glowing Doberman as far as I was concerned.

A few years ago, I had two large marks—which I thought to be pimples—just below my lip. I made an appointment with a dermatologist, which I despise doing. Me entering a dermatologist's office is like a very obese man entering a cardiologist's exam room. I get a lot of "Oh boy"s and "Cancel my next appointment," type responses on first sight, then it goes further downhill when they see my answers to their office forms:

"This says you consume more than six drinks a day, Mr. Flannery?" the doctor asked.

"No, it says I *average* six drinks a day. There are many days where I have less. Today I've only had four."

"Do you understand binge drinking is five drinks in a day?"

(The first three times a doctor told me this I laughed out loud.)

"Well, 'binge drinking' must be one of those words

where the general population is using it differently than experts," I pointed out, helpfully.

(Also, I said "experts" with air quotes, showing I questioned that number.)

There was a pause. I felt it necessary to elaborate.

"Like 'enormity' or 'data,'" I went on. "We use it one way, but [*air quotes again*] experts [*end air quotes*], use it differently. The people I know, when they say 'binge drinking,' they are talking about *a lot more* than five beers in a day." I gave a fake laugh, and added, "Are you saying every person I know is an alcoholic?"

The doctor visibly scanned me up and down.

"That's possible," she answered.

She looked at the form on her clipboard.

"This says, your family has a history of skin cancer, correct? On which side?"

"All four sides."

"You have a history of skin cancer on all four sides of the family?"

"Doctor, am I your first Irish patient?"

She laughed at that and started examining me,

"It's this bump here right?" she confirmed while looking near my lips, then stepped back uneasily,

"We are going to take that out, today," she said, before adding, "I'm going to use a scary word. But I don't want you to panic because this looks like something we caught early and it should not be a danger to you once removed. But I think it could be…*cancer*."

There was a silence, which she must have interpreted as shock on my part, as she continued, reassuringly: "But you are going to be fine. We caught this immediately and we are going to remove it right now."

I thought about it for a moment and answered, "Today's not good."

"What?" she reacted, a bit taken aback.

"I have some buddies in town."

There was a pause. I assumed she could deduce the rest, but she could not.

"We have Cubs rooftop tickets."

"What does that have to do with cancer?" she asked.

"I can't be on any meds tonight. The tickets include all-you-can-drink beer."

She tried to understand my intent, but ultimately trailed off, asking, "So you are saying..."

"It's a no-go," I clarified, as though I was ground control telling a pilot to find a different airport.

"We have a definite No-Go on our hands here."

She asked for one or two more confirmations and I explained that, if it was as harmless as she was saying, what's one or two more days? She eventually relented and told me to schedule an appointment with her staff.

"No problemo," I pledged, "see you soon."

"By the way," she asked while opening the door of the exam room to leave, "what else does 'enormity' mean?"

"It means something that is hugely evil. It has nothing to do with measuring size generally," I explained.

"Really?" she said, surprised, then left, shaking her head.

I collected my sweater and exited the room. The doctor was going over paperwork with a nurse in the hallway. I reached the billing desk and there was a line of people. I gave it about five seconds to move—it didn't—so

I walked straight out of the office and I'm pretty sure the doctor saw me refusing to wait ten seconds to make an appointment to remove cancer.

"Wow," she must have reasoned, "that is either the world's most impatient man or the world's most slowly-suicidal."

But, "What are two more days?" I thought. Plus, an appointment can be scheduled just as easily over the phone. I murmured all this to myself while leaving the office.

Except, I never made that call. The need to call, to have this operation, left my mind completely the moment I walked out of the building. Not so much because I am that absent minded—though I am very much so—but because, at this stage in my life, I truly believed I was indestructible.

I had survived so many injuries and accidents—walking off a roof; electrocutions (yes, plural); driving off a bridge; ribs pushed in and arms pulled out—that, to outlast all of that, I believed I could not die. Most of us have entertained unrealistic body goals: maybe you thought you could be a circus performer, or outfielder for the Cubs? Well, I thought I could be deathless, so I forgot to call a doctor to have them cure me of a tumorous growth on my face.

Now, I am not sure if it's because doctors have sworn to help you, or they just want to get paid, but I can say with a certain degree of confidence that no creature on Earth will hound you more doggedly than a doctor who thinks they can perform an operation on you. One time, a guy used my identity to steal a limo from a Florida airport and that airport and its bill collectors called me less regularly than this doctor.

Two weeks later I was at a bar called Hi-Tops near Wrigley Field with friends in town, drinking on a weekday afternoon before a Cubs game. One of my buddies was visiting with his long-term girlfriend and she had not met his high school "friends."

I put "friends" in quotes because, back when my buddies were a few years out of college and meeting women and considering marriage, the reaction from each of these ladies when they met us was, "That's how men treat *their friends?*"

To a woman, the male friendship looks more like fully-reciprocal bullying, than any kind of rapport:

"You guys let him get so drunk, he was vomiting into his dresser and you were laughing?"

"Yeah, it was pretty funny."

"Those are his clothes! You're supposed to be his friend!"

Every time I told Jessica a story from back home, about a person falling from a statue we told him to climb or hydroplaning from a flooded road we said his car could handle, or just being straight up abandoned in Hiawatha, Kansas by us, she would ask: "And this person is your friend?" in that tone women use when they aren't sure if your statement is inaccurate or merely to confirm that you really are that stupid.

I'm not sure how or why but male friends talk each other into situations that, on paper, look like they were designed by your worst enemy.

My buddy warned as much, saying his "friends" were a bit—I think this is the word he used— "nutty." We met at Hi-Tops. Back then, I would drink whatever was cheapest so that day I was drinking Jell-O shots. The bar made too many and were looking to unload them at the dangerous and quite frankly irresponsible price of twenty-five cents a pop.

While ordering the latest round of Jell-O shots for the group, I glanced at my phone and noticed that someone had left me a voicemail. We did the shots and I checked the messages.

It was the dermatologist's office again, reminding me to schedule an appointment to remove the tumors. My friends noticed that I was trying to listen intently to the message, which surprised them since I never checked messages.

"Who's calling you during a baseball game?" someone asked

"Oh, dude, I forgot: I have cancer."

They stared at me.

"Yeah, in my face," I elaborated.

My buddy's girlfriend who was meeting us did a spit-take, which, when you're drinking Jell-O shots is less like spit and more like a tiny barf.

"What?" she yelled.

"Yep. Right there, as it happens," I answered, pointing to the offending area of face.

I excused myself to call the doctor's office back.

For two weeks I had been putting off calling this doctor's office back, but this was the first time I heard the message drunk. I have an odd habit where, when I'm day drunk, I go out of my way to prove that being drunk in broad daylight won't affect my productivity. I end up completing errands I had been avoiding for months. In some ways, it's an efficiency boost, but, almost always, I complete the errand the way a drunk would and I only create three additional errands in order to clean up the mess.

I dialed and they answered, "Hello? Dr Lundy's office." It sounded like Jennifer, who had left the message.

"Hello, Jennifer, this is Sean Flannery, calling on behalf of...well, Mr. Sean Flannery."

I have a second, terrible habit when day drunk: if I'm talking to a sober person, I use inflated language in order to not sound drunk. I know other people that do this when drunk—try to interface with sober people in stilted language—and the best-case outcome is you sound like a British person with dementia. But usually, the other person just knows you are blasted.

"Mr Flannery? We've been trying to reach you."

"And so I've heard! I think my staff has been failing to relay all my messages. But, that's a conversation for another day. What day should I come in for this operation? This *abscission*? This, may I call it, *miracle*?"

"How's next Tuesday?"

"Beautiful!"

I hung up, got blackout drunk and did not show up the following Tuesday.

Eventually though, I did revisit that doctor's office, had two small, basal cell cancer growths removed, one under my lip and one under my ear. The growths were tiny; as I recall, I needed only a couple of stitches and was sent on my way.

Two years later, I was attending the wedding of my buddy and his girlfriend—the same couple I had met at Hi-Tops that day—in a conservatory in

Columbus Ohio.

"Gorgeous ceremony! What a location!" I said to the couple and they both laughed heartily and thanked me for coming.

Much later in the night, I ran into the groom at the bar and while we were talking I learned why they laughed so hard when I complimented the location.

"In a way, you chose the conservatory for us!" he explained. "We had been talking about marriage for a while, before you and the other guys met us that week in Chicago and we always said: art museum or conservatory. Then she meets you guys and—I told her you guys were 'nutty'—but at that bar, what was it called? Hi-Tops? Yeah, she meets all of you and, if you remember, we got loaded off Jell-O shots and as we are walking to the game she's like, 'I think we get married at the conservatory.' And I'm like, 'Oh, cool, why?' And she answered, 'I don't think we can invite your [*air quotes*] friends [*end air quotes*] to a wedding at the art museum.' And I said, 'I thought they were OK at Hi Tops.' And she goes: 'They just got absolutely loaded off Jell-O shots! And the guy buying most of the rounds had to be reminded he had cancer! We can not have them drinking next to a Renoir. At least *trees* can survive them.'"

The bartender slid him his drink. We were both laughing—hard—and he finished the story, with, "I think she always suspected my friends were jackasses but, when she met all of you! Hahaha! I think that's when the full enormity of it hit her! Ha!"

He returned to his guests, laughing. The bar was only serving beer and wine and, at the end of the bar, I saw other friends ordering wine to be filled into espresso cups to be drunk as shots.

"Shot of red wine?" one of them inquired.

"I believe it's called a rouge-iato," I joked back, accepting it and shooting the wine.

They immediately ordered a second round and it occurred to me: I don't think my buddy, the groom, knew the actual, correct definition of "enormity," but in this context—as we wait for another round of table wine to be poured into espresso cups—he pulled it off.

Cleveland Public Auditorium
Cleveland, OH

I attended The Midwest Beer Fest at the Cleveland Public Auditorium ("Public Hall") in 1997 or thereabouts, back when the Internet and craft beer barely existed. My friend heard of the fest on the radio and asked if we wanted to go.

"What's a beer fest?" I asked.

He explained that, as he understood it, for a single $12 ticket you would spend all day going booth-to-booth drinking beer.

I was incredulous.

"Is that legal? Why would they want to do that?" I ask.

"I don't know, but it's real," he answered. "It's basically," he continued, "the Louisiana Purchase of beer drinking."

"OK, sounds amazing," I conceded, "but, just remember; I have to start a new job the next morning so, I can't get too crazy."

"You can't get too crazy at an all-you-can-drink event?"

"I can get crazy. But I have to get back to Akron! I can't stay in Cleveland."

We met at Mitch's Lounge in Akron, to drive up to Cleveland from there. Mitch's Lounge was my "college bar." I put that in quotes because, though it was on the campus of my university (Akron U); I was usually the only person under the age fifty who would go there. Mitch's was a proper dive bar: a bar that would be unsustainable in the age of Yelp.

It had a huge sign outside that said "Mitch's Lounge and Restaurant" but the bar did not have a kitchen and, what's better, the sign was *never* a problem. In all my years drinking there not one person walked into Mitch's asking to see a menu. The bar was so visibly dank and questionable from the outside, everyone simply assumed that sign was wrong.

> [*EDITOR'S NOTE: We contacted several of Sean's drinking buddies from this time and while most agree it had no kitchen, there are some claims of a cook occasionally showing up at Mitch's and making food. In fact one claims that he and Sean got "sicker than dogs" after splitting a lobster bisque there one night. Sean says, "There's no way—even if it had a kitchen—I was ever drunk enough to order seafood from it," and that, "If we did puke, I'm sure it was the fifty beers we drank."*]

Signs You are in A Dive Bar:

1, *It opens very early.*

Most dive bars are thirty-plus years old which means they opened back when America still built things, which in turn means people were working at all hours. The night shift would exit at 6 a.m. looking for a beer. Dive bars accommodated these workers by opening early.

Nowadays we all work for the same market-research company and no bar created in the last decade opens before 5 p.m. because, God-forbid, a modern worker might have a drink with lunch which then might cause them to answer a question honestly during the next PowerPoint presentation, like: "Who cares what our mobile strategy is? We sell butter!"

2. The bar (i.e., the serving counter itself) takes up most of the space.

This is because everyone at a dive bar is drinking alone; there is no need for tables. Nobody goes to a dive bar on a date or to close a business deal. They are there to sit down by themselves and try to forget the last 10 to 500,000 hours of their life.

Plus, this (long bar) is how taverns were set up many years ago, which pleases the customers at a dive since everyone at a dive bar is ancient. In many ways dive bars are a time-warp to a previous era, which is why you see so many old people in them. Nothing scares the old more than change. Old people have lived through wars, poverty, high crime rates, and none of those things frighten them. But ask an old guy to pick a beer from a drink menu that's organized into countries, brew styles, and flavor profiles, and—oh by the way, "This is not where you order, sir, this section is growler pickup"—he will *panic*. He would rather disarm a robber.

3. Bad TVs.

Mitch's had a very old TV and it was behind chicken wire. When I enter a bar that someone calls a "dive" and see a huge, flat-screen TV behind the counter, I know the place is not a real dive. Why? Because the owner of this joint trusts their customers. They believe their customers are rational enough to understand that if a last second fumble happens or the umpire blows a called third strike, the customers' anger is not with the device broadcasting the event, but the event itself, hundreds of miles away. The owner of a dive has no such faith; They assume the TV will be pelted like it made the call.

We had a couple drinks at Mitch's and then drove to the beer festival.

We entered and paid and the woman at the ticket box explained the rules: We would each be given a lanyard with twenty squares on it. We were told that each vendor is pouring four ounce "tasters" and we could ask for tastes from whichever vendors we liked but every time we asked for a drink, the vendor would place a check in one of the boxes and, after all twenty squares were checked, you couldn't have any more beers. We did the math quickly: four ounces times twenty…It was about a six-pack. Well short of The Louisiana Purchase we were planning. We objected, saying, "We were told it was unlimited."

"That brings us to the fine print," she explained. "Technically, it *is* unlimited because you can come and get a new lanyard and you can keep getting lanyards—they can be unlimited—*if you pass a sobriety test*. You must pass a police-issued sobriety test to get a new lanyard."

Most attendees were upset upon learning the fine print of having to pass a sobriety test, but we loved it. First off, our driver would no longer need to conjecture about their own level of sobriety—if they were OK to drive everyone home—because the Cleveland Police Department will provide a professional assessment. Secondly, we loved the absurdity of the plan:

"This guy failed! He's too drunk to be here. Throw him out!"

"This guy is semi-passable. Give 'em another six-pack!"

We walked to the convention floor. The beer landscape was much different back then. There were fewer than twenty vendors and, of those, most seemed to report to huge conglomerates (Budweiser and Miller) and were not even offering beer. We saw booths for new wine coolers and ice coolers and spiked lemonades and noticed, to our surprise, this sugary nonsense had the longest lines; it was in the most demand; But we came to drink beer.

We went to the Great Lakes Brewery booth at which I filled up my entire lanyard. My friends were drinking at a slower pace, probably worried about not being able to pass the sobriety test but I was confident I would pass.

"Well, off to get my next lanyard!" I announced.

"Really? Flannery, you think you can pass a breathalyzer test?" they asked as I walked towards the ticket booth.

I reached the doors and turned around. "Yes, yes, I do," I responded coolly, then mule-kicked the doors open and entered the vestibule backwards. Now, I did not actually believe that I could pass a breathalyzer—I had been drinking for six hours if you included time spent at Mitch's Lounge—but I did believe, given how many people were at this event, there was no way they could actually administer sobriety tests in a timely way and that the whole threat was false. I believed they would, in reality, give each of us a new round upon request.

"Hi, need a new lanyard," I announced to the ticket booth while walking backwards.

"*Already?*" challenged a ticket agent, who was still hurriedly dealing with incoming customers.

"You got some good beer back there. Hoping you'll see a lot of me tonight," I answered.

The agent motioned for me to shut up, dealt with the current attendee, then screamed, "Wolf! Field sobriety test!"

A guy—clearly an off-duty cop—slid off his chair near the front door. Wolf was a frighteningly large, grey-haired man with a mustache, side pistol, and a tight-fitting yellow "SECURITY" jacket. He braced himself, as though about to start a battery of federal safety checks, then asked me, "Name four Cleveland Browns linebackers."

Back then the Browns ran a 4-3 defense so Wolf was essentially asking me to name one backup linebacker.

I named five.

Wolf turned to the ticketing booth, pointed to me and hollered, "PASS."

They gave me a new lanyard for twenty more drinks and I *ran* to my friends to share how easy the sobriety test was.

We kept drinking and getting new lanyards. As the night progressed and I got drunker, Wolf's questions became easier. At one point he asked me to name ten American cities. Not state capitals or cities with hockey teams: just ten *cities*.

A buddy said that Wolf asked him: "What's the difference between a burrito and an enchilada?" and according to my buddy, Wolf seemed to be genuinely asking it. Wolf must have always wondered what the difference is and was willing to give a new lanyard to the best answer.

Eventually we all got so drunk we slowly lost one another. This is by far the greatest improvement cell phones have made to drinking, maybe the only improvement.

Before cell phones, when a drunk friend became separated, going after them was like trying to find a bird that left from an unopened cage. You could only hope that, by chance, they might later land on the same bench you both previously visited.

So there I was, six lanyards deep at Cleveland Public Auditorium, beginning to feel a little worse for wear and with no idea where my buddies were and perhaps more importantly where our driver was located. I scanned around and most of the crowd was as lost and drunk as me. Wolf's easy trivia questions—God love him—created mass bewilderment; it felt like I was inside an airport where they just announced that every flight was canceled due to a blizzard; people were sleeping on the floor, others running to the exits, yelling, "I need to get to Beachwood tonight!" Nobody had a plan. Fortuitously though, I saw a buddy, Frank, who was not in our original group. Frank was attending with a separate set of friends and added that they had room in their car for me, if I needed a ride home.

"Thank God," I answered, "I was worried I wouldn't get home tonight! I'm starting a new job in downtown Akron in the morning and can't afford to be late."

I woke up in Huntington, West Virginia.

Frank and I had another friend who began working at Marshall University earlier that summer and we both intended to visit this friend in the past but each time it became delayed or canceled.

Apparently after dropping someone off in Portage Lakes, Ohio (which is about twenty minutes south of where we both lived) we miscalculated that we were at about the halfway mark to Huntington West Virginia and being halfway there, we convinced our driver to turn south, not north, so we could finally make this trip to Marshall University happen during what is clearly a convenient itinerary.

I looked it up on a map a few days later: we had miscalculated the halfway point by about 7,000 percent. We were twenty minutes into a four-hour drive, when we announced we were halfway there.

If time travel is invented, the inventors will want to know if the human mind can handle the pressures of such traveling and they will surely use drunks as their initial test subjects, as we have the most experience of waking up in an unfamiliar environment and piecing together where we are and how we got there from small clues. We have "The Right Stuff" for this mission.

We do it every weekend, and we solve it in steps, based on our senses.

The first is tactile: Upon waking up, you first notice you are not only not in your bed, but also not in a bed, period. You feel thick, bristly cords below you with no cushioning—you slept on a carpet—or your head rests on a piece of wood and the pillows below you have fused with your skin: you are on a couch!

Next is sight, which is when you apprehend the horror: you are not simply in the wrong room at your home, you are in the wrong home! Worse, it is rarely a hotel room or anything so recognizable or reassuring. No, you open your eyes to surroundings that are equal parts bewildering and horrifying; there's usually mounted deer heads or posters on the history of evolution or old, forgotten sports teams like the Baltimore Colts. A drunk person is never given rest near the hearth of the house: they are dropped into the least-used room, the room that used to the youngest child's room but was turned into a de facto storage space when they went off to California, surrounded by all the detritus and accoutrements the owner finds too embarrassing to place in the open.

You are put in these rooms mostly to reduce screaming in the morning. It's a bit like those family movies, where the kid finds Bigfoot or a friendly ghost or a caring robot and they want to put them in a room where no one will find the visitor before they can explain.

Last—and most debilitating—is your hearing, because this is when you learn that you're not even in the wrong home in your hometown. A moment after rousing, you hear a tugboat blow its horn just outside the window or a freight train building steam or the pilot announcing they will taxi to runway two.

On this morning, in Huntington, West Virginia, I awoke on the floor underneath a giant flag of the Notre Dame fighting Irish leprechaun. I lifted my head up and saw that I had fashioned a pillow out of my jeans and shirt. I was wearing boxers and socks. Frank made some noises on the couch and I asked where we were.

"Marshall, dude."

"*What*?" I screamed back in disbelief.

"You were totally in favor of the idea. You said you had nothing going on today."

I never did start that job. I returned to Akron two days and (what felt like) 5,000 beers later. The lady who recruited me for the job, who was a bit of a drinking buddy of mine, said she and the employer called my home to look for me and my dad answered and explained that I had not returned from a beer fest.

They told my dad that I was supposed to start a job that morning. My dad started laughing.

"Do you know when he will be back?" they asked.

"Well, it's definitely clear you haven't started working with Sean yet," my dad answered.

"So you don't know?"

"I don't ask Sean where he's going because that would imply he has a plan."

I don't know if this story is true or not, but I was told that my great grandfather, who was a firefighter, had an identical twin brother, who was a milkman, and that, when one was too hungover to work, the other would do his job. When it was first proposed my great grandfather worried more about being a milkman than his brother worried about being a firefighter:

"I don't know your delivery route! How will I know which houses get milk?"

"You don't need to know it!" his brother assured him. "The horse does! Every time the horse stops, deliver a bottle to that house! It's fool-proof! Literally!"

As I was getting screamed at by this recruiter, I thought about that story; about how, at the turn of the century in a small town in Ireland, two major infrastructure jobs were being conducted by hungover impostors with no formal training, and who were mostly dependent on horses being more competent than them. And, between screams and threats, I further thought, "God I'd love to have a twin brother; this wouldn't have happened if I had a twin. I'd be working day three at this job right now, after my brother showed up for the first two...Or, if not a twin, maybe a horse? God I'd love to have a horse. I probably could have gotten home on a horse. It would have known the way."

If I ever open up a brewery, I think that's what I will call it: Twin Horses.

Long John Silver's
Unknown Parts of West Virginia

Want to break a man? Send him on a three-hour drive with his family. There is something about the male psyche where it can handle illness and war and poverty, but it will absolutely snap when one makes bad time on a road trip. It does not matter how laid back your dad normally is; when you have reached hour two of a supposedly four-hour journey only just having passed the county-line—in other words, not even close to the halfway point—your dad will lose his mind. He will lose it like a dictator that was just told none of his armies showed up for battle.

And, like all collapsing dictatorships, he will reach the paranoiac's conclusion that it was his inner circle—his own kids—that orchestrated it. He will convince himself that those nearest and dearest to him had met privately and conspired to divide their bathroom breaks into the most inconvenient exit points. There once was a (now debunked) theory called "The McClintock Effect," that stated that when women live together their menstruation cycles become aligned. That has always sounded dubious to me, but I am somewhat willing to allow the possibility that it exists because I can tell you for a fact, that the exact opposite effect occurs on road trips involving children. Once the car hits the asphalt, your kids will immediately dis-align their bathroom cycles; they will make you stop at every exit along the highway. You will make worse time than a public bus.

My family lives in a bungalow with two bathrooms and there is always a line for one of them; my kids seem to consistently use them at the same time at home and will scream endlessly at each other about the delays. But, on a road trip, the converse is true. It's as though the excretory system of a child has evolved less for the purpose of removing waste and more so that the timing of everything annoys as many family members as possible.

One of the peculiarities of regular, repeat road trips with the full family—a sort of mundane *déjà vu*—is that you end up stopping at the same places for bathroom breaks. Due to how often we drive back to Ohio, I have visited the same Indy 500-themed McDonald's in rural Indiana more often than I have gone to my local post office. And we enter the same way each time, too: I hold open the door as one kids bursts through, grasping their crotch and hysterically scanning for the bathroom, then a second kid enters a bit more casually, looks around, and screams: "WE HAVE BEEN HERE BEFORE!" If the staff didn't have such a high turnover, they would surely recognize us; it's also possible the latter has something to do with the former.

One of my kids has a kind of photographic memory for these places, which is *not* an advantage. Once, when driving through West Virginia (we travel to North Carolina every few years to see the ocean and visit my father-in-law's grave) we stopped at a Long

John Silver's. My wife sat with our youngest at a table while me and the two boys waited for the food at the counter. We got the food and one of my sons dropped his fork on the floor and yelled, "DAMNIT!"

The south is very weird about swearing. I have been in bars where men punched each other in disputes, loudly threatened each other—or entire creeds of people—and the staff mostly ignored them or politely asked them to settle down. But use the word "fuck" at anything above a whisper and they are impossibly offended: "Hey, hey, fellas, if you can't clean up the language, you're going to have to leave. It's not that kind of place."

With this in mind I was quick to chide my son for his outburst before the staff could object. "Hey! We don't swear in this family," I admonished.

"Actually, mom swears all the time," my eldest chimed in from afar.

"OK, well, mom is an adult and sometimes she uses adult words, but look at me; I never swear."

There's some truth to this: I almost never swear at home if the kids are around. Swearing for me is a conscious act. I select the word with deliberation, and although I swear when performing stand-up or with friends or coworkers or my wife at a bar, I don't even *accidentally* swear in front of the kids; a hammer could fall upon my toe, and I would not cuss if the kids are present. So I was, at this time, entirely convinced that none of my kids had ever heard a swear word from me.

My eldest—the one with the steel-trap

memory—disagreed:

"That's not true, Dad."

"What's not true?"

"That you don't swear. You've sworn once, Dad. And...it was at *this* Long John Silver's."

Internally, I began to feel terror: my eldest is never wrong when it comes to memories. Plus, as I glanced, some of the fixtures of the place began to look familiar: the aquarium containing unhealthily large fish, for one.

"It was three years ago, Dad."

He was talking in the kid "Fact Voice," the voice they use to tell you stuff like: "TECHNICALLY, IN ORDER TO BE A DINOSAUR, YOU CANNOT FLY." The voice where they scream, as if they have acquired data and knowledge that will rewrite history. Everyone in the pirate-themed seafood restaurant could hear him. The staff started to congregate around the register, smiling, fascinated with my son's oral history of the restaurant.

"The staff screwed up our order four times," my son recounted loudly, "and, when we got back to the table, you told mom, 'West Virginia makes shitheads like Ohio makes mosquitoes.'"

The staff erupted in laughter. First of all, probably none of them worked there three years prior. And as such took no slight from the criticism, but more importantly, these employees—who regularly had to tolerate customers attempting to embarrass and belittle them—finally got to see a customer get wholly embarrassed by his own kid.

I started laughing. "Well, Ohio doesn't have quite as many mosquitoes as you'd think," I equivocated, and waved to the cashiers abashedly.

We walked back to our table with the food. My wife noticed me smiling and the employees laughing.

"What's going on?" she asked.

"We've been to this Long John Silver's before," I answered.

"Yeah! And dad swears!" my youngest added.

Bathroom breaks are what finally caused my dad to snap. My dad was a social worker; he worked with the homeless, the addicted, the infirm, the victimized. Either despite or because of the fact he had that job on top of being father to half a dozen kids, he never lost his cool.

Until, that is, we left for a vacation on an island in Lake Erie. It was a ninety-minute drive but on this occasion, we were two hours into the drive, and yet not halfway there. The delay was due entirely to bathroom breaks, and my dad, who had arranged to get the keys to the cottage from the owner at a prearranged time, was freaking out about the tardiness. Dads reach a certain age—or rather, they reach a certain number of *kids* (usually three or more)—where they start to believe that the most disrespectful thing you can do to another man is make him wait. Sleeping with his wife would be less of an insult.

Also, this was back before the widespread availability of cellphones, so he couldn't notify the guy that we were running late. Back then if someone was waiting for you, they would just have to stand at the rendezvous point, like a statue being slowly chiseled into an expression of increasing anger.

Whenever we were the late party, my dad would scream, "A man is waiting on us!" in an attempt to motivate us kids into the car faster. He'd scream it like we were smuggling a spy across an enemy border and the sentries were closing in. As opposed to the real mission, which was usually something like dropping off a wet/dry vac. My dad was even more melodramatic when the positions were reversed, and we were the ones waiting for the other party to show.

"Honey, maybe we should leave," my mom would suggest after a thirty-minute wait.

"No, he might arrive any second," Dad would counter. "What if we left, then he arrived ten seconds later?"

"I think at this point he couldn't expect to still get the dresser."

"Oh, I don't care about the dresser," Dad would snap. "You can burn the dresser for all I care. No, I want to be here when he gets here, because I want him to see my face when he arrives so I can tell him exactly how late he is. How he *ruined* our afternoon!"

"So," my mom would summarize, "it's more important for you to shame this guy about being late, than to head home and enjoy as much of your remaining afternoon as possible?"

"Exactly."

My dad would do this often, after my mom

had sarcastically distilled how ludicrous his plans were. Instead of recognizing that she was making fun of him, he would take it at face value, as if someone finally understood what he was getting at. "Yes! We *are* going to ruin *more* of the day, so I can potentially have two seconds of vengeance. I'm glad someone gets it."

    Back to the trip: Due to the persistent bathroom breaks, we were running late, and my dad was getting increasingly concerned about a "man waiting on us." So he did something that was uncharacteristic for both him and our vehicle (a 1979 Ford Econoline Van loaded with eight people, four coolers, and an inflatable raft): he started speeding. After about thirty minutes of cornfields blazing past our windows in a verdant blur, we were pulled over by a state trooper. The trooper came up and my dad exited the car, pointed to the trooper's vehicle, and suggested, "Shall we chat?"

    Several minutes later my dad re-entered the car with a long yellow ticket, and told us they got him for speeding "up there." He went on to explain that the giant white rectangles painted along the shoulder of the road were actually markers for planes operated above by the Ohio State Highway Patrol, and that from these airplanes they would time you to the next marker to see if you were speeding. If so, they would radio for a patrolman to ticket you.

    My dad had just received a speeding ticket he could not afford and I was at that annoying age—old enough to have adult thoughts, but not old enough to correctly read the room—so as he began merging back on to the highway and the state trooper passed us, waving, I asked:

"Dad, would you admit this ticket shows we live in a police state?"

"Sean, it's just a speeding ticket."

"Yes, but it was assigned BY A PLANE!"

"Well, I should not have been speeding. And, it's good to have people slowing down. We need to be safe."

"I get that Dad," I continued, undeterred, "but that would be achieved by the cop just sitting in the middle of the road doing radar. In fact, that would slow more people down, because they would see the cop and drive safely. But, Dad, instead… *they put a PLANE in the air*! They don't want you to actually slow down! They want the tickets! They want you to drive as fast as possible while a cop in the sky fines you! We live in a police state!"

My dad started shaking his head back and forth, then noticed my littlest sister sleeping. He handed me a diaper.

"Put that on your sister. I don't want to do another stop because she peed on her car seat."

"But, Dad, you admit we live in a police state!"

At this point my mom got involved, suddenly screaming back at me, "Sean! We don't admit anything! We will never admit anything! Because we are more concerned about your sister peeing on the bucket seats!"

I put a diaper on my sister—she continued to sleep through it—and, not ten seconds later, one of my brothers announced, "I need to pee."

My dad looked at the ceiling of the car for about ten seconds—traveling at highway speed with eyes pointed away from the road—and muttered, "My God."

Dad looked back into the van. "WHY DIDN'T YOU PEE WHEN WE LAST STOPPED?"

"Dad, when you last stopped I thought you were getting arrested, and I shouldn't get out and pee," he answered.

"A state trooper doesn't care if a five-year-old pees!" Dad yelled back.

"They might be looking for it 'up there,'" I chimed in, "given that this is a police state".

Dad pulled over at the next exit. As a current parent, I now recognize that this is the hardest delay—the most difficult exit-pill to swallow—because it is a stop just after another stop *while* two of the kids are sleeping. As all parents know, a kid can sleep through the car running over a deer, a traffic stop by the police, a loud fight by siblings; but decelerate into a gas station and they will wake up with a collective "I want to buy something!"

My dad pulled into the station. All the kids were now awake. Dad walked across, forcefully slid the van door open and screamed:

"ERRRYEEE UNN! ODDA DA CAAR!".

My dad would occasionally reach what I called his "anger accent state," where he was so furious each word sounded like it came from Boston or Liverpool. We all obediently exited the car, even though only half of us needed to pee. My youngest brother, Brendan, piped up, "I can't go."

The other kids immediately shot him that older-sibling advice look, the one that says, "Are you sure you want to pick this moment to bring up that point?"

"Juuuussss gooowwww!" my dad yelled back, rage causing his vowels to once again drown in the mid-Atlantic.

"Dad," Brendan responded calmly, "I can't go. I'm trying to go *right now*. I'm seriously trying to pee my pants and it's dry. I can't go."

We all went to the restroom, loaded back into the van, and got back on our way. My dad was hoping against hope the man is still waiting for us. He accelerated up the entrance ramp and, before we even merged with traffic, we heard Brendan say from the back, "You're not gonna believe this."

We all knew what was about to happen next.

"I have to go," he repeated desperately, adding, "and it's an emergency!"

Driving with your dad for more than three hours is a lot like being in a submarine with a captain that is slowly going insane from the depth.

Upon hearing about Brendan's urgent bathroom situation, my dad stopped looking at how to merge on the highway, and instead started looking at the floor. For a good five seconds he had his head bowed, as he mumbled, "This trip, this trip, this trip."

My mom tied to snap him out of it, yelling, "Honey, we are going to have to merge".

I am convinced that, in that moment, my dad had a stroke from pure anger. If Apple watches had existed back then, the biometrics would have registered him as legally dead for at least a second. Fortunately his dad-brain kicked in, and reminded him that an accident might happen that could affect the resale value of the van. His mind re-booted just in time for him to merge onto the highway; even more impressively it did so as he simultaneously lost his shit, conceived of a plan, and began executing it:

"OK, Sean, pass him up!" Dad barked.

"What?" I asked.

"Pass him up! He has an emergency! Pass him to me!" then added, "Oh, and Sean? Close the windows back there!"

This was met with a Midwestern Greek chorus of "What?" None of us quite understood what was going on.

"I'm going to dangle his ass out the window," my dad answered, "and he's going to piss or shit into the highway."

What's weird about being Irish Catholic is that it's such an ordinance-based religion that I remember thinking: "I can't believe Dad said 'ass' and 'shit'" and not: "I can't believe my dad wants to shove my brother's bare rear end out of the window of a car that's moving at speed down a major thoroughfare."

"Brian!" yelled Mom. "You can't do that!"

"Shelia, no, I got it," he replied, "that's why I'm having Sean close the windows."

In other words, my dad thought Mom's issue

with having a three-year-old relieve himself from the window of a moving van was not that he could die or be traumatized, but that the shit could float back into the van. Which, in turn, would affect the resale value.

About forty-five minutes and two stops later, we reached the man my dad needed to meet for the keys. No one was dangled out of the window. The man was good-humored about the delay.

"I have four kids myself," he commiserated while laughing, "I remember those road trips." He then added, "A guy in my neighborhood drilled a hole in the bottom of his van for his kids to use on road trips. Bragged that he could make any state park in under two hours!

"I heard the same thing about a fella one town over from me!" my dad replied, excitedly

In the mid-1980s this seems to have been a suburban myth passed on from tardy dad to tardy dad; tales of a fabled, audacious man one town or one block over—no one had ever met him directly, they had only heard lore—who could caravan faster than so many geese because his kids would piss and shit through a hole in the car.

The tardy dads were never sure if they wanted to do it with their own kids—have them dangle their genitals or orifices six inches above pavement flying past at 70 miles an hour—and they were certain that their wives "probably wouldn't allow that." But still, damn, the time savings would be massive. You could make the trip times of a single man.

One could tell my dad was mulling the idea over as he walked back to the car.

My mom cut off his train of thought. "You don't think a giant hole that's been used as a toilet by six kids in the bottom of the van might affect the resale value?"

Taco Bell
Akron, OH

Drunk driving is a terrible scourge, killing over 10,000 Americans a year. To put that number in perspective, it would take hurricanes almost 600 years to kill as many Americans as drunk drivers do in twelve months. Yet we are so terrified of hurricanes that we name each one and track it in real time like a marauder from outer space, even though hurricanes kill fewer Americans (about seventeen per year) than the average sauced-up bowling team does after getting behind the wheel.

Which leads me to the following unpopular opinions:

In the great horror of drinking and driving, there are three villains: the car, the booze, and the driver. And

History will judge the greatest of those villains to be the car.

Humans have consumed alcohol since day one. In fact, it's been suggested that we began consuming booze (as rotting fruit that had fermented) even before we evolved into humans; back when "we" were chimps. And we—that is to say, the branch of primates that eventually gave rise to the beer-swilling, Chevy-operating homo sorta-erectus you see before you today—will continue to consume alcohol until our last day. When the asteroid finally hits, or robots become conscious and attack, we will be drinking a margarita at the mall- our final words being, as doom descends upon us, "I prefer mine with more salt." But the car—by which I mean the motorized vehicle that we steer—will probably only last three, four, maybe five generations?

I am of the even rarer opinion that not only will the car be viewed as the worst culprit in the driver/booze/vehicle pyramid, but children in the future will hear our stories of driving sober and be amazed any of this was ever considered a societal norm:

"You actually drove the car, grandpa?"

"Oh yeah, sometimes, we had to drive it into the setting sun—it was blinding and you couldn't see anything—but we just accelerated. You didn't want to hold up traffic. Some people were drunk."

"Was it safe?"

"Mostly. See, we were so bad at driving, we had safety belts all around our bodies. Kids were strapped in—like astronauts—and accidents happened so often every car had giant balloons that inflated once you hit a wall or tree. When you destroyed the car, you barely felt it."

"Destroyed the car? How–"

"Oh we destroyed them all the time! Half the businesses in my neighborhood were shops for fixing damaged cars. We got in so many accidents, little buddy, you had to purchase this paper called 'auto insurance' that basically said, 'When I shatter someone else's car, this company will buy them a new one.' It was illegal to drive without it."

"That sounds so dangerous. Not like today at all."

"I suppose you're right, little buddy...Now go tell that robot of yours to make me another margarita. And not to forget the salt this time!"

Technology I Like: *Self-Driving Cars*

When we think of a world with self-driving cars we tend to think of a business Xanadu, where the car picks us up outside the front door and drives us into work, while we relax with the morning news or get a head start on today's reports. The self-driving cars move like a flock of birds, crowded, but with no congestion and delays. And, though that sounds optimistic, we overlook the real, life-improving advance: The car can now pick us up outside of any bar and even though we don't remember our name or where we live, will get us home safe.

Like all new, far-reaching technologies, we know the industries that self-driving cars will disrupt—delivery drivers and auto body repair specialists, who will be put out of a job—before we see the industries it will help. We are gonna sell a fuck-ton of booze if these things ever take off.

A 2017 study by Morgan Stanley estimated that self-driving vehicles would lead to an additional $100 billion in alcohol sales a year, if current drivers just had one more beer a week! Which I find hilarious, that the New York millionaires who work at Morgan Stanley think drivers in Wisconsin will just have four more beers a month if they don't need to worry about DUIs. The global market size for all alcohol sales, according to the same Morgan Stanley study, is $1.5 trillion and, honestly, I wouldn't be surprised if Wisconsin and Illinois alone doubled that $1.5 trillion if DUIs are off the table. Ya know: a fuck ton.

And the alcohol industry knows this. In 2018 the liquor industry's largest lobbying group joined The Coalition for Future Mobility, the largest lobbying group for self-driving vehicles, which must have been an amazing call:

"Coalition for Future Mobility, how may I help you?"

"Hi. I'd like to join." [*The sound of rock ice clinking within a glass is heard*]

"We're flattered to hear that but we have the top leaders from the automotive *and* software industries. At this point, we are not accepting new members. We have all the leadership we need, to show how great this product is to both federal and local leadership."

"Yeah, you think so? Well, this is Ed Anheuser the Fifth..." [*the PHHHSST from a beer bottle being opened is heard*] "...and I have forgotten more about buying off politicians than you eggheads will ever learn. And I know how to sell a product that is GOING to be part of Saturday night. So, you might want to think about taking this call."

When self-driving cars finally reach U.S. cities, people assume we will need more engineers and robotic experts but, in reality, it's mostly bartenders we will need to hire. And there's already evidence for that, based on how ride-sharing apps affect the cities they enter.

A 2019 study from economists from The University of Louisville and Georgia State University showed that, when Uber enters a city, binge drinking increases and it corresponds to a higher demand for bartenders. But ride-sharing apps reduce drunk driving incidents so greatly that we don't complain about the increased binge drinking.

This why self-driving cars are so important to the alcohol industry: they would not only increase sales, but also absolve them of the sin of drunk driving.

When Uber returned to Portland after a four-month absence in 2015, alcohol-related car accidents fell by 62 percent! The same year, the San Francisco police department made only two DUI arrests on New Year's Eve, due to the popularity of ride-sharing. Imagine living in the second-most densely populated city in the U.S. and getting arrested for drunk driving, probably assuming you are one of countless, anonymous culprits, only to find out it's just you and *Walter*.

And, as much as I love to hear that only Walter and one other asshole were arrested on NYE in San Francisco, that does pretty definitely show which person has the most to lose by self-driving cars: The Shady DUI Lawyer. Auto body repair technicians, they can learn to repair the computers or batteries on self-driving cars. Auto Insurance companies can move into new risk areas: maybe rideshare liabilities? But Joseph Battilga, a successful DUI lawyer in Trenton—whose motto is "Don't Blow: Call Joe!"—he can't just start working for the Justice Department. Where are these shady lawyers going to go?

The good news is that most of those shady lawyers will probably make great bartenders.

About twenty years ago, I was in Akron, Ohio for a wedding.

This is one of those stories that when I tell in it person, my wife interrupts with, "This was before he and I were together!" When you are married, your wife divides your stories between the ones that happened before you were with her and the ones after you were with her; much as we do with the Old and New Testaments of the Bible. Your wife wants to clearly delineate the two periods so as if to say: This bullshit did not happen under my watch. Or maybe she is avowing: Believe me, I would not have said "yes" if I saw any of this bullshit.

The bullshit in question was: me and half the wedding party were nearly arrested after we breached, without a great deal of dexterity, a police barricade. In our defense, the police were barricading something one cannot resist after ten rum-and-cokes: A Taco Bell.

One must understand, back then, leaving a wedding presented two challenges that have diminished with time:

a) It was extremely difficult to get a ride home and

b) Small towns only had a single option for late night food: Taco Bell.

When I was in college, Taco Bell after midnight was the closest thing I got to entering a bar like the ones in a John Wayne Western: open, rolling fights; people dancing on tables; drunks passed out in corners. It was chaos, mainly because every customer was blind, raging drunk, yet the place was staffed like a deli.

Imagine pitching that shift to a bartender: "You are going to work the one venue in town that's open after last call and your patrons will be—exclusively—people that were thrown out of other bars." That bartender would insist you pay him more than the town sheriff and never schedule less than fifteen bouncers. Yet Taco Bell manages that same situation with three employees, all making minimum wage.

Which is why, in about one out of every three late night visits to Taco Bell, I saw an employee quit publicly, so he could fight a customer. The (ex) employee-vs.-customer boxing match was the highlight of any late-night Ohio Taco Bell visit because, first of all, you got to see someone quit a job they hate, which is always invigorating.

Every day we go to work and promise ourselves, today is the day we quit; we even tell our buddies on the job: "I swear to Christ, if Bert asks me to do Kenny's job again, because Kenny is too fucking stupid to do anything right, I'm quitting on the spot! I'm tired of doing two jobs for the pay of one!" And, sure enough, Bert's first words are: "I need you to go help Kenny, he's struggling with a customer install," and you never quit. When you are young, you dream of being a rock singer or astronaut but then you get older and you only dream of quitting your job and, the tragedy of it is, quitting your job is, for an adult, as unrealistic as becoming an astronaut is for a kid.

So, when you see a Taco Bell employee—at the height of the store's busiest period—quit in front of all the staff and patrons so he can punch a customer in the jaw, it's vitalizing. It's life-affirming. It's the nearest I'll come to witnessing an Oscar acceptance speech, in terms of sheer awe of personality and daring.

And the way that employee quits, throwing their cap and name tag into the ground as hard as possible, before they turn the corner and tussle, is great. I miss jobs where you could formally submit your resignation by chucking your hat across the counter violently.

And on this particular night, after this particular wedding, at this particular Taco Bell, things were particularly tumultuous. We had left the reception and made it to Taco Bell to find two police cars blocking the entrance, with their sirens on, with additional cruisers and additional sirens collected in the back. At any other restaurant and at any other time, this would have been considered a deal breaker and you would move on to find different food. Rarely, when you approach a dining establishment and notice a loud, active crime scene in its parking lot, do you say "Well, let's see if they are still open?" But this was Taco Bell at one in the morning in small town Ohio, which meant it was officially The Only Game in Town.

After you have been drinking, all greasy food tastes amazing but there are two meals that, in my experience, have a magical pull when drunk: burritos and gyros. You begin to crave them at a subconscious level. Some ineffable force compels you to find them, the way a bird is told to fly south when the weather cools.

And that voice, the voice that controls everything from bird migrations to the compulsions of your stomach, found its way to that Taco Bell parking lot and whispered in our collective ear: "You can fit your car between the two police cruisers attempting to block the entrance."

Someone at the front of the car asked: "How much have you had to drink?"

"I think I'd pass a sobriety test," answered our driver. Everyone nodded in agreement, so the driver let off the brake and we started to weave between the two police cruisers. The police cruisers were at an angle, splaying out so as to obstruct any attempted ingress, but they were not well-aligned; they more suggested that you should not enter, rather than being close enough to formally prevent it. We slipped between them slowly, correcting every few inches so as not to bruise the wing mirrors. Our driver was employing the kind of slow precision seen during a space station docking. Eventually we reached the other side of this hazard and, in the parking lot, saw the full scope of the problem: a car was flipped over at the bend in the drive-through lane.

One of the police officers noticed us nearing the accident, so the officer began walking toward our car, clearly annoyed. After a step or two his annoyance gave way to dejection and he forcefully spiked his hat into the ground—a classic from the old "I QUIT!" playbook—and screamed, "God Damn It!" into the air. That's when we noticed that five more cars had also completed the vehicular Khyber Pass and were now behind us in the parking lot.

I exited the vehicle from the back and the cop yelled at me to stay in the car.

"Exercising my Constitutional Right to a burrito, officer," I said and gestured toward the restaurant to indicate that it was still open and serving. I was still at that young age, an age some (white) men never outgrow, where you think that if you add the word

"Constitution" to any sentence, no officer will dare stop you.

He waved me past—he had bigger problems to worry about—so I entered the restaurant, ordered and ate a burrito. I exited a few minutes later only to encounter a fresh new obstacle: several of the doors to our car were open and, at the rear of the vehicle, a cop was banging hard on the trunk.

As I got closer to the vehicle one of my buddies stopped me:

"We have a real problem."

"What?" I asked.

"We have no ride home. No driver."

"What?"

"The driver is gone."

Another member of our group stepped in to give me more detail: "Locked himself in the trunk of his own car."

"What?"

"Trying to get out of DUI."

"But..."

"He thinks they need a warrant to open the trunk."

I could hear loud banging from the police and demands to "exit the vehicle" followed by our driver's muffled reply (from inside the drunk of his own car) : "Affecting my constitutional right to domicile, officer!"

The good ol' Constitution.

I have seen guys (again, to be clear: white guys barely out of college) surrounded by bouncers, being told they need to leave the bar and how do they invariably respond? "The Constitution says I don't have to go anywhere."

Bouncers usually pick the guy up and throw him to the sidewalk, but, just once, I want to see a bartender respond:

"Which Amendment?"

"What?"

"Which Amendment to The Constitution affords you the right to stay inside a bar for as long as you want, no matter how drunk you are? When did we ratify the right to not be ejected?"

(Though it would have been badass if, when America decided Prohibition was not working, rather than passing the 21st Amendment as a straight-forward repeal of the 18th Amendment, it instead guaranteed THE RIGHT TO GET SHIT-HOUSED.)

"Open the trunk!" the cop yelled again. His partner approached the driver's side door and snapped at our friend in the passenger seat: "Release the trunk!"

"What?" came the reply.

"The trunk! Passenger! Citizen! There should be a lever to the left of the driver's seat to open the trunk!"

The moment he said "citizen" half the people in the vehicle laughed, but at least one person was composed enough to say:

"Officer, this is a 1985 Toronado. I don't think it has modern features like 'trunk release.'"

At which point we heard our driver's voice exclaim, indistinctly, from the rear of the car: "I got both sets of keys in here."

Under Ohio laws—possibly under all state laws, I don't know, the Constitution—a tow truck cannot tow a vehicle with passengers in it. Even if those passengers are in the trunk, refusing to exit. So our problem was not going to be solved easily. The police announced they were getting a crowbar to force it open, which once again, elicited laughs from my group. Not that we didn't think it was a legitimate threat; rather we had information that the police did not. For example, we knew that opening that trunk would reveal there were at least four people in there.

Why four? One, because we were the last car leaving a wedding, which meant other people packed into that car like it was the last convoy out of town before a hurricane hits and, two, a 1985 Oldsmobile Toronado is about the size of a modern jet. The trunk was so huge we were able to fit four people inside it and I'm convinced that was mostly due to how big the mafia was back then. The Toronado was a two-door, seventeen foot long vehicle with a trunk that's nearly as big as the passenger compartment; those dimensions make no sense for a car, unless you believe that a sizable part of the economy is devoted to hiding bodies.

The cop walked away to get a crowbar when someone yelled, helpfully, "Wait, officer, the rear speakers in this car pop out! What if we remove the speakers and he hands the keys to us, from the trunk, through the speaker hole?"

The cop turned, performatively set a timer on his watch, and replied:

"You have exactly two minutes to get those keys out; otherwise I crowbar it open."

Which, frankly, was a pretty sizable conciliation from a cop. Usually you don't get to propose a "plan B" to the police. The only way I can think to explain it is that the cop was a father, who realized that the car in question probably belonged to one of our dads, and thus he was bound by the unspoken covenant that unites all American dads, no matter their line of work: "Thou shalt not affect the resale value of another dad's car."

A couple of people from our group pulled the speakers out and squeezed their fingers into the tiny hole left behind, shouting: "Get the keys to my fingers! Work together!"

The police likely found that an odd way to instruct a single person to hand you the keys.

This was also the point at which my parents showed up.

At some point prior it had occurred to me (to a few of us, in fact) that we would be not getting home from this Taco Bell in the same car in which we had arrived. Our driver was in the trunk, furiously and incorrectly quoting the Bill of Rights and, even if we were somehow to get the keys back and arrange an alternate driver, ahead of us was a car stuck upside down and behind us was a stalled caravan, honking rapaciously for tacos. So, this, again, being before rideshare services or even—given the hour and area—taxis, I called my parents.

When I was a teenager, I would stand in the hall, waiting for friends to come pick me up for a Friday night out, and my parents would dutifully issue the same speech, time and time again:

"We do not want you drinking, nor do we want your friends drinking. But, if something happens where you can't get home safely, if you or your driver is drunk: You can always call us and we will come pick you up. We will always give you a safe ride home. No questions asked. We won't be mad. You can call us and we won't be mad."

My friends and my siblings—almost everyone I knew growing up—received some version of this speech, and we were all skeptical. I could never picture my parents, after being woken up at 3 a.m., dressing quickly and then saying goodbye to the other (one of them would have had to stay home due to the other five kids still sleeping in the house) leaving with: "I'm so happy he called! This is a really proud moment for us!"

But, on the other side, I don't think our parents expected us to make that phone call at thirty years of age:

[*RING RING*]
"Umm, uggh, hello?"
"Mom?"
"Sean? It's 3 a.m."
"Yes, sorry. I think I need a ride home."

[*Long pause*]
"Sean. You live in Chicago."
"Yeah, I came home for a wedding. Remember how I said I'd be home in three weeks for my buddy's wedding? I was wrong; it was today. I screwed up the dates and had to catch a last-second flight."
"Where are you? The airport?"
"No, I'm at Taco Bell."
[*Another long pause*]
"Our driver," I elaborated. "He can't drive home."
"Is he drunk?"
I took a second and thought about how to explain that our driver was in the trunk of the car, with three bodies between him and the hole in the speaker we needed him to reach to free the keys.
"At this point, I don't even know if it matters," I answered.

My folks did not live far from the Taco Bell, so they arrived quickly. Due to the chaos in the parking lot, they parked on the street and walked into the lot to find us, which—upon locating us—is when my mom pretty clearly invalidated their earlier speeches from my teenage years:
"I have never been more mad at you in my life!"
"Mom!" I screamed back. "What are you yelling at me for? I'm not the guy in the trunk!"
"Oh! Thank God I raised the smart one!" my mom snapped back ironically.
"Got it!" someone screamed buoyantly from

inside the car. The keys were successfully passed back. A buddy exited the car, ran around to the rear and triumphantly showed the officers that the crowbar would not be necessary.

The lead officer took the key and went to open the trunk.

"What's going on here?" my dad asked.

"Dad," I replied, "I believe this is what magicians call '*the prestige.*'"

The cop popped open the trunk and four, distinct humans were now waving at him.

"Hello," they said, in a kind of unison.

"What the fuck?" another cop exclaimed.

"Why didn't you tell us there were four people in the goddamn trunk?!" screamed the leading officer.

"Constitution says we don't have to," someone replied.

"*Which of you is the driver*?" yelled the officer as the quartet began climbing out of the trunk.

"Legally, there's no way to prove that," someone answers.

My dad, watching all of this by my side, leaned in and whispered to me confidentially and confidently: "Not a good idea."

The cop in charge exploded.

"Do you shits honestly think we don't know who this car is registered to? And do you morons honestly think after we breathalyze him and he fails, he won't tell us exactly who was actually driving?"

That must have gotten through, because our driver stepped forward and said: "Officer, this is my car and I was the driver."

"YES" to Bars, "NO" to Cars:
A History of Drunk Driving Laws.

In January of 1897 the Daimler Motor Company began selling cars in London. A few months later, George Smith, a twenty-five-year-old taxi driver, was fined twenty-five shillings for drunkenly driving into a building. It was the first DUI in recorded history.

I wonder how drunk you have to be, to get a DUI in London in the 19th century? This is a city where people drink seventeen bitters for lunch, then ride a horse into a river. For you to be so drunk that a London copper shows up and invents a new crime on the scene, I don't think merely hitting a building is sufficient. I suspect that George Smith was not only the first drunk driver but also one of the very drunkest ever and, like most drunks put into a tractable situation, he talked his way into jail:

"Ah ha! What do we have here?!" asks the first officer on the scene.

"Fuck you! You stupid bobbie! This motor-wagon costs more than you make in a year!!"

And, with that greeting, the charge of Driving Under The Influence was born.

A few decades later the state of New Jersey

made drunk driving illegal, in 1906. It was the first U.S. state with such a law, but many states followed, with some fining as high as $1,000 for a violation (equivalent to $25,000 in today's money). Everyone agreed drunk people should not drive and, if they caused accidents, should be prosecuted more aggressively but it was difficult to prove a driver was inebriated. Convictions relied upon eye-witnesses testimony—bar patrons who recalled the driver ordering so many whiskeys—or anecdotal police tests, where the officers challenged the driver to stand on one leg or say tongue-twisting phrases correctly. Juries often acquitted, feeling there was no hard evidence against the driver.

In 1919 only about one in every three households owned a car. Then came Prohibition, so, even though—during the 1920s—car ownership grew by over fifty percent, DUIs were not a major concern because the entire U.S. societal stack was pretending that drinking did not exist.

But, in 1930, the 21st Amendment was passed (THE RIGHT TO GET SHIT-HOUSED), Prohibition was repealed, and suddenly America was concerned about the 31,000 people that were dying in car accidents. Luckily for prosecutors across this great country, a chemist at Indiana University, Dr. Rolla Harger, developed a portable test where suspected drunk drivers blew into a balloon-like device and it flashed if they were drunk or not. That device permanently changed DUI convictions by providing police with on-site, scientific proof the driver was drunk and, yes, you are completing the sentence in your head, assuming Harger's invention is the breathalyzer, but, no, amazingly (and hilariously) Harger called it "THE DRUNK-O-METER."

When one looks at all the phraseology choices America made—the terms that were lost to the sands of time—none seem more tragic than our decision to call the device that arrests drunk people "The Breathalyzer" rather than "The Drunk-o-meter." Imagine a world where a friend says they were arrested for a DUI and you ask, "What did you drunk-o-meter?"

The Breathalyzer came to replace the Drunk-o-meter a few years later in 1936, when an Indiana State Police Officer, Robert Borkenstein, worked with Harger to improve the drunk-o-meter so it was smaller and more portable. The new, cheaper and easier-to-use test was called the breathalyzer and was quickly adopted by law enforcement across the country. The device became so common that states could legislate DUI laws based on BAC (Blood Alcohol Content) figures rather than vague standards of inebriation.

Based on advice from the American

Medical Associate and the National Safety Council, most states declared the legal limit for drunk driving was 0.15 BAC which, when read today, is amazing. That is almost twice the current, legal limit. In fact, if you blew 0.15 today, you would qualify for "High BAC" charges in most states, meaning you are to be charged less like you were driving a car around town drunk and more like you were riding a missile around town drunk.

This is what happens to the human body at 0.15 BAC: your sense of balance has mostly failed and your brain struggles to responsively control muscles. Vomiting is common. At my weight, I can have seven shots of whiskey and pass a 0.15 BAC, which is amazing to consider that, in 1938, I'd be one of the safer drivers on the road.

America's response to drinking and driving remained, on sum, unchanged for almost half a century until in 1980 when a chronic drunk driver killed a 13-year-old girl, Cari Lightner, in a hit-and-run in Fair Oaks California. Cari's mother, Candy Lightner, created Mothers Against Drunk Drivers (MADD) in her daughter's memory and that movement did more to reduce drunk driving fatalities than the previous century's worth of breath inventions or legislation.

MADD was so successful in changing the dialogue around drinking and driving—in recognizing the scope of its danger—that, when you look for tables on DUI deaths in America, usually the numbers and graphs start in 1980, when MADD made it a priority. And, in that year (1980) about 26,000 Americans died in car accidents caused by drunk drivers; it was the leading cause of death for people under thirty-four years of age. Over the next decade, due mostly to the successful lobbying efforts of MADD, those numbers were nearly halved. MADD was instrumental in:

» Raising the minimum drinking age from eighteen to twenty-one
» Lowering BAC standards for a DUI to 0.1 from .15 (and then lowering it further to .08 in 2000).
» Disallowing open alcohol containers in a car.
» Deploying sobriety checkpoints across the U.S.
» Rebranding "The Breathalyzer" back to its old name, "The Drunk-O-Meter."

Alas, if only that final point were true.

Our driver agreed to a breathalyzer and blew a 0.07.

In all my years of watching sports in Cleveland, in seeing fans dejected by fumbles and interceptions and bad pitches, I don't believe I have ever heard a more crestfallen sigh than the ones those cops emitted when they realized our driver was legally allowed to go home.

"Ugggh...You're kidding me," the officer administering the test whined, after reading the device's final verdict.

"What's the problem?" asked the lead officer.

"Point! Zero! Seven! Sir"

"*What?*" asked the lead officer, puzzled. "Why didn't you just come out of the vehicle if you're sober?!"

Our driver shrugged.

"It was surprisingly dark and crowded in there," one of the trunk pilgrims added.

"So...I guess we will be on our way," another trunk denizen suggested. My friends and I used that phrase often back then—"I guess I will be on my way"—as a kind of *détente*, after we broke glassware or walked through a screen door; a proposal that suggested that if we were leave now, in that moment, perhaps we could consider this incident closed? A lawyer later told me that phrase, while maybe problematic at social gatherings, is perfect for dealing with police: always propose that you should leave and see how they react.

Everyone filed back into the car, except for me of course. I gave some hugs and goodbyes and explained that I should probably drive home with my parents, what with them waking up and traveling down to Taco Bell in their night robes.

    My folks (they obeyed the police barricade) parked on the street. We were walking to my parents' car, when I saw my friends leaving. Two police vehicles parted, to allow my friends to pass from the rear blockade. My friends passed between the cruisers, exiting to the intersecting road.

    As they departed, a new car rushed into the parking lot before the two police cruisers could reclose the bulwark. The cruisers honked and ran their sirens, but the new vehicle entered where our car just left, creating a brand new problem. The lead officer throws his hat to the ground. A passenger in the car, fell out of the rear window and ran into Taco Bell while the police descended on the vehicle.

    "They should pay those people more," my dad said while pulling into traffic.

    "Police?" my mom wondered. "I think they are paid pretty well by Akron, honey."

    "No," my dad responded, "Taco Bell employees. They oughta make more than astronauts."

Lake County Memorial Hospital
Cleveland, OH

I am the oldest of six kids. My wife is an only child.

When physicists explain the Big Bang, they say things like:

"Time and Gravity didn't exist until a few movements after the Bang, when elements cooled enough to create order. Prior to that, the universe is best thought of as pure chaos that we cannot understand."

My wife looks at my family as something that was born in that tumultuous inferno, before organization and gravity took hold.

When Jess first met my parents, she mentioned that there were only ten guests at her parents' wedding. When my mom heard that, she gave a bellowing laugh and said, "Oh, honey, I think that many people were kicked out of our wedding!"

Many of my current habits are due to growing up inside the loudness of a large family in a small house. I speak too loudly; I eat food too quickly; I take curiously-short showers; but, most of all, I am completely unbothered by injuries.

Someone was always getting hurt in our house. You would hear laughter and play outside, then a kid would enter the house with a branch sticking out of their eyeball.

The sounds of the injuries had structured movements, like a symphony. First was the raucous banging and crashing and laughing: *The Overture*. Then a crash, inordinately louder than all previous crashes: *The Accident*. This is immediately followed by *The Silence*, which is the scariest part- because silence is the most unnerving thing you can hear from a child. Silence means they have either hurt themselves so badly that we're all taking a trip to the hospital, or they have broken something so expensive, they are left speechless. Silence means they are processing consequences.

Next we have *The Crescendo*, when one of the non-injured kids runs down the stairs, a screaming herald, announcing: "Mom! Dad! Mom! Brendan just broke every bone in his body!"

A parent will run in, asking for more details, which then leads to: *The Reveal*. Brendan descends the stairs slowly with a clearly broken wrist. "Shit!" your mom yells knowing she has to pack up six kids and go to the emergency room. The Injury Symphony always ends with the same Carol: the herald yelling, "It wasn't my fault! It wasn't my fault!"

If you were to hear only the sounds of that house, you would think the world's most happy, yet accident-prone construction crew was constantly renovating it. This was back when kids could hurt themselves; the final years of The Era of The Great Whoopsie-Daisy, which stretched from the start of humanity to the late 1980s—before the introduction of childproof bottle caps and car seats and helicopter parents —when kids still had some level of independence, which they used to, almost exclusively, injure themselves.

Throughout history, the story of kids playing is a story of each generation being amazed at how much more danger they got in than their progeny. Every story I've heard from an adult about his or her childhood concludes with a laugh, a pause, then the same universal thought:

"Wow, you would get arrested if you let kids do that now."

Everything our parents allowed us to do a mere two decades ago would land them in jail today. My father-in-law built a functioning guillotine for my wife's third grade class Halloween party. When I asked him if it worked, he answered, "It could have decapitated a horse."
My siblings and I would often be driven four towns over in the bed of a pickup truck, like pumpkins being shipped to the market. Nowadays, I honestly believe if a helicopter were to crash and explode in the middle of a highway it would generate fewer 911 calls then if people saw a man merge onto that same highway with six kids in the back of his truck.

My siblings and I often tease our parents about allowing these activities—"We could have died!"—and they always respond with, "We didn't know any better! Back then it was normal." And then, in what is a better defense, they share a story about how their childhoods were even crazier. My parents have insane stories about playing hide and seek in active factories in Cleveland, being bitten by actual junkyard dogs, or falling through ice. Each of my uncles has a story of plunging into a frozen body of water.

"What?" we'd inquire, "how did you fall through ice, Uncle Marty?"

"Well, your grandpa got home," the reply would start, "—he was a window washer you know—and he liked to relax with a beer. And I started asking him questions. I think I was asking him what the difference between a toad and a frog was and he said, 'Why don't you and your brothers go play on that ice?' And the next thing you know: I'm trapped under one inch of ice."

Half the stories of my parents and their peers end with them chuckling, "I thought I was going to die!". It's a big escalation past our feeble, "We could have died, mom!" complaint.

But crazier yet are the stories of my grandparents being raised by their parents, my great-grandparents. My Grandpa Flannery only had one eye. He often removed his glass eye, and let it roll about on the table while he napped; he said the eye could watch us while he slept, like if Sauron just wanted a decent rest. He had seven brothers and I don't think any of them had a full set of eyes.

When I asked my grandpa how he lost his eye, he described his best friend shooting him in the face while hunting birds for dinner: "I thought I was dead," he finished laughing, somehow one-upping the old, "I thought I was gonna die!"

Then you go back further and further, until you eventually reach the Bible, where the parents are so negligent, most of their kids were killed by their own siblings or swallowed by whales. They grin, their final words being, as the lions encircle or the whale inhales, "Whelp, I'm dead."

That was the story of humanity: each generation grew up unsafely and, upon becoming an adult, raised their kids slightly more cautiously while laughing at how dangerous their own youth was.

But that makes me wonder: Now that the Era of the Great Whoopsie-Daisy is over, and a child is never alone for more than two seconds, what will this current generation laugh about when they grow old? What could my kids possibly look back on and say, "Wow that was dangerous; I can't believe we were allowed to do that."

My best guess is: peanuts. Peanuts might be banned in forty years.

They will still exist, but it will be like buying cigarettes, where you will need a photo ID to get them and, like smoking, you won't be allowed to consume them in public. In fifty years, if you eat a peanut in a public park, police will descend on you like you just exposed yourself to a group of joggers.

A few years ago, I sent one of my kids to school with a peanut butter and jelly sandwich and the school—with no exaggeration—reacted like I packed a sandbag full of live grenades.

"What were you thinking?" my wife asked me incredulously that night.

"It's peanut butter; not actual peanuts, babe," I responded.

"It doesn't matter, Sean. There are too many

allergies."

"It's a *sandwich*! People have been eating PB&J's for centuries without a problem. Plus, it comes from a grocery store! Everything in that fucking store is just made out of corn syrup dyed to the right color! But, even if there were peanuts in it, I ask you: Where did all these kids with allergies that sensitive come from? Where were they when I was growing up? Did a prolific seducer with a peanut allergy"—I was gyrating my hips at this point, like the seducer—"travel America and father an entire generation of peanut-allergic kids?"

"I don't care!" she snapped, "I don't care where it came from. Just don't make a PB&J for his lunch! I don't want to get called into the principal's office again."

"Did they ever over-react to that!" I sighed and pondered, "You know, when *I* was growing up, if you hadn't studied for a test and you wanted to shut down school, you called in a bomb threat. But now, if I was a kid and I hadn't studied for a test, I would just pack myself a peanut butter and jelly sandwich. They would shut down that school like they just found a gas leak!"

"Jesus," said Jess, "don't tell our kids this."

"What part?"

"*Any of it*! You! I don't want them to know you don't believe in allergies or that you hated school. Or that you called in bomb threats!"

"Well what did you guys do?" I asked, genuinely curious.

"We studied!"

Whenever my wife yells at me during a disagreement, I never think it's due to the current debate as much as that the current debate revealed how big of a jackass I used to be, and she's alarmed that she is raising kids with such a person. I once used the word "exacta" in an argument and she asked what that meant, thinking it would be some Latin phrase I knew and she would benefit from.

"It's when you correctly predict the first two horses in a race, in the exact order," I explained.

"How do you know that word?" she asked.

"I used to skip high school and go bet on horses."

This was followed by a full minute of silence and her staring at me.

"You didn't know that about me?" I asked, eventually.

My wife knows me better than anyone and most of that knowledge comes directly from our conversations; sharing what bands we enjoy or stories of how our families celebrated Christmas. But my wife does not fully understand how big of a disaster I used to be, or, if she does, she has deduced it indirectly, the way an archaeologist understands a past civilization by looking at bones.

For example, at the first family wedding Jessica attended with me, I broke my ribs drinking with my brothers the night before the wedding. Jessica was flabbergasted, less by the injury, but more by how normal my family considered it.

Places I Can't Return To

The four sides of my family are Flannery, Murray, Donovan, and McGinty, and I would say, at any wedding on any one of those sides, at least ten percent of the guests are attending with a bone they broke in the previous twenty-four hours.

When you are in a family like mine, bad injuries and trips to the hospital blend together the same way trips to the beach seem to most families: realistically, you were there often but only the biggest trips are remembered. These are the three I best remember:

1. When my brother Paul broke his arm.

My wife and I obviously have a lot of divergent customs, me being the oldest of six and her being an only child, but none separate more than how birthdays are treated. The way my wife explains how her birthday was celebrated growing up sounds like how the Soviet Union celebrated the birth of Lenin: a month of parades and bowing and gifts. And the best way to sum up how my family treated birthdays is to point out that for the first nine years of his life, we celebrated my brother Paul's birthday on the wrong day.

Paul broke his arm. Or maybe it was his wrist or a finger; no one really recalls what he broke, only that during the admittance process at the emergency room—as they consulted their records—we discovered that Paul was born on a completely different date than the one we had been celebrating. And we were not off by a day or two; it was a completely different season.

He went from a winter birthday to a summer birthday.

"Thank God you don't seem to be much of an astrology family," the nurse said. An understatement, considering that one of the kids just had his birthday moved half a year ahead.

In most families, where your birthday is tied to your identity this might have been a more traumatic experience, but Paul cut right to the meat of the matter:

"Does that mean I'm actually older?"

"Yes," my parents answered.

"So, my real birthday already happened?"

"Yes."

"So, hmm..." he pondered as he hopped down, his arm now in a cast, "...can we get a cake?"

"Yes."

Paul exited the room, managing his cast, announcing "GUYS! I have great news!" His arm was in a splint and he was holding an X-Ray. "We are getting a cake!" he proclaimed.

"YES! Hooray!" we yelled back. "Is it because you were so tough about the injury?"

"No! It's because the doctor says I'm a year older!"

"You're not seven anymore?"

"Nope!"

We looked at each other puzzled, not sure how to interpret that, but behind us was a teenager with road rash and I heard the kid's dad whisper, "What the hell kind of operation did *that* kid have?"

2. When my sister Eileen got into the medicine cabinet.

I remember the first time my mom and dad left me and my sister Sarah in charge of the other four kids while they went out for an evening. I was probably around eleven or twelve and my sister was a year younger. It was the last time I was part of "management." Sarah was placed singularly in charge after this incident.

Like all people who have been fired, I maintain I was let go because I took instructions from management "too seriously."

As my parents were leaving, they left a note detailing what restaurant they would be at and the phone number to it so they could be contacted if anything happened (again, before cell phones).

"But don't call unless you really need us!" my dad added.

"Brian! We want them to call if something is wrong!" my mom corrected him. She assured us that she wanted us to call if there was an emergency but to not bother them with small bickering. While she was explaining this, my dad shook his head "no" at me, signaling he just did not want to be bothered. I give him an "I got it" look.

They left.

About an hour later, Eileen—who was two or three at this time and who we thought was sleeping—walked downstairs to see us. She was blue and swollen to twice her size.

"What happened to you?" Sarah asked, concerned. Eileen held out a canister of medicine.

"Oh no! She ate medicine!" Sarah yelled.

"Well, hold on," I responded calmly, "it could be fiber or something. Let's not panic."

Sarah grabbed the bottle and read it. "It's dad's back medicine!" she exclaimed, "I'm gonna call mom and dad." She started walking to the phone and I ran in front of her.

"Hold on, they asked us not to bother them," I reminded her.

"Sean, she's a baby that ate adult-back-pain medicine."

"Sarah, I think we can all agree she's learning a valuable lesson."

"What?! We need to call them!"

"We were specifically instructed not to do that."

"That was for bickering! This is an emergency!"

It should be noted that by this point Eileen was now, physically, the biggest kid in the house and blue. She was laughing and having a good time and did not appear sick.

"I agree this isn't a great situation. But I don't think we should bother them," I opined.

Sarah shook her head, walked around me, called the restaurant and described my parents so the hostess could locate them and inform them they had a phone call.

When I watched movies as a kid, it was common for one of the characters to get a call at a restaurant. A tuxedoed waiter would interrupt a party and apologize, explaining a phone call was waiting for them; our heroes would answer and learn that their lead witness was just shot or that France has tested a new type of nuclear bomb. It always seemed so fancy and important to receive a phone call at a restaurant, but you eventually grow up and realize that when people get a phone call at a restaurant in real life, it is the babysitter saying one of the kids just broke their shoulder.

There was a pause as the hostess looked for our parents. Eventually I heard Sarah say, "Mom? Eileen ate dad's back pain medicine."

Sarah listened for a few seconds, then started answering questions:

"She looks swollen, but is happy...We don't know how many she ate because she spilled the rest in the sink...I think most of the bottle is in the sink...it all just happened...Ok...OK!"

At this point, I felt the need to apologize to our parents for this overreaction and to let them know I was against it. I grabbed the phone:

"Mom? It's Sean. Listen, I told Sarah we shouldn't bother you with this. I know she is overreacting and everything will be fine."

There was a measurable pause, and the hostess at the restaurant answered, "Your parents already left. In a hurry."

Many years later, after our grandparents passed, we found a letter that my brother Paul mailed to our grandma. It was an assignment at school to write and mail a letter:

"Hi Granma,
I LoVe you. I loss 2 tooths and TooTTH Fairy came!!
Uh uh. I havta go Granma.
Eileen ate daddy'S medizine and is puprole."

3. When my brother Kevin swallowed paint thinner.

It used to be as easy for a child to open a can of paint thinner as it was for them to open as a container of milk—actually, no, that's not correct; it was actually *harder* to open milk because milk was shipped in a cardboard obelisk that was impossible to unfold. Paint thinner lids, on the other hand, unscrewed as easily as turning a doorknob. When I was growing up, it was easier to get into rat poison than a school-issued carton of orange juice.

One day, Kevin was in the garage with my dad, and stumbled across a jar that stunk of fumes. Kevin asked my dad what it was.

"The strongest whiskey in the world!" my dad joked. My brother Kevin, being obsessed with pirates and reasonably confident that he had once heard that pirates drank mostly whiskey, replied, "Ahoy, matey!" and, in one motion—before my dad could intervene—opened the paint thinner and chugged a huge mouthful.

My dad scooped up Kevin, and ran inside the house yelling, "POISON CONTROL!"

To understand the rest of the story—and why I probably remember this incident so vividly—you must know that in the mid-1980s, my home city of Cleveland, Ohio did not yet support the national 911 emergency line. Meaning that when your kid decided to drink paint thinner like a buccaneer trying to dull a toothache; or even when you got mugged or your uncle accidentally lit the pergola on fire, all of those required that you look up the local number for the correct fire department or police.

It was chaos.

And the phones reflected that: everyone had giant, yellow stickers on their phones with the local numbers for various emergency services; police, fire, hospital, poison control, veterinary services, etc. Your phone had more warnings and emergency instructions on it than the emergency escape door on a plane.

The stickers in question were the national, mass-produced kind, just a label marked with an icon—a cross for the hospital, a flame for the fire department, etc.—and you wrote the relevant local number for your city next to them and affixed the completed sticker to your phone. Meaning that, in the moment of the emergency, someone was going to need to read a handwritten number off the phone then dial all ten digits with no mistakes.

Like I said: *chaos.*

"Poison Control!" my dad yelled, holding Kevin.

"What happened?" my mom asked, grabbing Kevin and hugging him. He started to vomit.

"He drank paint thinner!"

"What?" my mom gasped.

My dad grabbed the receiver off the phone and barked, "It's a long story!" which is hilarious because it's genuinely one the shortest stories I've ever heard: my dad told his son that poison was potable, as a joke. I have learned, through both my dad's actions and my own, that when a father brings home an injured child with the excuse, "it's a long story," he is really saying,, "I grossly underestimated several risk factors."

My dad was trying to read the handwritten number on the receiver while simultaneously dialing the digits on the rotary, and was visibly struggling.

"Sean, read the poison control numbers!" he barked.

"Got it dad!" I responded.

"I already dialed 216," he said, referencing the area code.

"Got it. 878."

"Dammit! Ok, 878."

"5461."

"5461. Done."

"Hi! Poison Control?! My son just drank paint thinner!"

There was a very short pause, followed by my dad hollering, "This *isn't* poison control?!"

My dad had apparently dialed the wrong number.

Meanwhile, Kevin had stopped vomiting and now seemed fine; he was explaining how he came to drink paint thinner, the whole pirate/whiskey confusion.

"This isn't 216-878-5461?" my dad snapped, trying to verify the phone number.

Another aspect that will baffle young people about pre-smartphone telephony was that when you dialed an incorrect number it wasn't like today, where you just apologized and hung up. No, it was a mystery that needed to be solved. Did I dial the wrong number? Or did I dial it correctly, but the number is written down wrong? Or is the person answering the phone just an asshole? A short interrogation would follow.

Also at this moment, my brother Paul was loudly explaining to Kevin that pirates don't drink whiskey, they drink rum.

"What? Are you sure?" Kevin asked back.

"Of course! Everyone knows pirates drink rum. You're thinking of leprechauns. Leprechauns drink whiskey, you moron!"

My dad put his hand over the mouthpiece and screamed at the kids, "Stop talking about liquor for a moment!" He waited for silence, and returned to this call:

"216-878-5461? Right? What? And it's not poison control?"

This meant that my dad had dialed the number correctly, but we had seemingly written down the incorrect number for poison control in the first place. Dad hung up, saying, "Let me see that phone, Sean."

I gave it to him, and he re-examined the number.

"Sheila, is this a 'one' or a 'seven' at the end? I

can't read your writing."

"It's a seven," my mom said without even looking.

"How do you know?"

"We dial it once a week."

WinCit Finance
Chicago, IL

On September 11th, 2001, I was fired from my job as a software developer.

After the terrorist attacks. That's an important distinction to make, because workers that are merely unproductive or sub-par don't get fired on such a day. You have to be a pretty terrible employee—a top-to-toe jackass—for your boss to remember to fire you a few short hours after learning the world is ending.

In my defense, there were extenuating circumstances: I was hungover. I have worked full time since the age of sixteen and this is the only time I have lost a job due to a hangover. Which, when you consider how much I used to drink, is uncommonly impressive. It's like an airline with a single late arrival in its history.

Often, when I arrived at work, the first words I would hear would be something like, "HOLY SHIT! I did NOT expect to see you today!" from some coworker who was out with me the night before. I often learned how crazy my night was from others, never my own memories. That's not to say I blacked out—I usually remembered everything—but I consider one's own memories a useless gauge because, in the Great Play of Drinking, there are only two characters: *Self* and *Other*. And Self always thinks it's doing just fine.

Self believes that it is always speaking with the

perfect touch of humor and nimbly moving between topics.

Other says that you are repeating the same story over and over, so loudly people three rooms away are afraid to become stuck talking to you.

Self feels proud, happy for kicking the party into a higher gear by starting a dance floor.

Other yells that you are knocking over drinks and that this is a studio apartment, not a bar.

Self thinks one more bar—a night cap!—would be the perfect ending.

Other screams that you start work in four hours and are missing a shoe.

See, there are two things you can't effectively do to your own body: One is tickle it, and the other is rate how drunk it is. (Side note: If you *do* manage to tickle yourself, you're probably pretty shit-faced.)

In order to self-assess one's level of inebriation, you must deduce your state of drunkenness from what The Other says. If people are repeatedly asking you questions like, "Don't you have to work tomorrow?" or "Please tell me you aren't driving home!" you are drunk, no matter what *Self* is telling you.

Science Time:
Meet the Players Behind Your Buzz

Hi. I'm the Cerebral Cortex. I cover the top parts of your brain and am the most complex, sophisticated part of the entire organ. I'm in charge of decision making, risk assessment, language skills, consciousness—I'm basically what makes you human instead of an ape—and I'm the first thing that is shut down by drinking beer.

You probably know alcohol is a depressant, right? And that this is the reason that you shouldn't drive drunk because it slows your reactions. What you may not realize is: The only reason you are even considering driving drunk is because alcohol already slowed me, the cerebral cortex, so much you can't even calculate how bad of an idea it is.

You are a fucking *idiot* without me.

Take me out of the equation and you are basically a heavy, land-based goldfish that can't make decisions or predict consequences. If I did not exist and you owned more than one dog, your dogs would be in charge of the house.

Are you one of those people that think you can speak perfect Spanish when drunk? Well, I would like to assure you, as the part of the brain that's normally in charge of reading other people's reactions, that you sure-as-fuck can NOT. Instead, what's going on is: you have flooded me with so much alcohol, I can't assess how people are reacting to you and, since you are not hearing any negative feedback from me, you drunkenly assume you are pulling off perfect Spanish.

You slur words when drunk because I am

in charge of language. After five margaritas, it takes me more time to assemble the syntactical units that make up a sentence but your impatient, drunk ass won't wait for me so you blurt out half-assembled, mispronounced nonsense that makes us both look like morons. The reason you fight more when drunk is because it takes me more time to determine if someone is agreeing with us or not and, again, your drunk ass won't tolerate that delay so you just throw a punch or scream "Fuck you, Rob!" rather than wait for an accurate answer.

I'm the chaperone of the brain. Come to think of it, I'm more a warden than a chaperone because this institution would be chaos without me. Without me, the rest of this organization we call a brain would be a right shithole.

No one around here fully grasps the challenges I face in just keeping you alive when you drink. As though impairing me with a bottle of wine wasn't enough, booze also increases the production of dopamine!

Dopamine is the brain's reward system, the party center; it creates euphoria and is the only neurological facility that accelerates when drinking. The best way to describe what happens when you get drunk is that you have locked me, the warden, in my office and you have emancipated the prison's craziest, least well-adjusted inmate:

Jimmy "The Dope" Dopamine. And all of the other inmates have elected him leader.

Have you ever wondered why you fall out of chairs laughing at stories when drinking? Why you are staying out five hours later than you planned? Why you are eating gyros as the sun rises? Because fucking dopamine is in charge! You think I would allow any of that? We have an ulcer for Christ's sake.

I don't expect you to absorb any of this. The curse of being the Cerebral Cortex is that I'm sophisticated enough to understand that you hate me. You despise the doubts and anxiety I cause by reading other people and wondering about the future. You want to burp and giggle and hold french fries down from your lips to imitate a beaver for your friends. That's why you drink.

But I want to point out: if not for me, you wouldn't exist! Not just you specifically, but the whole fucking human race! Did you know, when we started, there were dire wolves and sabre tooth tigers and bears that could run faster than cars? How the hell do you think we made it past all that? With our spleens? With dopamine? No, it was me!

So, I guess what I'm saying is: Show some respect next time you are drinking and ask yourself, "Is everything going as awesome as I think it is right now, or have I just shut out the best thing

> in my life and the only thing that tells me the truth?"
>
> Thank you.
>
> EDITOR'S NOTE: In the interest of equal time, we asked Dopamine to respond to this essay, but they did so by sending a recording of AC/DC's "Let There Be Rock" on a Maxell UR-90 cassette tape.

What we forget about September 11th, 2001, is that September *10th*, 2001, was like any other day; which meant I was doing what I usually did in those days: drinking until dawn. When I explain that I was out until sunrise the night before the attacks people often respond, "Wasn't September 11th on a Tuesday?"

"Yes," I reply, "yes it was."

That day I woke up an hour past the start of work and immediately panicked. I was supposed to be giving a presentation in twenty minutes' time. I did not know it but The Twin Towers had already been hit by planes and the rest of America was dealing with the knowledge that the country was under attack.

As far as I was concerned, the main danger that I was facing that day was imminent dismissal from my job. I jumped out of bed, put on some deodorant and the clothes from the previous night, brushed my teeth and then Febrezed my entire body. Back then you could smoke in bars so your clothes stunk if you wore them the night before. You could always identify the drunks at work because their clothes smelled like a bonfire, but not mine, after spraying them, my clothes smelled like a lemon tree. A lemon tree that someone had set on fire the previous night.

I ran out the door and boarded the train within five minutes of waking up. This is how I used to "get ready" for work, like a fireman answering a three-alarm blaze. I wonder what it must have looked like to my neighbors. I ran out of the apartment every morning like I was escaping a gas leak. There was never time for breakfast or coffee or to even verify that socks and shoes matched. One time I got to work, went straight into a meeting, and while I was answering a question, a pair of underwear and a sock dropped from inside my pants and onto the floor.
I had put my pants on so hurriedly that morning, I didn't notice the underwear and socks were still inside the legs.

So there I was, on the train, riding to downtown Chicago with about a hundred, confused, afraid Americans who are all processing a tragedy. And then there's me: a wholly-clueless, uninformed man with a terrible hangover.

For me, the main effect of a hangover is that I lose my wits. The world doesn't seem any slower to me—I know it's spinning at the same rate—but I cannot observe, interpret, or react to it at my normal speed. It's as though my eyes, ears, and brain have aged fifty years overnight. I always beam when people say I'm smart. Not because I'm insecure and need validation but because I consider it a great compliment when you realize that I wake up every day as a moron. When I was growing up, my brother Paul had a large, impressive train set that spanned across a model city he had built. Every morning our youngest brother Brendan would wake up first, play with the set, and in doing so, destroy the entire thing. Hours later, Paul would wake up and fastidiously rebuild it again. That's also how my brain works: I rebuild it each morning.

A specific example of that dimness: I did not notice our answering machine was blinking with a new message as I rushed out of the apartment, slamming the door blindly. This was back when cellphones were less common and, usually, when I left the apartment I looked at the answering machine in the hallway to see if I missed a call; to see if my plans would be changed. That day I did not look at the machine, and therefore did not hear that new message until the following day.

It was my roommate, calling to warn me:

"Hey Sean, it's Paul. Calling from work. I know you got in pretty late last night so you might be just waking up and... A major attack is going on. Planes have flown into the Twin Towers. It's pretty bad. Your office might already be closed: you should check. Anyway, mostly wanted to share just, so, ya know, you don't make an ass of yourself."

That last line proved to be prophetic.

The train moved underground and I began to feel unwell, like I might pass out. I only had one more stop but I was worried I would vomit before we reached the station. I pushed my way to the back of the train to have more space and buckled over against the back wall.

A very young man, probably college-age, saw me struggling and in a community-spirited kind of way, sought to reassure me:

"Hey, sir, hey sir: You're gonna be OK. OK? We all will."

He was, of course, talking about the 9/11 attacks.

But as I knew nothing about that, I assumed he had merely recognized that I was hungover and sought to give me some solace. As we pulled into my station, I turned to the guy, smiled, and said:

"Pal, this isn't even one of my ten worst mornings." and walked off the train.

As I exited the station, I started to piece together why I was feeling so unwell. It wasn't so much a hangover, not directly. I noticed a distinctly prophylactic smell emanating from me as well as white marks where the color has been rubbed out of my slacks. It was then I realized I had not Febrezed my clothes: I had grabbed the wrong bottle and sprayed OxiClean over everything. Thanks to haste and hangover, I did not notice that the first thing I did that morning was to cover myself in an all-killing bleach.

When I look back at all the peacock-ish mistakes I've made in life, I sometimes wonder if the bystanders remember the events as vividly as me. For instance: The kid who tried to reassure me that everything would be okay. He had to be left wondering, "What in the hell kind of life has this lunatic businessman lead to emphatically state that planes flying into buildings, the country in a panic, does not crack his top ten shittiest mornings?"

I climbed the stairs, and upon reaching street level and the fresh air, began to feel kind of normal again. My clothes looked ridiculous but I figured if I had good luck with the elevators, I should only be a few minutes late for my first meeting. I felt optimistic, until I saw the mad rush of people I would be working against to reach the office.

My building was a block past DePaul University's Loop Campus which had just canceled classes due to The Attacks. So at that point there was a large, mad rush of students pushing against me and trying to get on the train, while I marched to the office in the opposite direction. As I passed through the mass, I overheard disconnected statements of fear and worry as well as a phrase which I thought was "bomb threat." But even then, I concluded they were referring to the "Old College Bomb Threat." You know the one: Some fraternity slacker didn't study for their finals so they forced a pledge to phone in a bomb threat to cancel school and give them another day to cram.

I reached the office and was immediately pulled into a large conference room. Our CIO was standing in front of and addressing a large group of people:

"This is a scary morning. No one knows what's

going on. Some of you are hearing different things. We feel the appropriate response is to close the office. Go home, be safe and be with your families."

Now of course for the CIO, this was a solemn duty: Trying to discharge and provide comfort to a room full of nervous, dejected people; worried about the events unfolding on the news and what that meant for the future of the country. But as far as I was concerned (and blithely assumed everyone else was on the same page) he was overreacting to what was clearly a fake bomb threat next door at DePaul.

Believing myself to be the beneficiary of some moron's attempt to get out of test, I yelled, "YES!" and raised my hand for someone to high five me; possibly, the most inappropriate high five ever requested.

Because I'd entered late, I was situated near the front of the conference room, behind management and visible to everyone. I turned to the engineer nearest me, my arm still raised, still asking for a high-five, and announced almost-giddily: "Oh yeah, my man! Home by noon!"

The guy really didn't want to high-five me but I forced the issue.

The room was quiet except for my one happy yelp. I remember the CIO staring at me in bewilderment, along with my immediate boss, the head of eBusiness. I started walking towards the door, exposing white zebra stripes up and down my clothes where the cleaning agent had eaten away the color. Just before exiting, I turned and broke the silence with:

"Boys; I'm gonna get a haircut."

Then I walked out: first from the conference room, then the office and, eventually—as I learned a few hours later—that entire corporation.

A few hours after leaving, I learned of the attacks and when my boss called to fire me later, I considered it important that he knew that I did not know about the terrorist attacks during that meeting.

"Christ, Sean, I know that. You're not an asshole. You're being fired because you show up an hour late every day. And if you're wondering why we picked today; it's not even the awkwardness of how you acted. It's more that you are the Head of Software Security and the *entire office* just saw that you somehow made it to work, as the *head of security*, without learning about the biggest terrorist attack in modern history."

"Also," he added, "if we are leveling with each other: that weird, disappearing ink outfit you were wearing didn't help."

Acknowledgments/Thank Yous

I hope the book made you laugh.

I'd like to thank you for buying it. I'm from the Midwest which means one out of every four sentences ends in either a thank you or an apology so, if you liked the book: thank you.

And if you hated it: I'm sorry.

I'd like to thank the following people who helped me make both the book and the stories in it:

My wife, Jessica, who always supports me, is the love of my life and a great mom to our three kids.

My family—my five brothers and sisters and my folks—who cracked me up my whole life and have, in later life, become an important comedy network where they text me the latest, craziest thing my dad said (the last one was: "I DROVE BY YOUR CHILDHOOD HOME AND SAW GUTTER DAMAGE. TRIED TO INTRODUCE MYSELF AND TALK ABOUT IT. DID NOT GO WELL.").

Pat Brice and CJ Sullivan and all the guys behind "The Visitor's Locker Room." The best comics I met who taught me that great comedy starts not with the premise or the punchline but the right beer.

Tyson Lowery and all the Walsh guys: Jeff (x 4?), Tim, Willy, Ted, Brad, Sturz, Eric, and more. Half of these stories were created with you and, despite the bruises and hangovers we still do it again each year.

Adam "The Cane" Burke who edited this book. If you were to put The Cane on the border of Illinois and Indiana—not too far from where we live—and you were to say to The Cane, "You are to swat every bug that enters Illinois! We do not want them!" The Cane would respond, "I can do that, because I corrected every spelling mistake in Sean Flannery's book, which is like swatting every bug on Earth!" The Cane is the best: funny, brainy, and sunny; the book wouldn't have finished without his edits, insights, encouragement, and optimism.

All the Chicago comedy venues that provided me with opportunities but, in particular, The Comedy Bar and The Lincoln Lodge, both of which had a lot of faith in me and gave me a lot of leeway. And, in particular, The Comedy Bar, which had so much faith in me they allowed me to sign a life-time, "Never pay for a drink" contract. Hopefully this book enhances my profile because, if we are being honest, Comedy Bar is losing their shirt on that deal.

Steve and the whole team at JWT (Aaron, Dan, Dion, Erich, John and more). My comedy career, given some of the health challenges my family had, is mostly possible due to the great support I had at my day job. Also, those nerds somehow drink more than stand-ups.

The bars that elected NOT to throw me out, which I guess, when I think about it, is only two: Galway Bay and Pipeworks Brewery. Nolan and Jay of Galway bought me about a thousand Guinnesses and I know they always bought it because I made them laugh and they knew I had no money; but I appreciate that they lied, "It's an investment; you'll be a rich comedian some day and can promote us." And Bobby Minnelli of Pipeworks, who, besides introducing me to some of the world's greatest beers, had funnier stories than mine and encouraged me to start writing everything down.

Colin Lenehan for his tireless work editing the audio book (that guy erased out a lot of ice cube clanks), along with his past tech help at my live shows. Rudy Schultz for all the great artwork on this project and past ones. And Chris Ocken for the photographs.

I'm also debating about thanking COVID. It's not that I feel grateful to it; COVID upended my life. Society ended. I gained twenty pounds. Because I couldn't perform stand-up comedy -- where drinks are comped, I had to pay for my drinks which meant, not only do I have no money, since I can't perform but now I'm paying retail for gin (!) which was bad. But, I did write this book under lockdown and maybe that's the closest thing to a 'win' COVID can put on the board; that it slightly improved teleconferencing software and some Irish jackass finished his memoirs on basement bar experiences.

Finally, I'd like to end on a thank you to a big group of people who were usually side-by-side with me in most these stories and did their best to help me recall the details. If people were to ask, "How true are all these stories?" I feel I can confidently answer, "No book has ever been truer, given this level of whiskey." Thanks for the stories:

The Guys From Blerds and all the Chicago comics from way back then: Mikey O, Joey V, Ricky, The Puterbaughs, Ken, Brady, Josh, Kro, Joyce, Jonah, Kumail, Matt, Klinger, Emily, Nick, Meg, Matty, Aaron; The Cleveland Crew in Chicago: Monica, Meg, Jay, Paul, Frank, Gina, Angie, Doug, Joe; The Cap E&Y guys: Rich, Dave, Joe; The Comp USA people: Steve, Carl, Tom (x2), Joe, Josh; The Cleveland Crew: all my cousins and aunts and uncles, Homey, Kross, Bertsch, Steve L.

Made in the USA
Middletown, DE
17 December 2022

18959726R00201